WAS JESUS MARRIED?

WAS
JESUS
MARRIED
?

The
Distortion of
Sexuality
in the
Christian
Tradition

WILLIAM E. PHIPPS

1817

HARPER & ROW,
PUBLISHERS

New York, Evanston, and London

LIBRARY OF CONGRESS CATALOG CARD NUMBER: 74-126282

CONTENTS

Preface   ix

I. TACKLING A TABOO QUESTION   1

    The timeliness of this inquiry

    Past positions on Jesus' sexuality

    Hypothesis clarification

II. SEXUAL ATTITUDES IN ANCIENT JUDAISM   15

    The genesis of sexuality

    Hebrew marital customs

    Sexual asceticism and Jewish Scriptures

    Lifelong celibacy and the Essenes

III. THE SEXUALITY OF JESUS   34

    The argument from silence

    The conception of Jesus

    Joseph and Jesus

    Jesus, the Essenes, and John the Baptist

    Jesus and asceticism

    "Tempted in every respect"

    Marital testing and human maturation

    Jesus' relations with women

IV. TRADITIONAL ARGUMENTS FOR JESUS'
     CELIBACY   71

Jesus' spouse is the church

Sexual desire is evil

Celibacy is prerequisite to discipleship

Jesus advocated the eunuch way of life

The angelic life should now be copied

V. PAUL AND SEXUAL RELATIONS   99

The marital status of church leaders

The de-married apostle

Paul's general sexual outlook

Review and preview

VI. SEXUAL ATTITUDES IN SECOND-
     CENTURY CHRISTIANITY   120

Greco-Roman moral dualism

Sexual asceticism in Gentile Christianity

Hermas and "spiritual" marriage

Marcion and Cassianus

Justin and Tatian

The Valentinians' married Jesus

Athenagoras and Irenaeus

VII. SEXUAL ATTITUDES IN EARLY
      ORTHODOXY   142

Tertullian's sexual asceticism

Clement's biblical perspective

Origen the eunuch

Jesus the bridegroom

Virginity the chief virtue

Pagan roots of monasticism

VIII. SEXUAL ATTITUDES IN ROMAN
CATHOLICISM   164

Jerome's horror of sex
Augustine's antisexual attitude
Aquinas' block against sexuality
Effects of medieval celibacy
Sin and sex in modern history

IX. THE SIGNIFICANCE OF THE QUESTION   187

Residual asceticism and docetism
The offensiveness of celibacy
The relevance of Jesus' marital ethic
Notes   197
Indexes
  Biblical texts   235
  General   237

PREFACE

There are a number of people to whom I owe a special word of gratitude. I am indebted to the Davis and Elkins College community for fifteen years of living in an atmosphere of academic freedom. My perspective on human culture has been widened by teaching a broad range of subjects and by the interdisciplinary conversations that are a part of everyday life at that liberal arts institution. More specifically I am deeply grateful to Dean Thomas R. Ross, who initiated the sabbatical leave program that has permitted the leisure for researching this book. My Religion and Philosophy Department colleague, Professor Donald Walter, has given perspicacious advice from the inception of this study onward.

I acknowledge also my indebtedness to Princeton Theological Seminary, where my embryonic ideas on the subject of this book have gestated. I would like to thank President James McCord, who invited me to Princeton as a Visiting Fellow; Dr. Charles Willard, who provided for my research needs at Speer Library; and Professors Bruce Metzger, Karlfried Froehlich, and David Hay for their helpful criticisms and encouragement.

Finally I thank Martha Ann, Charles, Anna, and Ruth, who have confirmed for me that "it is not good for man to be alone." I dedicate this book to my wife who, like the biblical figure who shares her name, has learned from Jesus that "man does not live by bread alone."

Bill Phipps

Elkins, W. Va.

Chapter I

TACKLING A TABOO
QUESTION

Most Christians have the unquestioned belief that Jesus renounced marriage and that celibacy must therefore be a holier way of life, at least for some people. This perspective is also the considered judgment of the vast majority of Christians scholars. For example, Philip Schaff, a conservative Protestant church historian, writes: "The Son of God and Savior of the world was too far above all the daughters of Eve to find an equal companion among them."[1] D. Sherwin Bailey, a liberal Anglican scholar, speaks of Jesus' "choice of the single life as a necessary condition for the fulfillment of his messianic vocation."[2] Although his study is well-documented, Bailey gives no evidence for that categorical statement. Helmut Thielicke, a contemporary German Lutheran, maintains that "Jesus himself was unmarried. He also demanded of his disciples the renunciation of family ties."[3] The traditional Roman Catholic position has been expressed anew in a 1967 encyclical by Pope Paul VI:

Christ remained throughout his whole life in the state of celibacy, which signified his total dedication to the service of God and men. This deep connection between celibacy and the priesthood of Christ is reflected in those whose fortune it is to share in the dignity and mission of the Mediator and eternal Priest; this sharing will be more perfect the freer the sacred minister is from the bonds of flesh and blood.[4]

These clerical positions on Jesus' marital status harmonize well with attitudes expressed by Christian laymen. This was amply demonstrated by the letters I received in response to an initial brief article in a theological quarterly, in which I advanced the hypothesis that Jesus married.[5] My views were picked up by an international newsmagazine and widely publicized in the newspapers and over the air for their sensational appeal. From the general public came a voluminous and overwhelmingly negative response. Quite a few people expressed disgust at the suggestion that Christ came "down" to our human level. They reflected either an implicit or explicit belief that celibacy was a better way of life for the truly spiritual person. Only common men, they claimed, should have physical association with women. One asked, "Does not the word Jesus mean passionless and sexless?" An Australian Mormon, evidently not realizing her church's historic position on Jesus' plural marriages, asserted that Jesus could not have been capable of reproduction since he was essentially a neuter spirit.

In addition to theological objections, many people expressed strong moral objections to the idea of Jesus being married. And there was the underlying assumption that sex in itself is necessarily sinful. "Minds which are in the truth and not in the gutter," said one, would realize that a perfectly sinless creaure could not have married. Another urged me "to love Christ as the Supreme and Holy Being who is all good, and certainly incapable of love affairs and other lowly things." Still another respondent maintained that "marriage is a holy sacrament only when the couple has chaste intentions to live together without sex-life."

Also included in the potpourri of responses are people who take for granted a deep cleavage between Jewish and Christian norms of sexual morality. In my article I quoted from the records of ancient Jewish tradition in the Mishnah and Talmud in describing the moral environment that Jesus inherited. Some critics held this to be an illegitimate procedure, saying that Jesus repudiated Jewish tradition as worthless and felt no constraints from the culture in which he was born and bred. One respondent claimed that Jesus was crucified because he rejected such Jewish cultural institutions as marriage. The most antisemitic rebuff came from one who challenged the report that I was a Presbyterian. He thought I was really a Jew who was attempting to slander Jesus by assuming that he would have followed the "corrupt" marital standards of Judaism.

Just the thought of inquiring into Jesus' marital status alarms many Christians. One wrote: "Even if Jesus was married, why bring up this smear now?" More than one letter called my conjecture that Jesus was sexually alive a greater sacrilege than the declaration by some faddish theologians that God is dead.

Attitudes such as these, on the part of laymen and theologians alike, show that the belief is widespread in contemporary Christendom that celibacy was chosen by Jesus, and is for that reason a superior way of life. Because of that choice many have wondered if sex is in some way inherently defiled and counter to man's purest nature. Any amount of writing to the effect that sex is a potentially wholesome part of God's good creation loses it's impact on anyone who continues to think of religious celibates as demonstrating a better way. Such views convince me of the need to clarify the biblical outlook on sexuality and Jesus' relation to it. Consequently, in this book I will study seriously and thoroughly the question: Was Jesus married?

THE TIMELINESS OF THIS INQUIRY

An inquiry into Jesus' marital status is at once both compelling and forbidding. It is compelling because it involves a theme relevant to our time: the sanctity of the physical. There is a growing awareness now that a healthy integration of mind and body— which was characteristic of biblical culture—has been generally lacking throughout the history of Western civilization. Moral dualism has been pervasive, causing Western man to try to separate his godly spirit from his devilish flesh. Ascetic renunciation of those sensual impulses that give pleasure when gratified has been considered essential for those who exemplify pure spirituality. Yet Jesus belonged to a culture that emphasized the psychosomatic wholeness of personality. Thus there is an urgent need for Western man to raise basic historical and theological questions about Jesus' sexuality, that is, his involvement in the broad range of male-female interactions.

But such an inquiry is forbidding because there is no already beaten path prepared by the explorations of previous scholars. Few have ventured to blaze a trail into this obscure area because it is overgrown with cultic taboos. Even though Jesus is the most influential figure in the history of mankind, and though sexuality is a vital part of us all, there is a conspicuous void of studies that focus on Jesus' sexuality. The subject is overlooked not only by the many devotional treatments of Jesus' life, but also by the critical studies that stress Jesus' humanity. On virtually every other aspect of Jesus' life painstaking and detailed monographs have been written. Indeed, there are more scholarly books treating his life than years since his death. But an examination of literally hundreds of "lives of Jesus" that have been written in various European languages reveals only a rare raising of the question of Jesus' sexual viewpoint. Moreover, reasons are usually not given by those who accept the dogma that Jesus rejected marriage. Evidently they assume, quite unscientifically, that either private intuition or hoary tradition makes that dogma indubitable. This absence is especially enigmatic since marriage was the one social institution that Jesus blessed and used in his parables to illustrate the Gospel.

Two factors in current scholarship make this an appropriate time for an intensive probe into the relationship between the historical Jesus and marriage. One is the recent lifting of the scholarly moratorium on the study of the historical Jesus.[6] At the turn of the twentieth century Albert Schweitzer brilliantly exposed the shallow scholarship of European theologians who wrote so-called lives of Jesus.[7] He found that nearly all of them uncritically assumed that Jesus' outlook mirrored the worldview of Western man. They shared the egocentric predicament of human nature that is continually in conflict with scientific inquiry. When they looked down through the murky well of history at the founder of their religion, they were predisposed to see little more than a reflection of themselves at the bottom. But thanks to the heightened self-consciousness resulting from social science studies, we are becoming more aware of our prejudices and are better prepared to combat them. As a result there is a renewed interest in objective studies in the history of religion.

Viewing the life of Jesus with objectivity is an unattainable ideal even if the historian's bias is diminished. The main problem is that the writers of the authoritative records about Jesus had little biographical interest. The Gospel evangelists and the apostle Paul were not preoccupied with a quest for the historical Jesus. However, it is possible through biblical scholarship to establish a modicum of solid facts about Jesus, to find a considerable amount of empirical data about his culture, and on the basis of these two factors, to assess judiciously some probabilities about his life style that we would not otherwise know.

The findings of modern social and biological research in the whole area of human sexuality are the second factor that makes an inquiry into Jesus' sexuality pertinent today. Apart from the latent assumption contained in most treatments of the life of Jesus, it has been generally recognized throughout history that sexuality is not an elective that a man can voluntarily take or leave. Even the medieval monk Thomas Aquinas recognized that only the instinct of self-preservation is rooted more deeply in human nature than sex.[8] He believed that by nature man is even more a conjugal animal than a political animal.[9] In this century Sigmund Freud has inferred on the basis of clinical observation that the sexual impulse is not only inseparable from human behavior, it is the basic ingredient in human nature. He has broadened the concept of sexuality to apply to prepuberty development as well as to adult male-female interactions. At the same time the science of genetics has shown modern man that sexuality is fundamental to highly developed plants and animals and is a quality intrinsic to every cell composing the human organism.

Emil Brunner is indebted to modern studies of sexuality when he writes:

We cannot say that humanity is divided into the "sanguine" and the "choleric" temperament, into extroverts and introverts, into white or colored races, into geniuses and non-geniuses; but humanity certainly is divided into men and women, and this distinction goes down to the very roots of our personal existence. . . . Sexual disposition is not something purely natural—as is, for instance, the digestive system. It helps to determine the whole psychical and even the spiritual nature of the man and the woman.[10]

In another work he follows up this point of view with the declaration: "Without sexuality there can be no full humanity."[11]

Since this neo-orthodox theologian accepts the Chalcedon formula and thereby believes that Jesus is "complete in manhood," one would expect him to discuss Jesus' sexuality in his systematic theology. But there is no such treatment even in the chapters devoted to the humanity of Jesus.[12] Rather, Brunner shows that the European mores he has inculcated have given him a mental block: "Shame accompanies . . . sex-relations in marriage. . . . We cannot think of our Lord as married."[13]

Brunner is not atypical of those who write in the field of Christology. They generally agree that someone from whom masculinity or femininity was absent would not be a human personality. They also believe, at least in theory, that Jesus was fully human. If pushed, they might follow their logic and admit that Jesus was not sexless. Yet the practical implications of the weighty proposition that Jesus was sexual are hardly ever worked out. Instead, conventional theologians discreetly keep Christology and sexology in separate compartments.

Hence two lines of approach for a study of Jesus' sexuality emerge. The inductive historical approach consists of judiciously examining the biblical and extrabiblical records related to Jesus' life. It includes probing ancient documents that give insight into the sociology of Palestinian Judaism in Jesus' time. The other approach is a priori, deducing the libidinous implications that are contained in the affirmation that Jesus was a real man. Neither of these basic modes of reasoning has been systematically applied to the study of Jesus' sexuality. Both approaches will be utilized here, although the historical and empirical approaches will predominate.

PAST POSITIONS ON JESUS' SEXUALITY

A look at the few furtive treatments of Jesus' sexuality that have been made in modern history will serve as a springboard into this study. There have been a handful of iconoclasts from a variety of historical and cultural backgrounds who have suggested ways in which Jesus may have expressed his sexuality in his life situation. One of these has hypothesized that Jesus may have been homosexually oriented, and several have held that he had a heterosexual pattern of behavior.

At an Oxford conference in 1967, Canon Hugh Montefiore, an

Anglican theologian, suggested that Jesus may have had homosexual tendencies.[14] He drew this conclusion from coupling the
assumption that Jesus never married with the fact that he had
close masculine companions. Montefiore stated his point in a
vague way:

It is precisely my concern to show Christ's complete identification
with mankind that raises for me a question about our Lord's celibacy.
I raise it with reference to those thirty "hidden years" at Nazareth
when it seems as yet he did not know either his vocation to be Messiah
or his status as Son of God. . . . Why did he not marry? Could the
answer be that Jesus was not by nature the marrying sort? I want to
make it crystal clear that when I suggest this possible answer, no question of Jesus being less than perfect was or is involved or implied. It
is of course important not to confuse temptation with sin. . . . This
kind of speculation can be valuable if it underlines . . . how God in
Christ identifies himself with the outsider and the outcast from society.[15]

If some find Montefiore's speculation plausible, it may be due
to the effeminate way that Jesus has sometimes been represented.
Artists have sometimes used women as models for paintings of
Jesus in order to capture his tender qualities on canvas. The
Madonna figure, which has been dominant in Christian art, also
conveys the notion that Jesus was always in the hands of his strong
pure mother but out of touch with Joseph. Such a pattern of
parental relations is often symptomatic of homosexuality. Donald
J. West states: "Males who have had a combination of dominating,
possessive, sexually prudish mother, and a weak, absent or aloof
father, risk developing sexual difficulties in general and homosexual
orientation in particular."[16] Another association that may cause a
suspicion of homosexuality in Jesus is the condition of some who
profess to imitate him closely. It is no secret that the celibate
priesthood attracts a significantly larger number of people with
homosexual tendencies than most other vocations. Marc Oraison,
a physician-priest, has written:

Clinical findings sometimes give us pause. In an important French
seminary a specialist who conducted psychological examinations ascer-
tained that seventy per cent of the young men—median age of twenty

one—had no father psychologically speaking, a widowed mother, a weak father who was hardly "present," or a sick and infirm father.[17]

If the prototype is assumed to be like clerics who have traditionally worn ladylike gowns, it is easy to see why some might wonder if Jesus were a homosexual.

Although some of the artistic and cultic expressions of Christianity do suggest that Jesus was effeminate, there is no biblical basis for this assumption. As will be described later, Jesus was considerably more independent of Mary and more associated with Joseph than artistic stereotypes indicate. Moreover, the Hebrews distinguished themselves sharply from such cultures as the Greek and the Roman by regarding homosexuality as an "abomination" and punishable by death.[18] There can be little doubt that Jesus, like Paul, regarded homosexuality as a perversion of the created order.[19] Had Jesus by some quirk of his early home environment become a latent or patent homosexual, it is hard to see how he could have gained leadership in a culture where homosexuality was not tolerated. Or at the very least, if Jesus possessed such an extraordinary temperament, we would expect to find some reference to it in the Gospels or in the early anti-Christian literature. As shall be argued later, it is the unconventional practices of a person that are more likely to be remembered and recorded. Montefiore begs the question when he argues that Jesus had a homosexual aversion to marriage since he never married.

Then there are those writers who treat Jesus as a man of normal heterosexual temperament. At least one scholar has conjectured that Jesus was sexually interested in women and married. Several writers show him to have had desire for the opposite sex even though they believe he did not marry.

John Erskine suggests that Jesus had a wife and children during those two decades of young manhood that are unmentioned in the Gospels. He speculates that the wedlock became a deadlock:

It does not seem improbable that he did fall in love and had some experience of parenthood. . . . He understood women very well indeed, with the special understanding of a man who has been hurt by one of them. . . . I think he early met someone who charmed but who was unworthy, someone he idealized, and by whom he was cruelly disillusioned. . . . The Gospels indicate that Jesus had an extraordinary fondness for children, and a special understanding of the relation between father and son. It is evident that he exerted upon women of various temperaments a strong fascination. . . . The father of the prodigal son is not a portrait of Joseph, but the record of human yearning for a child. Whether these emotions in Jesus ever attached themselves to particular objects, the story does not say, but his character renders it for me utterly impossible that his youth and manhood could have been unmoved by warm, human emotions. . . . If he really took our nature upon him and was human, then he had our equipment of sex.[20]

Tom F. Driver shares Erskine's general point of view although he does not carry the romantic reflections as far. With respect to the Gospels, Driver says: "The absence of all comment in them about Jesus' sexuality cannot be taken to imply that he had no sexual feelings." He further testifies:

It is not shocking, to me at least, to imagine Jesus moved to love according to the flesh. I cannot imagine a *human* tenderness, which the Gospels show to be characteristic of Jesus, that is not fed in some degree by the springs of passion. The human alternative to sexual tenderness is not asexual tenderness but sexual fear. Jesus lived in his body, as other men do.[21]

Some leaders of the early Mormon church believed that Jesus married and married often! Not long after the Mormon pioneers settled in Utah their president, Orson Hyde, argued that Jesus was a polygamist, having married a woman called Martha and more than one called Mary. He wrested biblical support that Jesus married and had children from the suffering servant passage of Isaiah. In Isaiah 53:10 it is prophesied: "He shall see his offspring." These words were interpreted as a literal description of Jesus, who would be born centuries later.[22] In a sermon delivered at Salt Lake City Hyde elaborated further: "There was a marriage in Cana of Galilee. . . . Jesus Christ was married on that occasion. If he was never married, his intimacy with Mary, Martha, and the other Mary also, who Jesus loved, must have been highly unbecoming and improper, to say the best of it."[23] The confession of one of

Brigham Young's wives indicates that the founder of the Utah colony agreed with Hyde:

Brigham Young, in one of his sermons . . . declared that "Jesus Christ was a practical polygamist; Mary and Martha, the sisters of Lazarus, were his plural wives, and Mary Magdalene was another. Also, the bridal feast at Cana of Galilee, where Jesus turned the water into wine, was on the occasion of one of his own marriages."[24]

How can this astounding speculation be judged? Polygamy was practiced by some of the Hebrew patriarchs and is never explicitly forbidden in the Old or New Testaments. However, monogamy was the usual pattern in Hebrew culture and polygamy was rarely practiced by the Jews in the era of earliest Christianity or afterward.[25] Even if the New Testament stated that Jesus was married, it would be unwarranted to assume that this meant that he had more than one wife.

The motivation behind this early Mormon view may parallel the motivation behind the traditional view that Jesus was celibate. The New Testament does not mention Jesus' marital status but the sociology of ancient Judaism shows that neither of the above views, and especially the latter, would have been at all probable for a Jewish man of Jesus' time. However medieval churchmen thought that holy men should be celibate. Consequently, monks with much zeal and little historical knowledge projected their ideal onto the New Testament Jesus. The same projection of cultural values was displayed in the early Mormon efforts to make Jesus the model man in the pioneer Utah community. In all of this there is an attempt to read history backward.

Others have assumed that Jesus had normal sexual impulses but renounced marriage. Nikos Kazantzakis presents Jesus as a continent bachelor in *The Last Temptation of Christ*. In his imaginative reconstruction some features are added to the traditional characterization. Jesus is not only the son of a virgin and one who raises the dead, but he is also one who struggles with sexual temptation. He desires to take Mary Magdalene, a prostitute, as his wife. A devilish voice speaks within: "Take her! God created man and woman to match, like the key and the lock. Open her. Your

children sit huddled together and numb inside her, waiting for you
to blow away their numbness so that they may rise and come out
to walk in the sun."[26] With a realism drawn from the peasant
habits of Mediterranean folk culture that Kazantzakis knew so
well, Jesus is depicted in anguish. His sexual instinct is at fisticuffs
with his godly impulse. Heroically Jesus resists his desire for a wife
in order to fulfill his spiritual vocation.

Catholic officialdom appraised Kazantzakis' novel as vulgar and
heretical and in 1953 it was placed on the Index of banned books.
Nevertheless, Michael Novak reviewed it favorably in a Roman
Catholic publication:

Since Kazantzakis pivots the narrative upon the relationship between
Jesus and Mary Magdalene (a mutual love which he in the main
handles with taste and respect), he reminds us that in fact we don't
understand very well Christ's sex life. . . . It is notable that Christ's
entourage in the later days of his public life consistently included
women. How did he feel towards them? How was his affection shown?
What is it like to be pure entirely? And without prudishness?[27]

In a Protestant journal Kyle Haselden also expresses appreciation
for Kazantzakis' treatment: "In a day when the sweet, lulling in-
cense of docetism is heavy in the theological air, we need the
artist's pungent reminder that our Lord was one 'who in every
respect has been tempted as we are, yet without sinning.'"[28]

Kazantzakis assumes that the Incarnate One combatted the
carnal, and he succeeds in depicting this better than most writers.
However he imposes a polarity between the impure flesh and the
pure spirit that is non-Hebraic. Kazantzakis betrays that the traditional Greek moral dichotomy between body and soul is still a basic
part of his moral outlook. By contrast, in the Gospels the real tension
within Jesus is caused by the impulse to carry out his own selfish
wishes rather than the will of God.[29] This is a matter independent
of the question of whether to marry. Selfishness or unselfishness
is no respecter of marital status. Perhaps the reason that there
is no allusion to Jesus' "last temptation" in the Gospels is that
Jesus saw no necessary opposition between responding to the
natural desire for marriage instilled in him by God the Creator and
responding to the divine mission inspired by God the Redeemer.

Martin Luther presented still another point of view. It seems that he thought that Jesus, along with unmarried men in general, was incontinent. In 1532 Pastor John Schlaginhaufen recorded this comment of his friend Luther:

Christ was an adulterer for the first time with the woman at the well, for it was said, "Nobody knows what he's doing with her" (John 4:27). Again with Magdalene, and still again with the adulterous woman in John 8, whom he let off so easily. So the good Christ had to become an adulterer before he died.[30]

Can this astonishing report be accurate? It has been included for centuries in the standard works of Luther, edited by various devout Lutheran scholars. As Arnold Lunn says: "No editor who was not mentally defective could include such a passage unless he was convinced that is was genuine."[31]

How could Luther have uttered such seeming slander regarding Jesus? Even though the comment was off-the-cuff "table talk," it fits into his attitude toward sexuality. Luther believed that the satisfaction of all physical appetites was necessary.[32] Consequently, he held that a vow of continence was as impossible to fulfill as a vow to create the stars, or to grow as old as Methuselah.[33] Sexual indulgence between a closely associated man and woman was as inevitable as the burning of dry straw when ignited.[34] He also maintained that women would be used by men either as wives or as prostitutes.[35]

If Luther's assumptions about sex are understood, it is easy to see how he could have declared that Jesus fornicated. Jesus' hunger for food and drink was substantially gratified throughout life, even though satisfaction was at times delayed or incomplete. If the need for the opposite sex is as demanding as the need for water by a thirsty man, then obviously every man, Jesus included, must satisfy the dictates of his organism.

Although it is possible to find some logical consistency in Luther's position, it should be recognized that there is no historical basis for his allegation that Jesus "was an adulterer." Luther's personal outlook on the unrestrainable nature of sexual desire tells us nothing about the actual conduct of Jesus. As in Montefiore's case, there is circular logic in Luther's position. He seemed to think that since Jesus was unmarried he must have been promiscuous. Neither theologian doubted the premise that Jesus was unmarried.

A nearly exhaustive range of possible conjectures on ways in which Jesus could have expressed his sexuality have been presented. The only common link that Montefiore, Erskine, Driver, Hyde, Young, Kazantzakis, and Luther share is the assumption that if Jesus was fully human he had sexual desire. The positions of these bold image-breakers have usually been ignored or rejected as absurd and obscene, and there has been little attempt to cultivate the seminal ideas that any of them has planted in order to understand the life of Jesus more adequately.

HYPOTHESIS CLARIFICATION

Along with all orthodox Christians I believe that Jesus was fully human and, endorsing the sciences of man, I think that sexual desire is intrinsic to human nature. I do not agree with Luther that this desire is so irrepressible among the heterosexually oriented that all must gratify it by coitus. However this means of gratification, in the context of marriage, has been the ordinary way in which most humans throughout history have attempted to deal with a basic psychological as well as physical need. The question that concerns me is whether there are sufficient grounds in the sources pertaining to the life and times of Jesus to substantiate the common assumption that he followed a different pattern of sexual behavior from that of most other humans.

The Gospels do not record Jesus as having stated either that he was a virgin or that he was the son of a virgin. Likewise, the earliest book of church history, Acts, shows that those who were closest to Jesus give no hint of knowing any special virginal conditions associated with him. In light of this it seems more plausible that Jesus and his family accepted the prevailing mores of his culture with respect to sex and marriage and that his earliest interpreters understood this to be the case.

Jesus was reared in the tradition of Palestinian Judaism that survived the destruction of the Jewish state in A.D. 70 and was preserved in the Mishnah and in the Talmud. As an adult, Jesus, like other rabbis, was sharply critical of certain aspects of that tradition. However, George F. Moore, the leading authority on Judaism in the first Christian century, demonstrates that Jesus' ethic was usually in line with the mores of the rabbis.[36] Samuel Sandmel, a Jewish specialist on that same period, agrees with Moore, and believes that the evidence from Qumran manuscripts does not make Moore's position obsolete.[37] He writes:

We can see in early first century Judaism the impulses which developed into Rabbinism and Christianity. Qumran, though, represents a dead end. . . . Earliest Christianity grew out of the Judaism of the synagogue. . . . Data about customs . . . culled from the Rabbinic Literature can help us understand many of the implicit suppositions of the Gospels.[38]

Rabbi Joseph Klausner, who wrote one of the most scholarly studies of Jesus' life, agrees with Julius Wellhausen's quip: "Jesus was not a Christian: he was a Jew." Even more forcefully Klausner says that Jesus "was a Jew in every respect" and "a Jew he remained till his last breath."[39] An eminent Christian authority on the New Testament, Frederick C. Grant, asserts: "Certainly Jesus was a complete and thorough Jew. . . . He was no Greek philosopher in disguise . . . or ascetic. The thorough Jewishness of Jesus is assumed by all present-day scholars competent to judge."[40]

Since there is scholarly consensus on Jesus' acceptance of Jewish moral standards, subsequent chapters will scrutinize biblical and extrabiblical literature concerning the perspective on sex and marriage of ancient Judaism and Jewish Christianity of the first century. Also germane is an inquiry into the probable impact upon Jesus of Joseph, John the Baptist; and the various women with whom he was associated. Within a chronological framework, the roots and the fruits of the doctrine that Jesus never married will be traced. The infiltration of Hellenistic asceticism into the post-apostolic church caused a dramatic switch in sexual values. It appears that many Christians still have in the back of their minds the Greek-originated notion that sexual passion pollutes purity. Finally, I will consider the potential impact of the contention that Jesus was married. If such an opinion becomes widely endorsed, it should have a beneficial effect on the Christian church and on the quality of life that Western man idealizes as truly human.

Chapter II

SEXUAL ATTITUDES IN ANCIENT JUDAISM

In reviewing the salient aspects of the Jewish traditions on sex and marriage, attention must be given to the Genesis doctrine of creation, in part because Jesus quoted from it when asked about marriage. This doctrine is also significant because early Christians believed that Jesus was the "last Adam," or "the second man,"[1] and that his destiny was to live out faithfully the life that God had originally intended for all men. Also to be considered are such sociological matters as the role of Hebrew fathers in arranging betrothals and the customary age of marriage. All extant records of ancient Judaism will be probed to see if lifelong celibacy was sanctioned by any groups or individuals.

THE GENESIS OF SEXUALITY

In the two Genesis accounts of creation, sex is seen to be a gift of God like the rest of the created order. Its potential for good is found not in the solitary male or female but in the couple who blend together to form a total human. It is significant that in both accounts the marital union of man and woman climaxes God's creative acts. This place in the order of creation indicates that human sexuality is endowed with more grandeur than other aspects of the natural world. It is provided for man's happiness and is judged by God to be "very good." David Mace shows how this outlook affected the ancient Jewish view of sex: "The Hebrews so ordered their community life that no one was likely to be left in the condition of prolonged sexual frustration. Sex was a gift of God, and it was given to be used."[2] Mace quotes a famous Jewish saying to express the characteristic outlook: "A man will have to give account on the judgment day of every good thing which he refused to enjoy when he might have done so."[3]

In the Priestly account of the sixth day of creation, the female and her mate are both infused with the "likeness" of God. The themes of woman's equality with man and of their incompleteness apart from each other are both struck in Genesis 1:27–28. Johannes Pedersen comments apropos this account:

Singular and plural are used indifferently about the same being. Man is a whole consisting of two parts, the man and the woman. Nothing is said of the relation between them, except that they are indispensable to each other, and not till they are united do they together form a whole human being.[4]

The Priestly writer also referred to man being in the image of God after the flood story, so he apparently thought of this original male-female relation to God as continuous in history.

In Genesis 1:28, the first blessing of God is associated with the union of the two sexes. This basic theme of the blessedness of sexual relations within marriage echoes throughout all subsequent treatments of sex and marriage in Judaism. Israel Abrahams, an authority on Jewish marital ethics, writes: "The act of sexual intercourse was consciously elevated . . . from an animal function to a fulfillment of the divine plan announced at the Creation."[5] Appropriately, the ordinary Jewish term for marriage, *kiddushin*, comes from a root meaning holy. Since holiness is related to wholeness in Jewish theology, the union of husband and wife sanctifies life.

The Priestly writer assumed that procreation was the prime purpose of marriage and that God's first command was: "Be fruitful and multiply." In Judaism this purpose became valued as a major reason—although not the exclusive one—for marriage. In the first century before the Christian era, the leading schools of Hillel and Shammai, while differing on many points, agreed on this: "No one may abstain from keeping the law, 'Be fruitful and multiply.' "[6]

To supplement the Priestly epic of creation, the Pentateuch editors included the "Yahwist" story. Recorded in Genesis 2:4–24, that story was an earlier and more picturesque composition, focusing on the creation of animate nature. Its setting is Eden, symbol of the perfect environment where YHWH and his creatures live harmoniously. Man, a compound of mud and divine inspiration, is a social being like the Potter who made him.

Considerable ingenuity is exercised to find man a partner (*azar*) that will satisfy his gregariousness. It is unfortunate that *azar* is usually translated "helper," an English term often associated with a servile position. Throughout Scripture *azar* refers to either a superior or an equal, but never an inferior. For example, in Psalm 46 an *azar* is an essential support and refuge for man. In Genesis 2, when the beasts and birds are passed in review, man finds no *azar* among them even though they come from the elements of the earth like himself. Those animals are treated as things to be named and classified—inferior objects, not subjects evoking delight. Only when a rib is removed from man's own anatomy is an *azar* created and man's celibate condition relieved.

The symbolism of the rib is important in understanding the Hebraic view of sexual relations. Coming from the bosom, it connoted an intimate friend. Just as we speak of a "sweetheart," the Semitic people speak of an affectionate "rib."[7] Unlike the other animals, this rib was on man's level, worthy of becoming his partner. Man, whose solitariness was now cured, bursts into song: "This at last is bone of my bone and flesh of my flesh!" The first words of man display his primary social preoccupation throughout history. His interest in finding a woman is even stronger than his interest in his parental home, so he leaves it in order to cleave to his wife.

The meaning of Genesis 2:24 is especially significant for the hypothesis being defended here. When asked for his views on marriage, Jesus quoted this verse, which affirms that the couple become "one flesh." He thus showed that he had no personal opinion that superseded the ideal presented in Genesis. The key to understanding Genesis 2:24 is realizing the many facets of the Hebrew term *basar* ("flesh"). Unlike the later Hellenistic concept of flesh, there was no Hebraic dichotomy between the tainted flesh and the higher soul. For the Hebrews a human was not a spirit wearing a garment of flesh; rather, the total self was called flesh. Thus, in Genesis 2:24, "one flesh" basically means one whole self. Other meanings of *basar* have subordinate bearing on this verse: the genitals, a kinship tie, and mortals in contrast to God.[8] By combining these varied meanings we find that this verse refers to a bond similar to that with blood relations—a union of genital organs as well as a psychological merging into one human life. The masculine ego and its feminine alter ego are spliced together in such a way that individuality is preserved.

The celibate Ruud J. Bunnik testifies that he finds confirmation here of the scientific judgment "that an unmarried person is in some way unfinished, and truncated; both his biological and psychological structure ask for a complementary partner."[9] On the basis of his findings in psychiatry, Sigmund Freud writes: "A man shall leave father and mother—according to the biblical precept—and cleave to his wife, then are tenderness and sensuality united."[10] Concerning the relationship between Freud's judgment and the Jewish outlook, David Bakan states: "Freud had as a norm the so-called 'genital' form of sexuality, most adequately realized in marriage. The Talmud and the whole orthodox tradition had pressed the marital form of sexuality into normative position."[11]

Thus the two creation accounts both affirm marriage, the older one stressing the companionship motive and the later one stressing the procreative aim. The rest of the Genesis saga continues to illustrate the ancient Jewish view of sexual relations.

What association is there, if any, between sex and the serpent's temptation? The common interpretation of the serpent as a sex symbol was given in the patristic era[12] and has subsequently become widespread in Christendom. It has inspired the quip that original sin was not caused by an apple on a tree but by a pear (pair) on the ground! This interpretation is based on: 1) the assumption that the serpent is used to represent the phallus; 2) the fact that sexual relations between Adam and Eve are not explicitly mentioned until after the serpent episode; and 3) the desire of Adam and Eve to cover their nakedness after grasping for the prohibited "knowledge."

It is true that in the mythology of fertility cults the serpent sometimes symbolizes the phallus. But there is no suggestion in the context of the Yahwist story that the serpent signifies any kind of mythological creature. Gerhard von Rad comments: "What distinguishes it a little from the rest of the animals is exclusively its greater cleverness."[13] Because if its sly movements, the Hebrews found the snake an apt symbol for shrewdness.[14] In response to the second reason above, there is implicit evidence of sexual intercourse before the encounter with the serpent. In Genesis 2:24–25 the husband "clings" to and becomes "one flesh" with his wife while both are nude. It was the prevailing Jewish view that conjugal relations in Paradise preceded the temptation.[15] Thirdly, the forbidden fruit does not signify sexual desire and its satisfaction. Rather, the story points out that the fruit symbolizes "knowledge of good and evil." That Hebrew idiom refers not to carnal knowledge, but to knowledge in toto.[16] Therefore, Genesis 3 tells of humans intoxicated by hubris, feigning omniscience. This arrogance causes alienation and guilt between man and woman. As a result they naïvely assume that they can hide from one another by wearing fig leaf aprons. This is as futile as their attempt to escape from YHWH by hiding among the trees. Thus there is no textual evidence here that sexual relations are intrinsic to human sin. Rather, sin is haughty pride that rebels against creaturehood status and uses irresponsibly the good gifts God has provided in the natural order.

Misogynist interpreters of Genesis 3 have agreed with Adam's plea that Eve is to blame for his succumbing to temptation. But it is improbable that the Yahwist writer agreed with his male character. He indicates that both characters knew about the prohibited tree. Woman is portrayed as putting up more resistance than her mate, who eats without qualm. Also he expresses feminist sympathy by contrasting the pre-sin and post-sin roles of woman. The sentence passed on woman following YHWH's interrogation implies that male supremacy in history is a result of human sin. As we have seen, the wife does not have a servile status in the ideal created order.

The Yahwist writer suggests that monogamy is the Creator's intention for humanity. Polygamy, with its concomitant lowering of a wife's equal status, first appears in Genesis 4:19. There Lamech, a bigamist, is portrayed as even more despicable than his ancestor Cain. For the Yahwist, then, woman's inferior role was the result of the disruption of God's purpose. In neither creation account is one sex esteemed superior to the other.

"Adam knew (yada) Eve his wife and she conceived." This four-letter verb in Genesis 4:1 and throughout the Old Testament in similar contexts is considerably more profound than our vulgar verb for copulation. Yada is not a euphemism that the Hebrews employed because they were too embarrassed to speak more directly and candidly about coitus. They purposely used the same term for intellectual, spiritual, and carnal knowledge to indicate that sexual intercourse is more than a fusing of genitals. It was literally an inter-course, a flowing through of personalities that afforded a deep knowledge of the uninhibited self. It provided a unique means of self-revelation: there was not only a physical disrobing but a concomitant stripping away of psychological barriers.

In Genesis 5:1–2 the Priestly writer reiterated his basic doctrine: "When God created man, he made him in the likeness of God. Male and female he created them, and he blessed them and named them man." This passage was also interpreted in classical Judaism as showing the psychological and physical commingling of marriage. It was observed that "man is not even called man until united with woman."[17] Also, "the Divine Presence rests only upon a married man, because an unmarried man is but half a man."[18] It was believed that the marital state afforded a fuller self-realization.

Due to the humanizing qualities as well as the reproductive potentialites associated with marriage, it was mandatory for every righteous man to marry. One talmudic commentary on Scripture goes so far as to contend that the neglect of marriage not only abrogates those qualities that make a man human, but is a crime as serious as committing murder. Genesis 9:6–7 is used to support this position, because in that passage a law prohibiting murder is followed by the imperative to reproduce. Not to procreate was, in effect, to take the lives of potential offspring.[19]

HEBREW MARITAL CUSTOMS

The patriarchal saga presents a number of customs that express the sanctity of human sexuality. The earliest patriarchs began the practice of infant circumcision that was prominent throughout biblical history. In the New Testament Jesus was circumcised, and Paul thought the rite had value for Jewish Christians.[20] Far from being considered an obscene organ, the penis, with its cut foreskin, became the distinguishing mark of a Hebrew male. Martin Buber muses: "Sex is hallowed by the sacrament of the circumcision covenant which survives in its original purity and not only confirms the act of begetting but converts it into a holy vocation."[21] The dignity of the genitals is also displayed in a procedure for taking a solemn oath. In Genesis 24:3 a servant is asked to place his hand under the "thigh" of Abraham and swear by YHWH that he will find on his master's behalf a Hebrew bride for Isaac.

Genesis 24, which tells the story of Isaac and Rebekah's betrothal, depicts clearly Hebrew sex and marriage mores. Marriage was a covenant initiated by the heads of two families and consummated conjugally by the bride and groom. It was not a cultic rite solemnized by a priest at a shrine. The fathers or their agents negotiated a betrothal agreement, whereupon the boy's representative turned over the dowry payment (the *mohar*) to the girl's guardians.[22] The bridal couple played only an insignificant role in the transaction.

Scholarly descriptions of Hebrew marriage show that Abraham's arranging for Isaac's wedding was typical of the general practice in the biblical period. Roland de Vaux states: "The parents took all the decisions when a marriage was being arranged. Neither the girl nor, often, the youth was consulted."[23] Alfred Bertholet agrees:

It is the business of the parents, especially of the father, who is the embodiment of the family power and the family tradition, to secure suitable marriages for his children, especially for his sons; and the leanings or likings of the individuals concerned have little to do with the choice made.[24]

In our equalitarian era it is difficult to realize the extent of ancient parental domination in all aspects of conduct. A Hebrew father could sell his daughter into slavery and a rebellious son could be stoned to death.[25] Capital vengeance could be meted out for striking or cursing a parent.[26] Thus it was highly unlikely that a boy would disrespectfully reject a wife selected by his father.

The centrality of the father in matchmaking was a principle that the Hebrews shared with other ancient cultures. In Mesopotamia, the Babylonian and Assyrian codes show that the father chose wives for his sons.[27] Among the earliest and most respected laws of Rome were those giving the father absolute authority over his sons, including the right and obligation to arrange their marriages.[28] The impact of this ancient practice is still felt in the Middle East. Raphael Patai describes the current situation:

> Since the wife of a son became incorporated into his father's family, the choice of a wife was, under usual circumstances made, not by the son, but by the father or one of his trusted representatives. This was the rule in biblical times and has remained the prevalent custom in tradition-bound circles in the Middle East to the present day. . . . To procure a wife for himself without the payment of the bride price by his father is well nigh impossible for a young man in the traditional Middle Eastern family setup where all the property is controlled by the head of the family. This being the situation, there is no intrinsic need to consult the young man himself; he can be assumed to be amenable, driven as he is by his biological urges to marriage and dependent as he is on his father economically.[29]

At what age were marriages arranged? E. Neufeld replies: "From the general circumstances existing in the East in ancient times it can be assumed that children were married at a very early age—even before the age of puberty—but it seems that marriage was usually entered into soon after puberty."[30] This expert judgment is supported by an examination of chronological data in the Old Testament historical books. From the records of some Judean kings it can be deduced that teenage marriage was common in ancient Judaism.[31] Although there was no biblical law establishing a minimum or maximum age for marriage, it was the practice to marry quite young.

A comparative study reveals that early marriage was and is still the custom among tradition-oriented people in the Middle East. In Hittite,[32] Persian,[33] Greek,[34] and Roman[35] cultures it was a firmly established standard that marriage should follow immediately after puberty. According to Arabic tradition Mohammed said, "A man who has a child should give him proper training and should marry him on reaching puberty. If the child was not married then and committed an immoral act, the father was to be blamed."[36] In this century, Hilma Granqvist, on the basis of a field study of a Semitic village in Palestine, reports that marriage is generally at the time of puberty.[37]

Early betrothals were the by-product of the parental mate-selection custom. Virginity in unmarried girls was prized, so the earlier a father with an eligible daughter could arrange her betrothal the less would be his anxiety over mishaps. Also, the bride would more easily accept the ways of the husband's family if she married young. Then too, parents no doubt realized that children were more docile before they attained adulthood and would accept with less resistance the procured spouse.

In this marriage system, a couple often did not encounter, much less appreciate, one another until the betrothal. Isaac, for example, was not acquainted with Rebekah until she was brought to his home. For this reason there was necessarily a reversal of the romantic wooing sequence that modern Western culture takes for granted. The story of Isaac's betrothal concludes with this comment: "She became his wife, and he loved her." Whereas in Western courtship love often cools after marriage, in non-Western cultures the warmth of affection can only intensify after the wedding. That this was true of one of the patriarchs is shown by the frank comment: "Isaac was fondling Rebekah his wife."[38] Thus, among the married, the Hebrews sanctioned sexual play. One of them suggested that love making should be enthralling:

> Have your pleasure with the wife of your youth;
> A lovable doe! A sweet little mountain goat!
> May her breasts always intoxicate you!
> May you ever find rapture in loving her![39]

The Hebrews valued sexuality so highly that draft deferments were granted to newlyweds so that a husband might "rejoice with his wife."[40] Unlike the value structures of some modern governments, the Israelites gave higher priority to the fulfilling of marital responsibilities than to the duty to fight for one's country.

One of the most sensuous love songs in world literary classics is the Song of Songs. Its editors considered it to be Solomon's loveliest poem. It is permeated with unashamed expressions of hungry passion. Far from assuming that physical intercourse is deplorable, allowed only to prevent the extinction of the human species, that song points out its delights. Robert H. Pfeiffer writes:

Song of Songs is an anthology of erotic poems; . . . they depict with brilliant imagination and consummate art the thrills, delights, torments, and dreams of love between man and woman—love in the bud and in full bloom—against the background of the charming Palestinian countryside in the springtime.[41]

The permanent psychological bond of love is integrated with ardent sexual desire in the climax of the book.

It blazes up like flashes of fire,
Incandescent as lightning.
Raging rivers cannot quench love,
neither can floods sweep it away.[42]

Due to the emphasis placed on premarital courtship in Western civilization, the Song of Songs is easily misunderstood as an expression of the libidinous cravings of the unbetrothed. However, those lyrics were probably collected to be sung at a wedding celebration.[43] The frequently mentioned "bride" responds in a pure and natural way to her spouse on their "honeymoon." A. S. Herbert states that underlying the poems is the conviction that "through love's fulfillment in marriage human nature reaches the greatest heights of earthly experience."[44]

The fact that this piece of literature was revered in Palestine as the composition of the wisest king of Israel is another major piece of evidence affirming that the ancient Jews considered heterosexual desire and its passionate expression in marriage a beautiful thing. There is no evidence that the book was originally intended as an allegory showing YHWH's love for Israel or that it was interpreted as such in first-century Palestine.[45] The Song of Songs, interpreted simply as an articulation of human love, was a part of the culture inherited by Jesus and his fellow Jews.

Elsewhere in the Old Testament marriage is also viewed as the ideal state. Women who were eulogized were virtually always married. This is illustrated in one of the earliest and in one of the latest poems. Judges 5:7 extols Deborah, who "arose as a mother in Israel" and led her panicky people to victory. Proverbs concludes with an acrostic ode in praise of the varied talents of the home-maker. It calls a good wife "the crown of her husband."[46] Also, in prose, the books of Ruth, Esther, and Judith tell of married heroines.

As a corollary, no Hebrew wanted to remain a virgin throughout life. The tale of Jephthah is a dramatic example of this attitude. Jephthah's daughter was not upset on learning that she would be sacrificed because of her father's rash vow. She lamented not her death as such, but dying a virgin. So she requested time to "bewail her virginity" with her companions.[47] To go through life unmarried received as negative a valuation for men as for women. Marriage was expected in every vocation, including the priesthood.[48] Refraining from coitus was not a requirement of the Nazirites, even though they took other temporary vows of abstinence.[49]

The high value that the Hebrews placed on marriage is reflected in their attitude toward producing progeny. Childlessness caused social reproach, jeopardized social immortality, and was regarded as a mark of God's disfavor. Consequently, the patriarchal wife articulated the longing of all women of her culture when she cried: "Give me children or I shall die!"[50] The levirate custom—the custom obliging the brother of a dead man to marry his childless widow—arose to relieve the shameful condition of the childless wife as well as to provide offspring to carry forward the name of the deceased husband.

In light of the universal practice of marriage, why was there no biblical law forbidding celibacy? Ancient legal prohibitions arose out of pragmatic community needs. They were directed not against what no one did, but against the deviant behavior of some within the group. For example, in one of the oldest documents of history there is a proverb condemning celibacy: "He that supports no wife, he that supports no son, may his misfortunes be multiplied."[51] This curse implies that there were probably some in the Sumerian culture who preferred and lived the bachelor life. Likewise, if there were in the Mosaic code a law against celibacy, it would also mean that a few adults who could have found a spouse neglected to do so.

Throughout ancient Middle Eastern cultures the unmarried status was considered inferior. In the Semitic civilization this outlook is reflected in its languages. Ludwig Köhler calls attention to the fact that the Old Testament has no word for bachelor, so unusual was the idea.[52] Arabs, who follow the married prophet Mohammed, call the unmarried azab, meaning lonely. According to Moslem tradition the bachelor was Allah-forsaken: "Mohammed asked a man if he was married, and being answered in the negative, he said, 'Are you sound and healthy?' Upon the man replying that he was, Mohammed said, 'Then you are one of the devil's brothers.' "[53] Alfred Guillaume, in an article entitled "The Influence of Judaism on Islam," states: "There is general agreement in principle that celibacy is disgraceful and contrary to the law of God: marriage in both religions is not merely a state 'commended,' it is obligatory."[54] In Persia, Zarathustra, the founder of the Zoroastrian religion, had a wife and children and believed that it was through marriage that moral excellence could best come to maturity. In the scripture of Zoroastrianism, the good God Ahura Mazda says: "The man who has a wife is far above him who lives in continence."[55]

SEXUAL ASCETICISM AND JEWISH SCRIPTURES

In the Old Testament licit gratification of sexual passion was encouraged and marriage was a religious duty that every man took seriously. Further, there was virtually no moral contamination associated with marital intercourse and there are no instances of lifelong voluntary celibacy in the entire Old Testament history. Several alleged cases of sexual depreciation will be examined to defend these categorical assertions. Some assume that the Torah declares sexual intercourse to be morally unclean. It has also been thought that a psalmist was prejudiced against sex. Furthermore, many think there is historical evidence that Jeremiah was a lifelong celibate.

There are a few verses in the Torah that associate "uncleanliness" with sexual intercourse. The most prominent example is Leviticus 15:18: "If a man lies with a woman and has an emission of semen, both of them shall bathe themselves in water, and be unclean until evening." If that verse is examined in its context, it is seen that the Hebrews were concerned about the possible connection between some bodily discharges and illness. Their hygiene was rather primitive, and they suspected all emissions of possible venereal infection. As a precautionary disinfectant, clothes or bodies were washed after exposure to semen or menstrual blood. The Hebrews recognized that the sexual functions were both vital and mysterious. Since discharges were occasionally irregular and contagious, concern for self-preservation made it necessary to be wary of pathological conditions. Also, blood was a symbol of life that belonged to God, so there were rituals to protect its holiness. It is illegitimate to deduce from this cultic and medical cleansing that coitus was morally polluting. N. H. Snaith rightly states that the section in Leviticus dealing with sexual cleanness "has nothing to do with ethical matters."[56]

In Psalm 51:5 a penitent confesses: "I was brought forth in iniquity,/and in sin did my mother conceive me." Such Christian sexual ascetics as Origen, Ambrose, and Augustine have used this parallel couplet to prove that sex is related to human depravity.[57] At first glance it does look as though the sentiments expressed go against the affirmation of the goodness of sex in the creation accounts. But this is not its only interpretation, and it was never the one given by ancient Jews. David M. Feldman states that in the entire Talmud the marital act is never considered as being evil.[58] In interpreting the poetry of Psalm 51:5 one should not assume that the penitent is focusing on the act by which he was generated. Rather, while feeling guilty over some transgression, he reflects on his sinful tendency throughout life.

Scholars today agree that abstinence from marriage was unheard of in Old Testament history apart from the isolated instance of Jeremiah. But if Jeremiah never married then our hypothesis that Jesus married is considerably weakened. Jesus and his countrymen considered Jeremiah to be a prominent figure in the development of Judaism. If he believed that it was the will of YHWH to renounce copulation and procreation for his life, it is reasonable to suppose that this might have had some influence on Jesus.

There is one particular passage that has caused some to assume that Jeremiah was a lifelong celibate. In Jeremiah 16:1–4 he testifies:

The word of YHWH came to me: "You shall not take a wife, nor shall you have sons or daughters in this place. For thus says YHWH concerning the sons and daughters who are born in this place, and concerning the mothers who bore them and the fathers who begot them in this land: . . . They shall perish by the sword and by famine.

There is no indication in Jewish and in the earliest Christian literature that this passage was interpreted to mean that Jeremiah never married. However, from at least the fourth century until the present day, this has been the common Christian interpretation. The celibates Jerome[59] and Cassian[60] maintained that Jeremiah was a virgin throughout life. Lucien Legrand's review of virginity in the biblical era begins with Jeremiah, whom he believes to have been the first Hebrew to renounce marriage.[61]

When Jeremiah 16:1–4 is set within the entire framework of the prophet's teaching and activity, one gains quite a different understanding of his marital outlook and condition. Jeremiah was confronted with a Jerusalem citizenry who stubbornly believed that their city was inviolable. It was firm doctrine that YHWH would never allow Jerusalem to be destroyed because it was the focal point of the religious establishment. Witness of this was its miraculous deliverance in an earlier century when Assyrians besieged the city. But Jeremiah was convinced that it was YHWH's will that the Babylonians conquer Jerusalem. Eagerly he sought to have his people surrender at once to the inevitable conqueror and thereby avert death by disease, starvation, and the sword. He attempted to communicate this political outlook, but his fellow Jews closed their ears to what they considered unpatriotic and subversive. In a further effort to get them to change their aim, Jeremiah attempted to dramatize their impending plight in nonverbal ways. For a time he walked about wearing oxen yoke to portray the bondage that would come if Judah did not reverse its military policy.[62]

Jeremiah's abstinence from marital relations was also calculated to have a shock effect. Since to be without wife and children was a terrible disgrace, the lethargic public that he was attempting to arouse would realize that he was intensely serious if he gave up the connubial life to make his point. Jeremiah was convinced that if the status quo prevailed there would be certain destruction. Thus his sexual abstinence was purely a warning of national disaster. That he truly would have preferred the married life is shown indirectly in this tragic oracle: "I will make to cease . . . the voice of mirth and the voice of gladness, the voice of the bridegroom and the voice of the bride."[63]

The temporary nature of Jeremiah's symbolic act is evidenced in the phrase "in this place," twice repeated in Jeremiah 16:2–3. His actions at the time of the siege show that his continence was intended only for the duration of the war.[64] He purchased a plot of land,[65] indicating that he planned to settle down to normal married life if he survived the destruction of Jerusalem. He probably intended to act himself on the advice that he gave to the exiles —to build homes, take wives, and bear children.[66] Jerusalem was destroyed and the Babylonian conflict was over not long after Jeremiah's peace demonstrations. When that tragedy had passed, there would have been no point in his continuing his protest, either by wearing the undesirable oxen yoke or by refraining from the desirable connubial yoke.

LIFELONG CELIBACY AND THE ESSENES

Was there celibacy in ancient Judaism apart from biblical history? There was a sect of Essenes living in Palestine, and it is usually maintained that some of them believed that a permanent state of virginity was a requirement imposed by God. If this were true it would show that some Jews had renounced the first of the 613 divine precepts in the Torah. It would follow then that Jesus, even if he were not a member of the Essene sect, might have adopted their view toward marriage.

The Essene sect flourished in the two centuries prior to the Roman destruction of the Jewish state in A.D. 70. Until the Qumran discoveries of the past generation, information about the Essenes came from three secondary sources of the first century A.D., Philo, Pliny, and Josephus. The earliest of these sources states: "No Essene takes a wife."[67] But Philo also pointed out that the Essenes "are all full-grown men, already verging upon old age."[68] In harmony with this description Pliny wrote: "They have no wives, having renounced sexual love."[69] Josephus spoke of two different orders of Essenes. The major group scorned marriage but did not condemn it on principle. The smaller group took wives because "Those who decline to marry cut off the main function of life, which is to perpetuate the race; and moreover, if everybody declined to marry, the race would soon cease to exist."[70]

These secondary sources have led to the assumption that most of the Essenes, like later Christian monks, permanently rejected marriage. Thus, when the Essene discipline manual was discovered at Qumran, scholars expected it to contain references to celibacy. Surprisingly, in none of the "Dead Sea Scrolls" is there any mention of a member of the community living in an unmarried state.

On the other hand, there is considerable evidence in the primary sources of marriage in the Qumran community. Female skeletons have been found in several cemeteries at Qumran, showing that women were not excluded. And one scroll refers to members of the community taking wives and fathering children.[71] There is no indication that those members were exceptions to any rule. Furthermore, monogamous marriage is stated to be the "true basis of nature."[72] Another scroll seems to imply that marriage was obligatory for all:

This is the rule for all who compose the community . . . every youth is to be instructed . . . in the ordinances of the covenant for a period of ten years. . . . At twenty he is to be examined preparatory to his admission . . . to the holy community. He is not to have sexual relations with a woman until he has reached the age of twenty, the age of discretion. . . . At twenty-five, he is to take his place in the formal structure of the holy community and be eligible for communal office.[73]

If the Essenes married, then how could the writers of secondary source material about them have all been impressed by their sexual abstinence? A clue is provided in the scroll on holy warfare. The Essenes thought of themselves as undergoing training for the eschatological battle between good and evil, and their community was therefore structured along the lines of a Hebrew army camp. Recruits were sworn in at the age of twenty, the enlistment age in earlier history.[74] Yet they could not fight in the crucial battle against "the sons of darkness" until they were twenty-five.[75] During the five years that they were awaiting "war" service, they "rejoiced" with their wives and had children in accord with the military regulations in Deuteronomy 20:7 and 24:5. After entering active service, sexual continence was required of the married warriors for the duration of the conflict. The marital law read: "Any man who is not pure with regard to his sexual organs on the day of battle shall not join them in battle."[76]

The purity referred to here is ritual purity, not moral purity, for there is no dualistic asceticism expressed in the primary sources. Ceremonial purification for holy warfare goes back to early Hebrew custom.[77] For example, when David requested holy bread at the shrine of YHWH for his soldiers, he announced: "Women have been kept from us as always when I go on an expedition; the vessels of the young men are holy."[78] Perhaps there was also a practical motive for requiring continence. By refraining from any pleasures they would be more eager to expedite the war. Samson would probably have been an abler warrior had he been required to refrain from his sexual exploits with Philistine women until the Philistine crisis was ended.

Not being sect members themselves, the first-century writers about the Essenes did not really know about their community life and were not aware of the military aspect of their training. Philo, who was immersed in Hellenism, and the Roman writer Pliny interpreted Essene continence in accord with pagan ascetic notions. In regard to Josephus' misinterpretation, Abel Isaksson says:

Full members of the community over the age of twenty-five are obliged, as soldiers mustered for holy war, to refrain from having any sexual cohabitation whatever with a woman. This gave outsiders the impression that all Essenes lived celibate lives. But the men aged between twenty and twenty-five did not live in celibacy. . . . These married members are not, as Josephus states, a separate group amongst the Essenes, distinguished by their special view of marriage. The married men are a definite age-group within the community, and the fact that they live with their wives and beget children is wholly in agreement with the community's conception of its own being, as an army living according to the laws prescribed for the holy war.[79]

In an independent study, Josephine M. Ford comes to a similar conclusion: "The Essenes probably married and produced children according to the Jewish law either before they joined the community or at the early stage in their membership in the community. . . . Some of them may have abstained from their wives after a certain age."[80] Essene marriage was somewhat like the Hindu *ashrama* practice—although it is improbable that there was any influence of one on the other. Sexual abstinence was required of the Brahmin student. Then, since it was man's foremost duty to raise a son for himself, he had children. Afterwards he could lead a continent life withdrawn from his family.[81]

Are there records of any ancient Jews in Palestine or in the Diaspora who did not conform to the marital requirement? It is sometimes maintained that there was one rabbi living in the second century of the Christian era, Simeon ben Azzai, who did not marry.[82] This assumption is based on a talmudic story. One time he spoke eloquently of marriage, saying that anyone who does not dutifully marry thereby diminishes the image of God. He was then criticized for preaching better than he practiced.[83] But other talmudic sources indicate that he had married the daughter of Rabbi Akiba when he was young but had divorced her at a later period.[84] It seems then that the rabbis, as their Hebrew forefathers, unanimously taught that every man ought to marry and that they lived up to their teaching. George F. Moore states their outlook concisely: "Marriage was regarded not only as the normal state, but as a divine ordinance."[85] Louis M. Epstein elaborates on this cardinal rabbinic principle:

The flesh and its legitimate pleasure are essentially good. . . . The most important corollary that follows from this teaching is the unequivocal opposition of the rabbis to celibacy. Marriage is a legitimate physical satisfaction; it furthers God's universal purpose in the perpetuation of the human species; it sustains the social unit, the family; it helps us toward our personal salvation in that it keeps us from sin.[86]

The greatest figure of medieval Judaism, Maimonides, also showed that asceticism has no place in his religion: "One might say: inasmuch as jealousy, passion, love of honor . . . bring about a man's downfall, I will therefore remove myself to the other extreme. I will refrain from meat and wine or a pleasant home or attractive garments. . . . This is an evil way and forbidden. He who follows these practices is a sinner!"[87]

Even those ancient Jews who were heavily influenced by Hellenism did not go to the extreme of rejecting marriage. For example, marriage is enthusiastically commended in the Wisdom of Sirach.[88] Moreover, nuptial consummation in emulation of Adam and Eve is the climax of the Book of Tobit.[89] Also, the Sibylline Books written by Alexandrian Jews affirm the sanctity of marriage.[90] Philo of Alexandria internalized the moral dualism of Greek philosophy, but even he married.[91] There was a syncretistic sect of Therapeutae in Egypt that practiced celibacy but, as we shall see, they seem to have been more pagan than Jewish in cultic practices.

Thus celibacy was rejected both in theory and in practice by the Hebrews. Hirschel Revel is not indulging in overstatement when he asserts: "The voluntary renunciation of marriage is a conception utterly foreign to Judaism."[92] It is not found in the Old Testament, the Apocrypha, the Pseudepigrapha, the Qumran scrolls, the Mishnah, or in the Talmud. The traditions that may have influenced Jesus are virtually all contained in these sources. But the Hebrews were much more positive toward sexuality than the mere avoidance of celibacy. They valued sex, in the context of marriage, for procreation, companionship, and recreation. The many-splendored purposes of connubial love were extolled and the extremes of undisciplined license and sexual deprivation were abhorred. One rabbi summed up the position of ancient Judaism, studding it with biblical quotes:

Any man who has no wife lives without joy, without blessing, and without goodness. Without joy, for it is written, "You shall rejoice in your house." Without blessing, for it is written, "Cause a blessing to rest on your house." Without goodness, for it is written, "It is not good that the man should be alone."[94]

Chapter III

THE SEXUALITY
OF JESUS

In the extant writings of first-century Christianity there is no overt statement regarding Jesus' marital state. Consequently, those who hold that Jesus never married must buttress their contention with an argument from silence. What are the merits and demerits of this argument?

THE ARGUMENT FROM SILENCE

The treacherous nature of the argument from silence is apparent when one examines what has been extracted from some other silences in the Gospel. The New Testament does not mention that Jesus cried as an infant. Are we then justified in assuming that the Chrismas lullaby is correct in asserting:: "The little Lord Jesus, no crying he makes"? Obviously that would be simply mere sentimentality, for a baby's crying is an important sign of normality.

What of an opposite inference based on the same line of argument? None of the evangelists record that Jesus either laughed or smiled. Is it legitimate to infer from the silence, as was done in the Middle Ages, that his contemporaries never saw him laugh?[1] Our knowledge of the role of laughter and humor in normal humans generally and in the Jewish culture in particular gives grounds for suspecting this inference to be absurd. More empirical evidence for rejecting it is the record of Jesus' amusing repartee, and his advice on cheerfulness.[2]

A rather perverse example of the misuse of documentary silence has to do with Jesus' excretory functions. As with the record of most historical figures, there is no mention of Jesus having a bowel movement. It was evidently from this silence that some second-century Christians deduced that "Jesus ate and drank in a special manner without giving forth the food again."[3]

A more common implication based on the argument from silence is that Jesus was always in perfect health. True, there is no record of Jesus being sick. But human physiology shows that it is virtually impossible to go through life without being subject to viruses, fevers, and aches. Had Jesus never been ill or had he been chronically ill it is probable that either of these conditions, which deviate widely from the norm, would have been remembered and recorded by his followers.

The illicit use of this argument is also displayed in scholarly writing. For example, Kaufmann Kohler asserts: "The silence of the New Testament about the Essenes is perhaps the best proof that they furnished the new sect with its main elements both as regards personnel and views."[4] This illogic is similar to that of Upton C. Ewing, who assumes that since the Jewish sects that opposed Jesus—the Pharisees and the Sadducees—are mentioned in the New Testament, those about whom the New Testament is silent must be the initiators of Christianity. Thus "the Essenes and the early Christians were the same sect."[5] This argument from silence might have some plausibility if there were an essential similarity between Essene and New Testament ideas. However, Theodor H. Gaster, a Jewish expert on Essene document, asserts that there is in the Dead Sea Scrolls "no trace of any of the cardinal theological concepts . . . which make Christianity a distinctive faith."[6] Moreover, Jean Carmignac, a Christian scholar, demonstrates the "radical opposition" between Jesus' doctrines and those of the Essenes.[7]

These examples show the absurdities that have resulted from wrongly employing the argument from silence. Does the hypothesis that Jesus married differ from them in methodology? Is it any more legitimate to use this argument to prove that Jesus probably married than to prove that he probably did not marry? We maintain that in historical biography it is valid to use the argument from silence if it is coupled with convincing evidence from normative patterns of behavior.

It is widely recognized that the Gospels were not intended to be biographies. Rather, they are collections of materials used by the earliest Christian preachers and recorded about half a century after Jesus' crucifixion. This loosely knit sermonic literature only incidentally supplies biographical information. Consequently, there is no New Testament record for about ninety per cent of the span of Jesus' life. Other than Luke's vignette, which affords insight into the twelve-year-old Jesus, the silence is unbroken from his infancy to his thirties.

The valid reconstruction of some basic features of Jesus' life involves delicately using conjectures for filling in the "hidden years." These conjectures must be based on what is known of human nature in general and what is known of his culture's outlook. Those who try to write about Jesus without closely attending to these factors often produce a freakish superman, isolated from any historical environment. Such monstrous caricatures are rejected by those who share the unanimous conviction of New Testament writers that Jesus was a real Jewish man.

What data about Jesus' mode of life would be more likely to be remembered by common men, passed on in oral tradition, and eventually recorded by an evangelist? Psychology shows that unusual behavior is more likely to become etched in the memory and transmitted to a subsequent generation. For instance, there is no record of Jesus' diet, but it is recorded that John the Baptist ate locusts and wild honey. This indicates that Jesus' foods were commonplace but John's were unusual.

Most scholars dealing with Jesus' early life make the sound conjecture that he received not only religious education from his parents as required by the Shema but that he was also instructed at the Nazareth school. Yet in the Gospels there is no comment on Jesus' education in Nazareth. However, Luke records that when Jesus was twelve the Jerusalem scholars were amazed at his understanding; he was also evidently literate enough to read Scripture.[8] Extrabiblical evidence can also be marshaled in support of the conjecture that Jesus attended an elementary school. From the time of Simon ben Shatah (around 75 B.C.) Palestinian villages had schools called the Beth ha-Sefer.[9] Allusions to elementary education in ancient Jewish records make it reasonable to assume that there was a synagogue school in Nazareth when Jesus lived there.[10] But why could Jesus not have received all of his education at home? In that day scrolls would have been too expensive for families of moderate income to afford. So if the carpenter's son learned to read, it is likely that he attended the village school.

Although the assertion that Jesus went to school can now be made without damaging the image that most Christians have of Jesus, this has not always been possible. As early as the second century some Gentile Christians found it appalling to think of Jesus not knowing at his birth, and even before, the whole range of universal wisdom.[11] Therefore they wrote some grotesque tales, reeking with docetism, that became a part of the apocryphal New Testament. In one episode a teacher offers to instruct Jesus, but this wonder boy scathingly proclaims that he is omniscient. The teacher, annoyed at Jesus' impudence, slaps him. To revenge this humiliation Jesus curses him, causing the teacher to drop dead.[12] It would be difficult to invent stories that more diametrically oppose the spirit of Jesus as presented in the earliest records than those outlandish apocryphal stories of Jesus' boyhood.

The hypothesis that Jesus received elementary schooling has been scrutinized because it affords an excellent parallel to the hypothesis that Jesus married. Both assume that as Jesus grew to maturity he participated in the major institutions of the contemporary Jewish society. But there is no explicit reference either to Jesus going to school or to his getting married. There is evidence that Jesus was keenly interested in the Books of Scripture, perhaps the only available scrolls in Nazareth. Likewise there is abundant internal evidence that Jesus endorsed marriage. This attitude, coupled with the knowledge that the marital obligation was enjoined by Hebrew Scriptures and observed by Jesus' fellow Jews, makes it highly probable that Jesus married. In the second century, those who denied the full humanity of Jesus could not accept that he ever needed to learn anything. In a parallel manner, some of those same docetics could not accept that Jesus had carnal relations. The tradition then arose, and has prevailed ever since, that Jesus was a lifelong virgin.

Why is there now widespread agreement by biblical scholars that Jesus was educated by his parents and at school but virtually no acceptance by those same scholars that Jesus was married? Actually there is no evidence that schooling was a requirement for all Jewish boys, but there is evidence that marriage was expected of all. New Testament interpreters not only do not suggest that Jesus married; most of them avoid discussing the matter at all. In subsequent chapters I shall trace how the many centuries of celibate interpreters have made this subject taboo. As a result, even otherwise objective and critical modren scholars have failed to deal with this vital concern.

Because of the tendency to accept blindly as a matter of fact that some New Testament personalities were celibate, Jean P. Audet's insight has special acuity. A Roman Catholic, he rises above the celibate interpretative bias endemic to church history:

> If the chance of her having a fever had not happened to bring Jesus to see Peter's mother-in-law, the gospel tradition would in fact have observed total silence on the disciples' marriage. Could we therefore conclude that not one of them was married? No, we could not. All we can say is this: the ideas and the customs of the time and place are enough to make it probable that most of the apostles were married; it is even quite possible that they all were, without exception.[13]

Had Audet followed his logic further he would also have concluded that Jesus was probably married.

Jesus and Elijah have received similar treatment with respect to marital status. There is no hint in Old Testament history as to whether Elijah ·was married or not. However, in the early church the tradition arose that Elijah was a celibate.[14] Tertullian, for example, claimed that it was because of Elijah's unsullied virginity that Jesus desired his presence on the mount of transfiguration. But now it is recognized that there is no evidence for assuming that Elijah did not follow the same marital standards as his fellow Israelites. Even Lucien Legrand, who in his anxious attempt to find celibates throughout the Bible distorts some passages, admits that historical sources do not suggest that Elijah abstained from the customary practice of marriage.[15] The day may come when a similar reassessment of Jesus will be established among biblical scholars.

THE CONCEPTION OF JESUS

All parents' perspective on marriage affect both the sexual consciousness and the esteem for marriage of their offspring. Thus it is appropriate to approach Jesus' sexuality by way of his parents' outlook, especially since most church members believe that Jesus was born of a virgin.[16] This belief heavily colors views of Christians toward the sexuality of all exceptionally holy humans. Because of acrimonious past controversy over the conjugal bond between Joseph and Mary, it is tempting to pass over the doctrine of the Virgin Birth and let the sleeping dogma lie. But the question of Jesus' lifelong virginity cannot be adequately discussed until there is a full recognition of what the New Testament says about his relations to Joseph and Mary from his conception onward.

In Matthew and Luke, the only New Testament books recording the circumstances of Jesus' birth, it is stated that Joseph was "betrothed" to Mary.[17] The customary translation "betrothed" is misleading for contemporary Westerners. To become betrothed or engaged today means to come to a preliminary agreement to contract marriage at a future date. In our culture the social sanctions on engagements are weak, so the agreement can easily be broken with impunity. By contrast, in the culture to which Joseph and Mary belonged, breaking a betrothal was so serious that it involved obtaining a bill of divorce.[18] In Jewish law if the fiancé of the betrothed girl were to die before the wedding party transpired, she became a widow and subject to the levirate.[19] Both in the Bible and in the Talmud betrothal legally effected a marital relationship.[20] It was sealed by a commercial transaction in which the boy's guardian paid an agreed sum to the girl's guardian. Thus betrothal and marriage were quite similar with respect to rights and responsibilities.

Within a short time after the betrothal covenant was completed the boy had the privilege and obligation of cohabitation with his spouse. In the case of the earliest tradition pertaining to Hebrew marriage customs, there appears to have been only a few days lapse between the betrothal transaction and the cohabitation.[21] The girl remained at the home of her father until the husband was ready to receive her. At that time there was usually a nuptial drinking party to celebrate the bride's transference to the groom's home.[22] Intimate relations by betrothed couples were not prohibited in Jewish Scriptures. The Mishnah and the Talmud indicate that Palestinian Judaism showed considerable tolerance towards prenuptial unions in the era of the New Testament, and children conceived as a result were not stigmatized as illegitimate.[23]

In light of these betrothal mores, what is the meaning of Luke's poetry regarding the "overshadowing" of Mary by the Holy Spirit?[24] Unfortunately, in the history of New Testament interpretation, scholars have drawn on Hellenistic myths to provide clues to what transpired. Ancient historians relate that eminent men such as Plato, Alexander the Great, and Augustus were sired by gods copulating with women.[25] Justin Martyr, who had a strong Hellenistic background, was the first theologian to attempt to establish a parallel between the conception of Jesus and various Greek heroes. In the mid-second century he wrote: "When we declare that the Logos, who is the first offspring of God, was born without sexual intercourse . . . we do not report anything different from your view about those called sons of Zeus."[26] Had Justin been more aware of the Hebraic theology of sex he would not have so glibly assumed that if God were present in human conception then the human sperm would be absent.

There is evidence that the Hebrews in their more poetic moods accepted what might be called a theory of dual paternity. They assumed that God was active in the generation of each individual: YHWH creates when parents pro-create. The psalmist was not thinking of his virginal conception when he said of YHWH: "Thou didst form my inward parts,/thou didst knit me together in my mother's womb."[27] Without embarrassment the poet thought of three cooperating in his conception. Elsewhere in the Scriptures a faithful Hebrew was occasionally referred to as God's son.[28] This double sonship outlook became established in Jewish tradition. One ancient rabbi said that human creation occurs in this manner: "Neither man without woman nor woman without man, and neither of them without the Divine Spirit."[29] In the first birth account of the Bible, Eve exclaims: "I have brought a child into being with the help of YHWH." This was interpreted by a rabbi: "There are three partners in the production of a man: the

Holy One, blessed be he, the father, and the mother."[30] In that talmudic assertion "the rabbinic theory of marital intercourse is summed up."[31]

Dual paternity notions were not unique to the Hebrew culture. The ancient Chinese, for example, had a similar view, as seen in this saying of Confucius: "The female alone cannot procreate; the male alone cannot propagate; and Heaven alone cannot produce a man. The three collaborating, man is born. Hence anyone may be called the son of his mother or the son of Heaven."[32]

Can the view of dual paternity be reconciled with the Gospel texts? In Mark, the earliest Gospel, there is no problem since Jesus is an adult throughout and there is no allusion to the mode of his birth. Also, one would gather from Mark 3:21–31 that Jesus' mother and brothers were unaware of the virginal conception of a member of their family. It is incredible that they would have attempted to dissuade Jesus from his mission if they had been cognizant of his miraculous conception by the Holy Spirit. Moreover, there is no indication in Mark or in any other New Testament literature of Jesus being aware of being born without the agency of a human father.

The two Gospels that do allude to the conception of Jesus also contain passages in which Joseph is referred to in an unqualifiedly matter-of-fact manner as the father of Jesus.[33] Lacking are statements indicating that he was the foster father or legal guardian of Jesus.[34] This being the case, why has there been such a controversy in church history over whether Jesus was or was not born of a virgin? The controversy was probably not begun by the original compilers of the Gospels of Matthew and Luke in the first century but by some scribes in the postapostolic era, who shared Justin's Hellenistic presupposition that sexual relations are tainted, and thereby interpolated the texts slightly. Also the craving of the prescientific mind for the fantastic and the spectacular, although irksome to Jesus,[35] has given popular currency to a supernatural birth tale that is essentially the same as some pagan myths.

In Luke's artistic account of Jesus' conception, the Holy Spirit should not be interpreted as a substitute for a male progenitor.[36] The doctrine of virginal conception in that Gospel rests on two Greek words in Luke 3 and four words in Luke 1 that were probably added by a prosaic scribe who misunderstood the Hebrew doctrine of dual paternity. The more obvious scribal insertion into the original work of Luke is a parenthesis in Luke 3:23, which is detected by its inconsistency with the clause to which it has been added. It reads: "Jesus . . . being the son (as was supposed) of Joseph. . . ." The phrase "as was supposed" renders irrelevant the aim that the genealogical compiler had in mind, namely the tracing through Joseph of Jesus' descent. A less obvious scribal addition is probably found in Luke 1:34.[37] When translated literally the verse reads: "Mary said to the angel, 'How shall this be, since I know not a man?' " The last clause of that question is incongruous in the context of Luke 1, which states that Mary was betrothed. Why would an intelligent bride be bewildered by the means by which she would become pregnant? If "since I know not a man" is deleted, then Mary's question sensibly refers not to puzzlement over the agency of fertilization but to the magnificent destiny forecast in the preceding verses for a peasant's son. Rudolf Bultmann follows B. H. Streeter who suggests that an old Latin version of this passage in which there is no reference to virginal conception may "represent the text as Luke wrote it."[38]

This prophecy of Jesus' birth is similar in style to the foretelling of the coming of a Hebrew judge, Samson, and a Jewish prophet, John.[39] In each case the conception of a child is announced by an angel. However, those stories have never been interpreted as being related to virginal conception, even though the texts do not explicitly state that the husbands performed a father's function. Zechariah is told that his son John "will be filled with the Holy Spirit even from his mother's womb." When Elizabeth conceives after an angelic visitation she remarks, "Thus the Lord has done to me." This episode shows that the Gospel of Luke follows the Hebrew mode of thought and exalts YHWH's participation even though Zechariah's role is assumed. It is characteristic of Luke's theology that the Holy Spirit works through the interaction of human agents, although the process by which this occurs is not fully articulated.[40]

The Gospel of Matthew gives an account of Jesus' origin that is independent of Luke's account. Because it stresses that Jesus is the fulfillment of Jewish history, it appropriately begins with a genealogy designed to show Jesus' Hebraic descent. There is no historical evidence that the Jews expected a virginally conceived Christ. Justin Martyr represented the Jewish hope accurately when he had his Jewish interlocutor state, "We all await the Christ who will be a man born of men." Further, the Jew followed the Hebrew prophets in affirming that the Christ will be descended from David.[41] Thus it can be assumed that the original compiler of Matthew did not intend an un-Jewish virginal-conception interpretation of his opening chapter. Charles Guignebert offers a judgment of sound scholarship when he writes: "The belief in the Virgin Birth is . . . unquestionably later than the desire to establish the Davidic descent of Jesus as Messiah."[42]

An ancient Syriac version probably follows the original manuscript of Matthew when it traces the lineage of Jesus through Joseph to David and Abraham. It states that Joseph was the physical progenitor of Jesus. Accordingly, Matthew 1:16 should be translated, "And Jacob was the father of Joseph; and Joseph, to whom Mary, a virgin, was betrothed, was the father of Jesus who is called the Christ." Moreover, in that same Syriac version the angel announces to Joseph: "She will bear you a son." If the last verse of Matthew 1 is regarded as a later addition to the original, then that entire Gospel can be interpreted in accord with the Hebraic theory of dual paternity.

There is no way to prove or disprove that the original texts of Matthew and Luke were tampered with because the earliest extant manuscripts date several centuries later than the lost originals. But it was during the second and third centuries that virginal conception became exalted among Gentile Christians as the only fitting way for the divine Logos to have become enfleshed. The eminent Nicene theologican Athanasius, who believed coitus was destructive to sublime holiness, articulated the settled patristic position when he stated that the Logos took a human body "directly from a spotless, stainless virgin, without the agency of human father—a pure body, untainted by intercourse with man."[43]

Virginity has been a prominent characteristic of many pagan religions, and was, as we shall see, an indispensable feature in Hellenistic cults. Sacred virgins who were "undefiled" by those sexual relations permissible for ordinary mortals were revered as symbols of holy otherness. Because of their lives of separateness from mundane bodily concerns, they became pointers to divine transcendence.

Frederick C. Grant ably argues that the notion of a virginal conception is totally Hellenistic, and is not a part of the earliest New Testament tradition. He states: "For the Gospels, and the New Testament writing generally, and their writers, it had little significance, and was probably unknown."[44] Emil Brunner agrees with this position and reasons cogently:

It can scarcely be thought that if Paul had known it [the Virgin Birth] and accepted it he would have expressed himself as he does in Romans 1:3: "born of the seed of David according to the flesh." It is highly improbable that he who wrote the Prologue to the Fourth Gospel, concerning the Incarnation of the Son of God, would not have mentioned that idea, if he had known or accepted this view.[45]

It is especially incongruous for Christianity, which is centered in the holiness of a flesh-and-blood person, to affirm a nonphysical insemination. A basic presupposition of Christian theology is that Jesus is Emmanuel, "God with us." Passages of Johannine and Pauline literature give the definitive New Testament treatment of this doctrine.[46] Its thrust is that God does not dwell apart from man, but radiates through the carnal. He is not so aloof that a hierarchy of angelic mediators is needed to bridge the gap between the spiritual and the material. The affirmation that God is immanent and manifested in the life processes of humanity is in irreconcilable conflict with a literalistic interpretation of the Gospel's nativity stories. The former emphasizes the sanctification of the flesh; the latter implies that human generation is an impure and unfitting way for the Ultimate to become intimate. One affirms that biological material reality can be the area of God's activity; the other holds that the "Son of God" cannot be the son of a male. Again, one maintains that the perfect expression of the image of God is associated with the heterosexual couple functioning in accord with the Genesis creation accounts; the other assumes that the original divine image has been so corrupted by some primeval "fall" that no human who is not miraculously generated so as to contravene the natural order can fully embody God's flawless purity.

Those who interpret the virginal-conception stories figuratively have no quarrel with modern science. The geneticist maintains that in the reproduction of anyone who is truly human the ovum is fertilized on receiving from the sperm a set of twenty-three chromosomes. But the biblical literalist has to make the unhappy choice between: 1) affirming that the spiritual God directly produced the male chemical genetic packet that included the sex designation of his offspring; or 2) denying the verified scientific theory that individual human reproduction only occurs when each parent supplies half of the chromosomes. The literalist's position drives a wedge between the Creator of the natural order and the God of Jesus.

The orthodoxy of the "ultraorthodox," who literally believe the virginal conception of Jesus to be a statement of historical fact, has properly been questioned. Brunner, a conservative, inquires:

Is a man who is born without a human father a "true man"? Does he not lack the most essential thing for a human being, the fact that he has been born in exactly the same way as we all are? There is a strongly docetic trait in this idea, and a negative valuation of sex procreation as such, which is more in accordance with a Hellenistic ascetic view than with that of the biblical doctrine of creation.[47]

He also asserts: "The majestic wonder of the Incarnation of the Son of God is not made greater but smaller by the biological theory of the procreation through one sex alone."[48] In a similar vein Paul Tillich rejects virginal conception because "it is theologically quasi-heretical. It takes away one of the fundamental doctrines of Chalcedon, namely, the classical Christian doctrine that the full humanity of Jesus must be maintained beside his whole divinity. A human being who has no human father has no full humanity."[49] Thomas Boslooper, in the most complete recent study of the birth of Jesus, concludes with another relevant criticism of "fundamentalists" of the J. G. Machen tradition.[50] He observes: "Those who insist that the story of the virgin birth be taken literally are simply admitting that they think mythically and are unable to perceive that in the name of history they are actually removing the origin of Jesus from historical connection."[51]

The endorsement of a doctrine of dual paternity has been rare

in church history even though it fits the biblical perspective well
and harmonizes with other doctrinal positions. In this regard Christians have tended to see the issue like Tertullian, who was trained
in Roman law. His legalistic and prosaic frame of mind made him
argue that Jesus had to have either Joseph or God for his father,
simplistically ruling out the possibility that he could have had
both.[52] Yet Christian theology abounds with paradoxes. The Chalcedon doctrine of the dual natures of Jesus demands the juxtapos-
ing of seemingly contradictory ideas. A similar paradox can be
found in Romans 9–11, where Paul claims that divine providence
and human decisions are both fully responsible for the course of
historical events. Clement, unlike his contemporary Tertullian, had
a profound comprehension of the Hebraic doctrine of marriage and
held that both earthly and heavenly fathers could be thought of
as working together in human conception. He even related a saying
of Jesus to dual paternity. In Matthew 18:20 Jesus assures his followers that "where two or three are gathered together" the divine
presence is in their midst. Clement suggested that the "two"
could be the married couple who are procreating, and the third
refers to the conception.[53]

I have argued that the earliest Christians probably established
no dichotomy that obliged one to believe that Jesus was either the
son of Joseph or the Son of God. Rather, they appealed to the
phrase "son of Joseph" in emphasizing his biological ancestry and
to the phrase "Son of God" in reference to his unique theocentric
character. In Judaism sex had been demythologized,[54] so it would
have been gross for one of Jewish heritage to think of YHWH in-
jecting the fertilizing sperm into Mary's womb.

JOSEPH AND JESUS

It is important to consider the father-son relationship of Joseph
and Jesus, especially since Joseph is a figure much neglected by interpreters of the life of Jesus. In reflecting on whether or not Jesus
was married, the focus should be more on the father than on the
son. Marriage was usually not a question that a Hebrew lad was
at liberty to determine. Neufeld asserts that in betrothals "it was
the word of the respective fathers rather than that of the parties
themselves which gave binding validity to a promise of marriage,

especially so as in many cases the parties themselves must have been minors."[55] In ancient Judaism the more liberal rabbis allowed that the age of twenty-four was the upper limit for marriage, but the more rigid said, "When a bachelor attains the age of twenty and is unmarried, the Holy One says, 'Let him rot!' "[56] The average age for "the bridal chamber" in the era in which Jesus lived was around sixteen for the boy, with the age of betrothal even younger.[57]

The Jewish imperative regarding parental duties, accompanied by New Testament information about Jesus' early family relations, gives weighty evidence that Joseph betrothed his children even as he himself had been betrothed. In his time a Jewish father's obligation to a son was clearly defined: "He must circumcise him, redeem him, teach him Torah, teach him a trade, and find a wife for him."[58] What evidence is there that Joseph fulfilled these five duties? Although there are only a few sentences in the New Testament about Joseph, even those show that he was faithful to Jewish standards. In Matthew 1:19 it is stated that he was "a just man," which meant that he regulated his life by the Torah. It is recorded that Jesus was circumcised and redeemed at the age prescribed in the Mosaic law.[59] In accordance with Exodus 13:11–15, a sacrifice was presented at the temple for the first-born son as a symbol of redemption from Egyptian bondage.

The uncanny ability of the adult Jesus to dredge up from memory relevant Scripture passages suggests that religious instruction began in his home as a child. And since both father and son are referred to as carpenters,[60] evidently Jesus was apprenticed in the craft at Joseph's shop in Nazareth.[61] At the age for job training, Jesus was obedient to his parents according to Luke 2:51; acceptance of the same vocation would have been a prominent way of displaying obedience.

A Jewish father completed his responsibilities to his son by arranging for his marriage. Abrahams quotes a first-century saying in discussing the ancient Jewish family: "He who loves his wife as himself, and honors her more than himself; who leads his sons and daughters in the straight path, and marries them near their time of maturity; to his house the words of Job apply: 'Thou shalt know that thy tent is in peace.' "[62] If Joseph betrothed Jesus, why is there no mention of this in historical records? Again, biographical silence with respect to a prevailing culture should be interpreted to mean that the individual concerned followed the normal pattern of conduct. The duty of becoming betrothed shortly after puberty was as axiomatic in ancient Judaism as celibacy was in St. Benedict's monastery. Consequently, there is no mention of celibacy in Benedict's *Rule* nor do the Gospels allude to marriage.

Would Jesus' awareness of his special mission have interfered with his participating as an obedient son in a marital arrangement? There is little reason to think that at the age when Jesus would have been betrothed he had fully in mind the career that a decade or so later would supersede his work as a carpenter. In summarizing Jesus' development, Luke 2:52 states that Jesus "increased in favor with God." Presumably this means that there was a gradual growth in Jesus' awareness of his unique vocation. Probably it was only at the time of his baptism, in the fourth decade of his life, that he felt constrained to leave Nazareth and become an itinerant teacher. Prior to that time it is reasonable to assume that Jesus was not unlike his other physical brothers with respect to participation in the dominant social institution of human society. According to 1 Corinthians 9:5, Jesus' brothers were married.

Those who speculate that Jesus voluntarily remained a bachelor because of his career as teacher and prophet in later life assume incorrectly that Jews did not marry early in life. For example, Louis Cassels states: "Jesus chose a life of celibacy for a good and obvious reason: he could not support a wife and children while carrying on an unpaid itinerant ministry."[63] But in light of our knowledge of the marital mores of the ancient Jews, this assumption bristles with improbabilities.

Joseph Blenkinsopp points out that "historically we cannot be certain that he [Jesus] was unmarried" because "we know too little about the period prior to his baptism in the Jordan to make the kind of generalization found so often in devotional literature." Yet he ventures to suggest that "Jesus was celibate because he was too poor to marry."[64] But it is actually the "devotional literature" that he criticizes that attempts to portray Jesus as coming from a home of dire poverty. Since Joseph and Jesus had the same work, it is likely that one could afford to marry as easily as the other. Hence there seems to be no reason to believe that carpenters of that time and place were not paid adequately to support a family.

JESUS, THE ESSENES, AND JOHN THE BAPTIST

With the discovery in recent decades of the scrolls and site of the Qumran community, there has been renewed speculation that John the Baptist, Jesus, and their disciples may have had ties with the Essene sect. The fact that this sect developed in the centuries immediately preceding the rise of Christianity has provided a basis for postulating causal relations between the two religious movements. These alleged associations deserve our attention because Essenes living at Qumran and elsewhere practiced sexual abstinence during part of their lives.

A few people have assumed that Jesus was significantly influenced by the Qumran community and shared its alleged marital mores.[65] Otto Betz, for example, asserts that Jesus was "closely related" to that community. The first evidence offered to prove this contention is "the fact that he was unmarried."[66] Although this circular reasoning can be dismissed as fallacious, there are some legitimate reasons for positing that Jesus' baptizer, John, emulated some Essene practices.

An Essene policy was to adopt children and instruct them in the rules of their communities.[67] This custom may help to explain the sketchy information given in Luke 1:80 on the early life of John the Baptist. Possibly he was orphaned and then taken nearby to Qumran in "the wilderness" of Judea to grow to maturity. John and the Essenes both ate "locusts and wild honey,"[68] and that common austere diet may indicate a close fellowship.

The teachings of John and the Essenes show remarkable similarities. John's thematic text from Isaiah 40:3, quoted in all the Gospels, was a prominent prophecy for the Essenes as well.[69] All were making moral and ritual preparations for the intervention of YHWH. The utilization of water baptism as a symbol of inner purification was also central for John and the Essenes.[70] Furthermore, both were gifted at hellfire-and-damnation oratory.[71] Thus it seems likely that John was influenced by the Essenes; possibly he belonged to the sect during his formative years.

Definite knowledge of John's attitude toward marriage would

be lacking even if John were a full-fledged member of the Qumran community. As we have seen, there is conflicting historical information on the Essene outlook on sex and marriage. However it is plausible to hold that the activities of John recorded by the evangelists and by Josephus[72] occur after he had fulfilled his duty with respect to procreating. If John were an Essene while in his thirties, he may have adhered to the Hebrew military code that required sexual continence. Perhaps John thought of himself as a warrior in the original salvation army, serving under the stern YHWH militant.

Turning from John to Jesus, it is tempting but unwarranted to assume that because John was Jesus' supporter in the Gospels, the Essenes therefore had a significant positive influence on both persons. The Gospels indicate that the Jews noted a marked difference in the temperaments and in the cultic practices of the two men.[73] For example, whereas John abstained from bread and wine, Jesus criticized and disregarded the practice of fasting.[74]

In response to a question regarding the reason for the dietary difference between John and Jesus, Aquinas wrote:

For Christ to lead a solitary life would not have advanced the purpose of the Incarnation; therefore he mingled in society: "The Son of Man came eating and drinking." It is most fitting that he should conform to the manner of living of those with whom he associated: according to the Apostle "I became all things to all men." Therefore he avoided eccentricity in food and drink.[75]

Aquinas was a corpulent imbiber of wine, so he was predisposed to think of the ideal man as one who consumed delectable foods and titillating drinks. But due to his personal aversion to women, he was predisposed against thinking of Jesus as indulging in marriage. Had Aquinas not been a celibate he might have extended his sound logic so that Jesus' conformity included having sexual as well as gastronomic satisfactions.

John and Jesus also differed in their attitudes toward people. John was a recluse who preferred dwelling in the desert to living in town. In this regard he may have deliberately followed the Qumran rule to "keep apart from all other men."[76] He did not go where the common people usually assembled; rather, the crowds came to the remote area to which he had withdrawn.[77] On the other hand, Jesus traveled widely and especially sought the company of the disreputable. He also frequented homes of the wealthy and accepted their hospitality freely.[78] Jesus welcomed social meetings with women and was fascinated by children. Unlike the Essenes, who abstained from the use of oil for anointing,[79] he was delighted when women applied the soothing emollient to his body.

The most striking witness to Jesus' conviviality is his participation in a wedding at Cana. According to John 2:1–11 he first "manifested his glory" by producing about 150 gallons of wine at the party. Erwin R. Goodenough documents that "dancing and merrymaking, including much drinking" were integral parts of the connubial ceremony in the ancient Jewish culture.[80] A century ago J. B. Lightfoot observed:

When we find Christ discussing the relations of man and wife, gracing the marriage festival by his presence, again and again employing wedding banquets and wedded life as apt symbols of the highest theological truths, without a word of disparagement or rebuke, we see plainly that we are confronted with a spirit very different from the narrow rigor of the Essenes.[81]

A striking reversal of Jesus' merriment at weddings is displayed in the crotchety criticisms of Cyprian, a key figure in the establishment of Latin Christianity. In a third-century treatise, he chastised those who diminished their purity by attending weddings. He asked: "What place is there at weddings for one who has no thought of marriage, or what can be pleasant and enjoyable in those occasions wherein desires and interests are so different? . . . By cutting away the desires of the flesh you are obtaining the reward of greater grace in heaven."[82] Cyprian believed that eternal vigilance is the price of virginity, and that indulgences in ordinary human pleasures form paving blocks along the road to perdition.

One of the ironies of history has been the unfounded assumption in much of church tradition that Jesus was a kill-joy, and that the Christians should therefore repress gaiety and withdraw from hilarity. Unfortunately there has been a tendency to project back on Jesus the repressive tendencies of many of his followers. In the nineteenth century Swinburne, evidently identifying the ethic of

Jesus with that of Victorian society, made the famous bitter admission: "Thou hast conquered, O pale Galilean; the world has grown grey from thy breath."[83] If he had examined the Gospels carefully, he would have realized that Jesus vis-à-vis his forerunner John was not a pale Palestinian.

John's humorless rhetoric was saturated with bad news of the coming doomsday, when the worthless people would "burn with unquenchable fire."[84] Jesus, although accepting the traditional Jewish theology of just retribution to the unrepentant, had a much more positive and life-affirming message. In his inaugural address at Nazareth Jesus quoted Isaiah 61:1–2 to affirm that he had been "messiahed" to bring good news to the oppressed and to emancipate them from their burdens.[85] John had serious misgivings about Jesus' unexpected approach and wondered if he had erred in announcing Jesus as the "Coming One." On learning of John's doubt Jesus affirmed that he was fulfilling what he considered to be the essential core of Jewish prophecy as articulated by Isaiah.[86] Unlike John, who expected a divine coup d'état, Jesus believed the messianic "kingdom" was partly present and gradually developing.[87] In a rather backhanded tribute to the prophet who "prepared the way" for this "kingdom," Jesus said: "Among those born of women none is greater than John; yet he who is least in the kingdom of God is greater than he."[88] He counseled that offense should not be taken if he pursued quite a different style of life than his forerunner had anticipated.[89]

In the light of Jesus' explicit rejection of some personal attitudes that were sanctioned by John and by the Qumran community, and realizing that Jesus championed a theology that celebrated the divine presence in the most unsuspected facets of ordinary life, one can conclude that Jesus thought Essene theology and practice deficient. Guignebert found in Jesus "not the faintest trace of Essene influence." To those who posit basic similarities between Jesus and the Essenes he responded strongly but wisely: "Short of admitting that the Synoptic tradition has grossly deceived us, to the point of declaring the exact opposite of the truth, concerning the type of life led by the Master and the spirit of his preaching, it is impossible to confuse his doctrine with that of the Essenes."[90] Lest it be thought that Guignebert's judgment, which dates from before the Qumran discoveries, would now need extensive modification, contemporaries like H. H. Rowley and others of similar expertise have likewise argued that a "vast gulf" separates the outlook of the Qumran community from that of Jesus.[91] Consequently there is no reason to think that Jesus felt constrained to imitate the continence of the Essenes.

There is no mention of either the Essenes or the Qumran community in the New Testament or in the massive tomes of rabbinic literature. This suggests that the Essenes were a peripheral offshoot of Judaism that was not to survive the destruction of the Jewish nation in A.D. 70. Unlike that sterile movement, rabbinic Judaism was virile enough to withstand its catastrophe and continue throughout subsequent history as a major influence on world cultures.

JESUS AND ASCETICISM

The comparison of Jesus' moral outlook with that of his more austere cousin and with the Essenes brings up the broader question of Jesus' relation to the ascetic concept in Greco-Roman culture. The Greek root of the term "ascetic" is *askēsis*, which first meant the training an athlete receives. Socrates used *askēsis* to refer to the self-discipline necessary for anyone desiring to become an educated citizen.[92] It later came to connote a life of abstaining from the natural enjoyments of life as much as survival permitted. Sensual pleasures, especially those received from sexual relations and from some foods, were denied. They were deemed inherently evil because they are stimulated by the flesh-craving part of man's psyche. In Hellenism the *askēsis* devotee consciously tried to rid his soul substance of the contamination incurred by contact with physical substance. For instance, in a chapter entitled "Concerning *askēsis*," Epictetus, the famous Stoic of the first century A.D., taught that the impulse to indulge in drinking, eating, and sensual love must be counteracted by an opposing discipline of abstinence.[93] Largely due to the influence of the Cynic-Stoic ethic, the notion of *askēsis* as moderation training was superseded by a strong negative emphasis. Self-purification through repression of bodily impulses came to have intrinsic value.

Because of the radically different ways in which *askēsis* was

used, it is confusing to label Jesus an ascetic. The original connotation of askēsis as employed by Socrates would have been appropriate to apply to Jesus' ethic. He certainly did not favor a life
of ease and intemperate self-indulgence any more than did Socrates.
Jesus told his disciples that "the gate is narrow and the way is hard
that leads to life."[94] He thought it indispensable to deny some immediate pleasures in pursuit of long-range happiness.[95] But when
askēsis is restricted to mean self-mortification as an end in itself,
it is a most inappropriate term for describing Jesus' outlook. The
word is absent from the Gospels even though it was popular in
the Hellenistic culture at the time they were compiled.

The term "ascetic" now generally refers to the more extreme
"No Thyself" imperative, and because of this the consensus of
scholars maintains that Jesus was not an ascetic. Adolf Harnack
wryly observed that many people are relieved by assuming that
Christianity means denial of the world "for then they know very
well that it does not concern them." But after an extensive discussion he concluded that "asceticism has no place in the Gospel
at all." Harnack said unequivocally: "We find nothing in the
apostolic age which suggests a community of men who were
ascetics on principle."[96] More recent German specialists in Christian origins agree. Rudolf Bultmann writes: "Jesus desires no
asceticism, he requires only the strength for sacrifice. As little as
he repudiates property as such does he reject marriage or demand
sexual asceticism. The ideal of virginity . . . is entirely foreign to
Jesus; he required only purity and the sanctity of marriage."[97] Hans
von Campenhausen further demonstrates that asceticism was alien
to New Testament Christianity.[98]

F. Homes Dudden admirably sums up the general view of Jesus
that he has culled from the Gospels:

Jesus nowhere teaches . . . that the gratification of the natural cravings is fraught with sin. He does not recommend men to treat their
bodies with contempt. He does not suggest that flight from the world
and disengagement from physical conditions is sanctification. He does
not say that those who, for duty's sake, renounce the world, are on a
higher spiritual level than those who do their duty in the world. He
does not hint that the only way of avoiding sin lies in an austere renunciation of all those things from which an occasion of sin might

arise. He nowhere implies that the lower goods are of no value in themselves, or that they ought under all circumstances to be foregone. The doctrine of Jesus is a doctrine not of annihilation, but of subordination. He admits, indeed, that special circumstances may make it incumbent on an individual to abstain from certain things which others, otherwise situated, may lawfully enjoy. . . . The Master who taught that matrimony was a divinely ordered condition, and emphasized in the strongest terms the sanctity of the conjugal relation, who practiced and inculcated the duty of filial obedience and love toward parents, who habitually used the symbolism of the family to express the profoundest and holiest truths of religion, certainly did not mean to teach that family life, as such, was irreconcilable with righteousness. He uttered no word in disparagement of it; he never implied that the married attain a lower grade of perfection than the continent. . . . Marriage in itself is not to be avoided as a thing debasing; it debases only when men refuse to subordinate it to the claims of the Kingdom.[99]

Jesus, in rejecting the premises and practices of moral dualism, was in complete accord with his Hebrew heritage. And concerning asceticism Moore shows that Judaism "is in contradiction with this philosophy at every point."[100]

"TEMPTED IN EVERY RESPECT"

Meeting at Chalcedon, an ecumenical council hammered out a Christological formulation that has been accepted ever since as fundamental by orthodox Christians of the Eastern and Western churches. It affirms that Jesus was "of one substance with us according to humanity, like us in all respects apart from sin." Apropos of this creed is Pope Leo the Great's declaration: "It is as dangerous an evil to deny the truth of the human nature in Christ as to refuse to believe that his glory is equal to that of the Father."[101]

These fifth-century positions are firmly anchored in the New Testament. All of the Gospels portray Jesus as expressing the broad spectrum of human emotions. He experienced the physical emotions of hunger, thirst, and fatigue.[102] Mentally and spiritually he expressed surprise, agonizing vocational struggle, and anxiety over death.[103] Jesus, like an ancient psalmist, felt despair and godforsakenness.[104] Socially, he was affectionate toward friends and acquaintances,[105] and he showed concern for his mother and his country.[106] Joy, grief, compassion, and anger were all part of his human nature.[107]

How human were Jesus' temptations? His three bizarre encounters with Satan, recorded as occurring at the beginning of his ministry, seem only quasi-human. What ordinary person is tempted to turn stone into bread, to gain control over the whole world, or to jump from the pinnacle of a temple in order to force guardian angels to come to the rescue? Although these do not seem to be realistic human temptations, they are related to several basic human motivations. Everyone is confronted with the impulse to use his personal abilities principally for the satisfaction of his own physical appetites. Most people have the urge to dominate other people and things even if devilish compromises with moral principles are involved. Then too, the thirst for popularity often drives people to perform ridiculous stunts to gain applause.

Hebrews picture Jesus "in the days of his flesh" coming to full maturity by withstanding distressing situations like a rugged "pioneer."[108] It affirms that Jesus "learned obedience"[109] by exposure to the same conditions as other humans. The author of Hebrews reinforces Luke's assertion that Jesus developed physically, mentally, socially, and spiritually.[110] Temptations are regarded as indispensable for moral perfecting. According to Hebrews 4:15, Jesus "in every respect has been tempted as we are, yet without sinning." Theodore H. Robinson comments on this verse: "He was tempted in every respect, on every side of man's complex being, and exposed to every peril of the soul. For he was like ourselves—exactly like us in his physical and spiritual constitution."[111]

Oscar Cullmann asserts that Hebrews 4:15 should lead us "to consider aspects of his [Jesus'] life with which we are not acquainted." He observes:

The full significance of this description of Jesus' humanity is rarely appreciated. The assertion that Jesus had to withstand as we is extraordinarily far-reaching. It obviously does not think [sic] only of the Synoptics' report of the temptations following Jesus' baptism. After all, they were messianic temptations which could be imposed only upon the Christ. . . . The author of Hebrews really thinks of the common temptations connected with our human weakness, the temptations to which we are exposed simply because we are men. "In every respect as we are" refers not only to form but also to content.[112]

Irenaeus, like the author of Hebrews, emphasized Jesus' exposure to genuine temptations under grim human conditions.[113] Jesus became "a child for children" and "a youth for youths, becoming an example to youths and thus sanctifying them for the Lord."[114]

If we take seriously these claims that Jesus ran the gamut of childhood, adolescent, and adult temptations, must he not have had sexual temptations? Along with the desire to eat, drink, and sleep, the sexual urge is among the more universal components of human nature. Humans even surpass beasts in libidinous desire, for they can be sexually aroused not for a season, but continuously. Plato went so far as to maintain that this desire is the most powerful of all human appetites.[115]

Frank biographies reveal that sexual desire is one of the deepest impulses in human nature. Even the early Christian saints were subject to disturbing sexual temptations. Anthony, popularly known as the father of Christian monasticism, was sorely tempted when "the wretched devil even dared to masquerade as a woman by night."[116] In that same fourth century Jerome admitted that he found his sexual desires agonizing: "When I was living in the desert . . . how often did I fancy myself among the pleasures of Rome! . . . I often found myself amid bevies of girls. My face was pale and my frame chilled with fasting; yet my mind was burning with desire, and the fires of lust kept bubbling up."[117]

Struggles such as these saints experienced seem to have been the rule rather than the exception among medieval Christians of exemplary morals. We are told that the pious Benedict, who founded the brotherhood at Monte Cassino, had excruciating trouble with his id:

He was seized with an unusually violent temptation. The evil spirit recalled to his mind a woman he had once seen, and before he realized it his emotions were carrying him away. . . . Just then he noticed a thick patch of nettles and briers next to him. Throwing his garment aside, he flung himself naked into the sharp thorns and stinging nettles. There he rolled and tossed until his whole body was in pain and covered with blood. Yet once he had conquered pleasure through suffering, his torn and bleeding skin served to drain off the poison of temptation from his body.[118]

Seven centuries later Francis of Assisi had a similar experience. While at the Sartiano hermitage he had "a most grievous temptation of lust." He beat himself with his tunic rope exclaiming, "There, brother ass!" This being an ineffective remedy, he resorted to more desperate efforts to cool his sexual desire: "Seeing that, in spite of scourging himself, the temptation did not leave him, though he had colored all his members with weals, he opened the cell, went out into the garden and plunged naked into deep snow."[119] If an overheated libido was combated by Francis, the "mirror of Christ," as well as by those who share less of Jesus' spirit, does this not imply that the one who has been tempted "in all respects as we are" was also confronted with sexual testing?

The struggle with sex is intense not only in celibates but also in couples who live in full heterosexual intimacy. D. H. Lawrence describes this situation:

A young girl and a young boy is a tormented tangle, a seething confusion of sexual feelings and sexual thoughts which only the years will disentangle. Years of honest thoughts of sex, and years of struggling action in sex, will bring us at last where we want to get, to our real and accomplished chastity, our completeness, when our sexual act and our sexual thought are in harmony.[120]

Although sexual temptation is inextricably tied to human nature, there has been much reluctance throughout church history to acknowledge that Jesus was fully tempted. Even Alexander Bruce, who keenly criticizes the church fathers who failed to accept Jesus' complete manhood, does not believe that Jesus' temptations were visceral. He categorically states: "A Christian . . . may have to do battle even unto blood with a lust or appetite, or old habit that wars against his soul. Christ had no such battle to fight."[121] Paul Tillich observes that through the ages theologians and popular Christianity have not been able to tolerate the thought of Jesus having the real temptations of man.[122]

Happily there is at least one contemporary theologian who tries to take seriously the full implications of Jesus' humanity. Tom F. Driver makes this point:

If the Man for Men was conceived to be without sexuality—was never, unlike the saints, even tempted by sex—then all would labor in vain who strove to prove that the Christian God looks favorably upon the sexual life of humanity. Hunger Jesus knew, and thirst. Death he endured. Pride, sloth, envy, desire for power, idolatry—all came close to him and were overcome in favor of the virtues of which they are the perversions. . . . To put it bluntly, a sexless Jesus can hardly be conceived to be fully human. . . . Lacking such a pervasively human element, the humanity of Christ tends to become a mere affirmation, a matter of pure dogma. Jesus is then man in principle but not in fact.[123]

MARITAL TESTING AND HUMAN MATURATION

There is a correlative aspect to the doctrine that Jesus was subject to a broad sampling of human temptations. It is naïve to assume that all or even most of the temptations related to marriage pertain to illicit affairs. Throughout history many have thought that some of the most difficult testing has been associated with problems arising from trying to live responsibly with spouse, children, and in-laws.[124]

Socrates' marital predicament with Xanthippe is a classic example. When asked how he could tolerate living with such a shrew, he replied that marriage to her had refined his character. He believed that learning to cope with her scolding tempered him for the peculiarities of all others.[125]

In the Roman era there were many, unlike Socrates, who did not appreciate or accept the moral testing afforded by the nuptial bond. Among Jesus' pagan contemporaries there was a growing distaste for married life because of the burdens it imposed. Indeed, the single life became so much in vogue in Rome that Caesar Augustus became concerned about the stability of the state. He issued a series of laws designed to impose penalties of property upon all the unmarried over twenty years of age. His decrees were considered so despicable by those who preferred the easier unattached life that citizens "insisted vehemently that he should repeal the law about celibacy and childlessness." Augustus then addressed the bachelors: "What am I to call you? Men? You have not yet proved yourselves to be men."[126]

Clement of Alexandria held that the married man is involved

in more exasperating tensions than the bachelor and therefore, if
he resolves them successfully, he has a superior moral excellence.
He wrote:

True manhood is shown not in the choice of a celibate life; on the
contrary the prize in the contest of men is won by him who has
trained himself by the discharge of the duties of husband and father
and by the supervision of a household, regardless of pleasure and pain
—by him, I say, who in the midst of his solicitude for his family shows
himself inseparable from the love of God and rises superior to every
temptation which assails him through children and wife and servants
and possessions. On the other hand he who has no family is in most
respects untried.[127]

Although Clement did not relate these thoughts to the life of
Jesus, his position would logically entail evaluating an unmarried
Jesus as not embodying the highest quality of life.

Some church fathers agreed with Clement's contention that the
married suffer more trials and tribulations, but they thought that
this factor sufficiently justified opting for the freer unmarried life.
Unwittingly they adopted a perspective similar to those pagan
Romans against whom Augustus railed. Saint Cyprian wrote:
"Virginity has no children; but what is more, it has contempt for
offspring: it has not fruitfulness, but neither has it bereavement;
blessed that it is free from the pain of bringing forth, more blessed
still that it is free from the calamity of the death of children."[128]
Chrysostom, the most famous preacher of the patristic era, offered
this advice to a friend who was considering marriage:

Would you have me speak of the domestic cares of wife and children
and slaves? It is an evil thing to wed a very poor wife, or a very rich
one; for the former is injurious to the husband's means, the latter to
his authority and independence. It is a grievous thing to have children,
still more grievous not to have any; for in the latter case marriage has
been to no purpose, in the former a bitter bondage has to be under-
gone. If a child is sick, it is the occasion of no small fear; if he dies an
untimely death, there is inconsolable grief; and at every stage of growth
there are various anxieties on their account, and many fears and toils.
And what is one to say to the rascalities of domestic slaves? Is this then
life, Theodore, when one's soul is distracted in so many directions,
when a man has to serve so many, to live for so many, and never for

himself? Now amongst us, O friend, none of these things happen. I appeal to yourself as a witness. For during that short time when you were willing to lift your head above the waves of this world, you know what great cheerfulness and gladness you enjoyed.[129]

Chrysostom's eloquent plea for the single life displays little more than egoistic hedonism. If this be the life of the unattached, then it can be demonstrated that a celibate Jesus would have been untested in some of the more strenuous situations with which most humans learn to cope.

In modern history there are both Christian and Jewish theologians who share Clement's outlook. Bishop Jeremy Taylor thought that marriage makes responsibilities heavier and therefore can produce sturdier character. To utilize Taylor's similes, the "celibate, like the fly in the heart of an apple, dwells in perpetual sweetness," but the married man lives like a bee, struggling to bring forth good.[130] From the standpoint of existential psychology Martin Buber held that salvation is forged through the conflict situations of marriage. There "the other as other" is experienced in a way that cannot be paralleled in other social life. Far from being an impediment to the holy life, true marriage essentially reveals the other in a profound way. Buber further stated: "Marriage is the exemplary bond; it carries us as does none other into the greater bondage, and only as those who are bound can we reach the freedom of the children of God."[131]

JESUS' RELATIONS WITH WOMEN

Assuming that Jesus had the testings, sexual and nonsexual, that are intrinsic to the major social institution of human culture, what were his relationships to women? Many women were attracted to his movement, but in the Gospels they are mostly anonymous.[132] Luke was especially fascinated with the interrelations of Jesus with women; he recorded six encounters not found in the other Gospels.[133] It is significant that Jesus is never represented by any writer of the canonical Gospels as being derogatory toward the opposite sex. He gave his disciples no warnings about the wiles of women. In practice as well as in theory he endorsed the created order of sexual equality. Paul displayed Jesus' viewpoint when he wrote that nationalities, classes, and sexes are equal for Christians.[134] Mary Daly is quite critical of antifeminism in Christian history, but she admits that

> there is no recorded speech of Jesus concerning women "as such." What is very striking is his behavior toward them. In the passages describing the relationship of Jesus with various women, one characteristic stands out starkly: they emerge as persons, for they are treated as persons, often in such contrast with prevailing custom as to astonish onlookers.[135]

The earliest records of Jesus portray an outlook that stands out in bold contrast to some later characterizations. For example, in the apocryphal *Gospel of Thomas* there is this conversation:

> Simon Peter said to them: "Let Mary depart from us because women are not worthy of the Life." Jesus said: "Look, I will lead her so that I will change her to male, in order that she also may become a living spirit like you males. For every female who makes herself male will enter the Kingdom of Heaven."[136]

It is instructive to compare Jesus' attitude toward women with that of Gautama the Buddha, founder of the most widespread nonsemitic religion in the world. He belonged to the Indian culture of the sixth century B.C. in which asceticism was prominent. According to early legend, the virgin-conceived Gautama renounced his wife and child during his third decade of life. After years of withdrawal and austerity he became "enlightened" and extinguished all sensual passion. Then he returned to instruct Hindu monks how they, too, could reach the state of Nirvana. Late in the Buddha's life a monk asked him for advice on the proper conduct toward the opposite sex. This exchange ensued:

"What should be our attitude toward women?"

"Avoid the sight of them."

"But if we should see them, Lord, what must we do?"

"Do not speak to them."[137]

Charles S. Braden, a specialist in comparative religions, rightly states: "The attitude of the Buddha toward women stands in sharpest contrast to that of Jesus. To the Buddha they are always inferior to men—a snare and a threat to men."[138] Gautama shared with his contemporary Confucius a depreciatory and suspicious attitude toward women. "Women and underlings are most difficult to deal with," the Chinese sage testified; "if we are friendly with them they lose their deference."[139] Confucius regarded women as little more than breeding organisms and servants.

Jesus dealt with both righteous and unrighteous women as individuals with specific concerns, not as cases illustrating some religious principle. He had compassion for the widow of Nain, who had lost her only son, and assisted her. Likewise he treated the woman caught in the act of adultery in a way that displayed empathy for her plight. Although her harsh accusers regarded her impersonally as a case involving the Mosaic code, Jesus did not get involved in legalistic arguments. He rose above their androcentric, hypocritical perspective by refusing to join them in expressing contempt toward the adulterous woman. In a therapeutic manner, without condoning or condemning, he dealt with her firmly but tenderly.[140] Nowhere did Jesus better express the way he had internalized the outlook that Isaiah had envisaged for YHWH's ideal servant: "He will not break a bruised reed/or snuff out a dimly burning wick."[141]

In another episode, Jesus showed unusual openness toward a Samaritan woman who had a similar problem.[142] Even his disciples were amazed to find that Jesus initiated conversation with a woman who was deemed inferior in several ways by their culture's petty social conventions. She was a member of a Palestinian minority from whom the Jews had separated themselves. Because she was a female, it was considered improper to converse with her in public.[143] Her apparent marital infidelity alone would have been reason enough for treating her like an outcast. The conversation shows that Jesus placed a positive value on permanent monogamous relations and a negative one on adulterous promiscuity. His method of dealing with her sexual problem shows a competence in interpersonal relations that is commended today in psychological counseling.[144]

In Luke 7:36–50 a parallel encounter takes place between Jesus and an unnamed "woman of the city who was a sinner." She was probably a prostitute[145] who had the boldness to enter the home of a certain Simon where Jesus was dining. She extended to him the courtesies that his host neglected, and Jesus was impressed by her profuse display of affection. As she washed his feet with tears and kissed them continually, he compared her ability to "love much" with the unforgiving attitude of Simon.

There is ample evidence, then, of Jesus' belief that outcasts have more potential for repentance than members of polite society.[146] Those who called themselves righteous were revolted by Jesus' acceptance of moral failures. But Jesus rejected the principle of salvation by segregation from those of ill repute. He did not assume that purity was preserved by isolation from those who were morally infected. Jesus introduced the principle of befriending sexual offenders and other wrongdoers in order to bring out the best in each individual.[147] Much to the consternation of the respectable of every era, he affirmed that his mission was to live not with the virtuous but with those who were aware of their moral sickness.[148] He aimed at extending the largest measure of trust possible to the dregs of society in order to restore in them healthy self-confidence as well as a godward and altruistic orientation.

Can the forgiven "sinner" of Luke 7 be identified with the woman named Mary and called Magdalene? There is some evidence for an affirmative answer. First, she is introduced in the paragraph immediately following the anointing episode. Second, it is stated that she had been cured of a serious disorder referred to as the expulsion of "seven demons." This could refer to healing a nervous and/or moral illness. Third, Magdalene could refer to her moral background. She may have come from Magdala, a fishing village along the Sea of Galilee that was noted in Jewish tradition for licentiousness, which resulted in the town's destruction.[149]

Mary Magdalene became one of Jesus' most faithful companions, for she did not forsake him even when he was crucified.[150] Possibly due to her deep insight into Jesus' mission, she was among the first to experience the triumphant Jesus on the day of resurrection.[151] It is significant that all the Synoptics place Mary Magdalene first in each listing of women,[152] just as Peter heads the listings of the apostles. Hence the earliest evangelists regarded her as the most prominent female beloved by Jesus. Because of this close association, some of the early Christians assumed that Mary Magdalene was Jesus' wife. That is the position taken in the recently discovered *Gospel of Philip*, which records a tradition at least as old as the second century. Chapter six will probe this Gospel more thoroughly.

It is also possible to relate the unnamed woman of Luke 7 with another Mary. Joseph N. Sanders cogently argues that the Luke 7:36–50 episode is one that Luke has shifted in time and place from the events of Mark 14:3–9. In both narratives Jesus accepts the kindness of an anonymous woman who anoints him during dinner in the home of a man named Simon. Sanders also suggests that John 12:1–8 is an account of the same event, which is independent of the Synoptics but equally reliable historically.[153] There the woman is identified as Mary, the sister of Martha.

Although Jesus was friendly with many women, the Gospels show that he had more intimate companionship with some. According to John, there were two particular women whom Jesus loved, Martha and Mary.[154] Perhaps he became acquainted with these sisters in Galilee and they traveled with him to Judea, staying with their brother Lazarus at Bethany.[155] Even though the relationship that Jesus had with them is not described in detail, it is apparent that he enjoyed visiting with them. It is also evident that Jesus had more rapport with Mary than with her envious sister, who was preoccupied with domestic chores. Showing an attitude uncommon in his day, he treated this woman with intellectual respect as she "listened to his teaching," commending her for having chosen what was best.[156] He appreciated Mary's devotion when she anointed his feet with fragrant ointment. When she was criticized for being extravagant, Jesus defended her gracious act.[157]

What was the quality of their companionship? Although his love is usually thought of as a one-way expression of concern for others, that characterization is inadequate for this relationship. Jesus and Mary gave and received love as is common among couples who delight in one another's company. Richard F. Hettlinger's comment on Jesus is true: "His love for his friends was not asexual. Our knowledge of the role of sex in childhood and adolescence, as well as the realization that all man-woman relationships have a sexual element, makes such a position absurd."[158]

It should also be pointed out that from at least as early as the second century there has been the assumption that the repentant "sinner" of Luke 7, Mary Magdalene, and Mary the sister of Martha form one composite figure.[159] The Latin church has continued that three-in-one identification.[160] Such a blend is found in a biography of Mary Magdalene by an unknown fourteenth-century Italian writer.[161] Because of this ancient tradition it is perhaps warranted for modern interpreters to use Ockham's razor boldly, and shave away the unnecessary multiplication of women whose special fondness for Jesus was reciprocated by him. J. H. Bernard and J. Middleton Murry argue that Mary Magdalene should be doubly identified with the unnamed "sinner" of Luke 7 and Mary the sister of Martha.[162] Dorothy Sayers, in a dramatic treatment of the life of Jesus, characterizes the unified figure thus:

Mary is vivid with vitality. Nothing—not even repentance—can quench her spirits for long. Once she loved the wrong things, now she loves the right things; but she does both passionately—nor is she going to pretend that the old, worthless pleasures were without their glamor. What she sees in Jesus is "the Life"—the blazing light of living intensely, which shows up the tinsel and the tawdry for what it is.[163]

Some Protestant scholars are reluctant to interpret the Gospel text so that Jesus' special friend is an exprostitute called Mary. For example, Francis Burkitt is considerably less forgiving than Jesus when he dissociates Mary Magdalene from the "sinner" of Luke 7 on the grounds that Jesus' itinerant band would probably not have admitted someone who had not always been respectable. He considers it "a psychological monstrosity" to identify Mary, the sister of Martha, with a notorious courtesan.[164] Such revulsion to postulating that a companion of the holiest of men could have been a woman with a record of sexual iniquity shows how radical Jesus' principle of accepting the socially unacceptable still is in our culture. That Jesus should fraternize continually with Judas, a potential betrayer, or with Matthew, who had been engaged in what was commonly regarded as an unethical racket, does not seem to bother interpreters nearly as much, since there is no evidence that they had a background of sexual irregularities! Sexual sin seems to be the unforgivable one for some Christians.

If Jesus married, what can plausibly be hypothesized regarding the identity of his wife? One conjecture that is intriguing because it blends with the basic biblical ethic might be: that Jesus married Mary Magdalene during the second decade of his life; she became an adultress; Jesus' love for her was unwavering and so a course of reconciliation rather than divorce was pursued; this expression of *agape* made her repent and become his faithful spouse again until the end; out of this experience Jesus came to believe that divorce should be opposed and that more emphasis should be placed on the permanent bond of marriage than was characteristic in his culture.

A second possibility is that Jesus married a woman named Mary, but that she was not his first wife. The accounts of Jesus' relations with Mary(s) are associated with his fourth decade, but it is highly improbable that he would have married for the first time at that age. Persons in their thirties were middle-aged in societies where life expectancy was not prolonged by scientific medicine. In light of such marital customs, it is possible that Jesus' first wife died, and that afterwards he married Mary during his itinerating years as a teacher. The remarriage of widowers was sanctioned and customary in Jewish culture.

Or again, Jesus might have been a widower during the years of his public ministry. If this were so, the lack of explicit reference to his wife in the New Testament would be understandable, for his wife would have existed prior to the period in his life when he became known by those who would transmit information to subsequent generations.

Another conjecture is that the wife whom Jesus had married as a Nazarene carpenter was alive when he was proclaiming the Gospel, but that she did not accompany him in his travels. A variety of speculations could support this case. She could have stayed in Nazareth to attend to child and/or parental care or to other pressing domestic responsibilities. Or her health could have been too frail to permit camping out with the traveling band. Or again, realizing that Jesus was alienated from his family,[165] and that there were citizens of Nazareth who would have liked to lynch him,[166] it is altogether possible that she had separated from him. And since Jesus rejected divorce, he would not have taken the liberty to remarry.

But there is a counterargument to the hypothesis that Jesus married. If Jesus married it can be presumed that he had children. The Mishnah shows that in Jesus' time the Genesis command, "Be fruitful and multiply," was taken with utmost seriousness.[167] Yet there are no allusions to Jesus' physical children in historical literature. It is incredible that the children of a person who was worshiped as a unique manifestation of God would not gain recognition.

However, in spite of a strong sense of duty among Jews to procreate, there were, of course, cases of infertility. So there is the remote possibility that Jesus was sterile or that his wife was barren. If such had been the case, it might help to explain why there is no reference in the Gospels to the Priestly creation account that stresses procreation, and why Jesus referred wholly to the Yahwist creation account, which does not associate procreation with the institution of marriage. Also, the children could have died before Jesus became an itinerating teacher. In ancient times the probability of such tragedy was much greater than today. Further, if Jesus did have children, they did not become prominent in the life of the early church and thus did not become memorable on their own merit. Jesus and his movement belonged to the prophetic stream of Hebraic tradition that did not ascribe significance to an individual merely because of his family status. Even though the prophets married,[168] in most cases no mention is made of their children. Isaiah's children were recorded by his disciples not because they inherited a charismatic mantle, but quite incidentally because their names happened to be titles of their father's sermons.[169] It is probable that Peter, as a married Jew, had children. But even though the early church elevated him to a preeminent standing among the apostles, there is no mention of any son of his in apostolic history. This demonstrates only that the activities of Peter's children were not significant enough to be remembered in the oral tradition and later recorded in the writings of the church. Any one of these three possibilities could amply explain how Jesus could have been married even though there is no mention of his children in extant literature.

How far have we progressed in answering the central question: Was Jesus married? The New Testament assumes that Jesus had normal sexuality and sexual desire, both of which are essential for humanness and prerequisite to marriage. Those biosocial qualities were indicated in the following ways: Jesus' male foreskin was cut; his general and individual relationships to the opposite sex display no sexual phobias; and his maturity was gained through exposure to the inevitable temptations of manhood. Jesus unreservedly approved of conviviality and connubiality and did not suggest that either was defiling per se. In view of no overt evidence to the contrary, it is reasonable that the silence of the New Testament should be interpreted to mean that Jesus internalized the Jewish mores pertaining to sex and marriage. Ancient Jews thought that sexual desire should always be channeled into a "one flesh" holy wedlock. By action as well as by teaching Jesus showed that a man could do God's will and eat ordinary food.[170] Can we not assume that his action and teaching vis-à-vis the usual marital diet were similar?

The New Testament silence on Jesus' overt sexual activity can be understood in the context of the Hebraic value structure. The Hebrews resisted both the deification and the debasing of sexuality. Although sexual mythology was woven into the warp and woof of many ancient religions, it was absent in Yahwehism. On the other hand, conjugal activity within marriage was not thought of as a sin and a shame. Apropos here is a comment of Tom Driver:

Over against the pagan gods and the pagan religions we may say that Jesus appears as the great neutralizer of the religious meaning of sex. He does not, it is clear, regard sexuality as a mystical force emanating from the God-head. Jesus is no Dionysus. But contrary to what many Christians have assumed, the Jesus of the Gospels is not plainly "anti-Dionysian" either. That is, he does not, as far as we can tell, regard sexuality as a force emanating from Satan.[171]

Ascetic renunciation of marital life and orgiastic extolling of unharnessed sexuality are both ways of calling more attention to sex than Jesus and his fellow Jews believed it deserved.

The Gospel accounts of Jesus' parents have been interpreted to show that they, too, fully participated in the Jewish matrimonial customs. Because of commitment to a Hellenistically inspired virginal conception dogma, some may wish to bifurcate the question of the sexuality of Jesus and his parents. However, as will be shown, the taboos regarding both have grown historically on the same ascetic stem. It is unlikely that the person who respects rational congruity will acknowledge that Jesus was totally involved in basic human institutions while maintaining that Mary was a virginal mother and that Joseph was not the full father of Jesus.

Unless more ancient texts are discovered that contain relevant information, it is unlikely that students of early Christianity will arrive at a general consensus on *who* Jesus married. While the question of whom Jesus married is intriguing, it is not nearly as significant for the church as is an affimative answer to the basic question of marriage. The positive arguments of this chapter coupled with the documented material in the next mean that Jesus most probably was married to a Galilean woman in the second decade of life.

Chapter IV

TRADITIONAL ARGUMENTS
FOR JESUS' CELIBACY

In defending the hypothesis that Jesus married, there now looms
the basic task of examining carefully those sayings of Jesus that
have been appealed to through the centuries as the highest possible
authority for proving his celibacy.

JESUS' SPOUSE IS THE CHURCH

*Jesus said to them, "Can the wedding guests fast while the bridegroom
is with them?" (Mark 2:19a).*

In the patristic era it was argued that Jesus was literally unmarried because he had a bridegroom-bride intimacy with the church.[1]
Accordingly, he would have been a bigamist if he had married a
woman. This unimaginative view still has currency, as seen in this
recent comment: "It would be better not to speak of the celibacy
of Jesus: if he did not take a wife, it is because he is the spouse of
the church."[2]
Actually there is little basis for assuming that Jesus even
thought of himself as a bridegroom vis-à-vis the community of his
followers. Joachim Jeremias shows that exegetical evidence favors
identifying the bridegroom figure in Mark 2:19a (and Synoptic
parallels) and in Matthew 25:1–13 with YHWH.[3] Moreover, the
disciples are compared by Jesus to wedding guests, not to the
bride.[4]

Jesus chose the marriage metaphor to refer to the quality of his relationships to his disciples. The prophets had asserted: "Thus says YHWH, 'I remember . . . your love as a bride' "; also, "As the bridegroom rejoices over the bride, so shall God rejoice over you."[5] In contrast to some of his contemporaries, who conceived of the religious life as a gloomy fast divorced from happiness, Jesus followed the strain of his Jewish heritage that accentuated its qualities of joy and love. It was the early Christians who introduced the bridegroom-bride imagery in reference to Christ and the church.[6]

SEXUAL DESIRE IS EVIL

You have heard that it was said, "You shall not commit adultery." But I say to you that every one who looks at a woman lustfully has already committed adultery with her (Matthew 5:27–28).

This saying of Jesus, as usually translated in the Sermon on the Mount, contains a verse that is appropriated by those anxious to demonstrate that Jesus had a distaste for sexual desire. For example, the Protestant monk Max Thurian employs Matthew 5:28 to fortify his assertion that Christians "must follow Christ in aiming at the pure love which renounces life."[7] Tertullian influenced the interpretation of that verse in Latin Christianity when he used it as the basis for castigating sexual desire expressed either by a man for his fiancé or by a husband for his wife. Either expression, he maintained, is of the essence of fornication.[8] Jerome also used the text as a basis for criticizing all infatuations by the unmarried or the married. He called anyone with ardent sexual desire for his spouse an adulterer.[9] In a treatise that earnestly advocates celibacy, Gregory of Nyssa interpreted Matthew 5:28 to mean that Jesus was denouncing those who have "employed any faculty in the service of pleasure."[10] Augustine believed that "the Devil sowed the seed" for libidinous craving, and quoted Matthew 5:28 to prove that its gratification is wrong.[11] If sexual desire is bad, as these champions of orthodoxy assumed, it would have been impossible for the superlatively good man Jesus to have had such desire.

Does the contextual meaning of Matthew 5:28 show that it can properly be used to prove that Jesus had an aversion to all expressions of sexual passion? In Matthew 5:21–22, 27–28 are found parallel sayings in style and content. In both Jesus quoted a Decalogue commandment and probed its inner meaning. He focused on the importance of rooting out the attitudes that can lead to the overt actions of murder and adultery. In the paragraph preceding those sayings Jesus declared firmly that his teachings were not intended to supplant the Torah. He came not to abolish the law, but to fill it full. Consequently Matthew 5:27–28 cannot be taken to mean that Jesus' teaching is contrary to the spirit of the Decalogue. In those Hebrew commandments there is no suggestion that sexual desire is immoral. On the contrary, the conjugal relations of husband and wife are given protection and dignity by the prohibitions against adultery and coveting another man's wife. In Matthew 5:28 Jesus is not advocating a novel interpretation but was, to use George F. Moore's words, "uttering a Jewish commonplace."[12] An ancient Jewish teaching shows this to be the case:

You are not to say that only he is called adulterer who uses his body in the act. We find Scripture saying that even he who visualizes himself in the act of adultery is called adulterer. And the proof? The verse "The eye also of the adulterer waitest for the twilight, saying 'No eye shall see me.' "[13]

Verses 27 and 28 of Matthew 5 both pertain to offenses against marital relations, but the latter verse refers to persistent thought of illicit sexual indulgence. Therefore the verse should be translated in a more restricted manner than has usually been the case in European languages. Textual authorities agree that *gunē* should be translated here as "wife" with "of another" understood.[14] It appears that Erasmus was the first European textual critic to recognize that *gunē* should be rendered in Latin as *uxor* (wife). In English, the Great Bible of 1540 properly translates *gunē* as "another man's wife." Another Greek term in Matthew 5:28 deserving attention is *epithumia*, usually translated as "lust." However, it is a morally neutral term meaning "longing," and needs to be modified by *pathos*, as in Colossians 3:5, if an evil connotation is desired. It has a good connotation in Luke 22:15, where Jesus confides, "I have earnestly desired (*epithumia*) to eat this passover with you."

There is no basis in Matthew 5:28 for maintaining that Jesus thought strong desire for someone of the opposite sex was in itself bad. F. C. Grant's judgment about this verse is right:

It does not forbid the natural desire of a young man for a young woman, or her desire for him, which leads to marriage; for the desire here denounced is one that involves adultery. . . . The fundamental Jewishness of the saying seems certain, and should be understood as forbidding the indulgence of the eyes and of the imagination, the covetous desire for another man's wife.[15]

William G. Cole's observation is also correct: "Those groups in the early church who interpreted this particular verse to mean that *all* erotic impulses are evil simply revealed their Hellenistic bias. They obviously misunderstood Jesus entirely, misled by their underlying dualism."[16]

Lactantius, a Christian rhetorician in the patristic era, was an exception among the Hellenized Christians, for he held that Jesus was criticizing only the ideas that precede adulterous conduct. Lactantius affirmed that sexual desire is sanctioned when it is an urge to merge in holy wedlock. "When God invented the plan of the two sexes," he stated, "he placed in them the desire of each other and joy in union."[17] Luther also correctly interpreted Matthew 5:28. Some who were puzzled by this verse asked him if it was proper for unattached men and women to have sexual desire for one another. He responded with the comment that those who ask such "silly" questions do not understand either nature or Scripture. He queried, "When would people marry if they had not desire and love for one another?" Trouble comes if such is lacking. He then explained the confusing verse by offering this terse maxim: "One is not to look at another as every one is to look at his wife."[18] More recently David Mace has remarked:

There have been people of fanatical zeal who have distorted this saying of Jesus. He obviously did not mean that a young man seeking a wife should experience no feelings of sexual desire as he contemplated an eligible young woman. Nor did he mean that the wholesome pleasure a man might feel in admiring a beautiful woman, or the delight with which a woman might look upon a fine specimen of manhood, was evil in itself. What he meant, surely, was that the best way in which we can all safeguard ourselves from unfaithfulness is to refuse to let the imagination dwell upon the thought of a sexual relationship which if it actually took place would violate a marriage, our own or another's.[19]

CELIBACY IS PREREQUISITE TO DISCIPLESHIP

If any one comes to me and does not hate his own father and mother and wife and children and brothers and sisters, yes, and even his own life, he cannot be my disciple (Luke 14:26).

This teaching of Jesus has also been exploited in order to identify him with the later celibate movement in Christianity. The Catholic theologian Edward Schillebeeckx explains it in this strong assertion: "That whoever belongs to Jesus' group in a special way cannot do other than leave everything and give up married life is an authentic biblical fact."[20] Surprisingly, not only those who belong to a celibate tradition interpret Luke 14:26 in this manner. Karl Barth cites this verse among those showing that "there are those for whom entrance into the married state is not only not commanded but temporarily or even permanently forbidden."[21]

If Jesus were advocating the celibate life for others, and if he, unlike those he criticized, practiced what he preached, then it can be concluded that he was a celibate also. But even a cursory examination of the verse shows that it is addressed to those who have wives and children, just as they have parents. It is actually a textual proof for those who maintain that Jesus' original disciples married. Moreover, one should not overlook that Jesus was not addressing just those who were to become ecclesiastical leaders. Could Jesus, speaking to the "great multitudes" in Luke 14:25, be laying down celibacy for everyone as a necessary prerequisite to discipleship? Certainly not.

What, then, does this strange saying mean? Jesus' hyperbolic style should first be considered. In order to make a point forcefully to those whose minds seemed Gospel-proof, Jesus frequently used conscious exaggeration.[22] He found some persons so hardened by routine religious practices that stark and jagged language was necessary to make them reassess their value priorities. When confronting the lethargic, Jesus used high voltage vocabulary, hoping that the shock treatment would cause some to alter their mode of living. This stark manner is like that of another ancient Jew who said: "If a man does not show himself as cruel toward himself, his children and his household . . . he does not succeed in acquiring Torah."[23] Jesus' teaching in Luke 14:26 is similar in style and content to his abrupt response to the person who excused himself from Christian discipleship because of a filial duty. "Follow me," Jesus enjoined, "and leave the dead to bury their own dead."[24] Elsewhere Jesus made his point without hyperbole when he said: "He who loves father or mother more than me is not worthy of me."[25] In Luke 14:26 "hate" is a Semitic idiom meaning "love less."[26]

Jesus did not harshly advocate the renunciation of one's family. In fact he maintained that the weighty Mosaic law, "Honor your father and mother," carried with it the duty to continue caring for them as they grew older.[27] It is altogether possible that Jesus, who was both literally and figuratively the "first-born of many brethren,"[28] was the breadwinner for his mother and siblings for some years. Since Joseph is not present in any of the Gospel accounts of the adult Jesus, he may have died while Jesus was between the ages of twelve and thirty. Perhaps one reason why Jesus delayed leaving Nazareth until he was "about thirty years old" was his sense of obligation to support a family of at least seven members.[29] Therefore, in the full context of the Gospels, Jesus certainly felt that family loyalty is an important responsibility. However, if it imposes obligations that seriously impede acting on the *agape* imperative, filial commitments should be subordinated. One's mother and wife are valuable just as one's hand and eye, but the natural desire for all of these should not separate one from the real true life.[30] Unless there is a malignancy, the actual cutting off of a troublesome part of the body displays little more than hysteria. Likewise, the abandoning of difficult relations is only an effective way of rooting out spiritual distractions in extreme circumstances.

Jesus believed that sex, marriage, and family life are not the be-all or end-all of life, and that his followers should become independent of any ties that were incompatible with religious dedication. Luke 14:26 follows immediately after Jesus' banquet parable, which tells of one invited guest who excused himself from participating in the festivities because of his wife. Dramatically portrayed here is the plight of the person who allows marital concerns to become greater than the sovereign claim of God upon his life.

Some Jews in Jesus' time argued thus: since the same term is used in Scripture for revering both God and parents, the two expressions of devotion are equal.[31] But Jesus endorsed the priorities expressed in the arrangement of the Decalogue.[32] Judging from his practices, he did not think that the love of God usually cut one off from a broad range of fraternal associations. Also, his Good Samaritan parable clarified that love is a sham apart from taking long-range responsibilities for particular individuals near at hand who need personal assistance. Jesus was not a mystic who believed that the command to love the Lord with all of one's self implied a solitary life. Indeed, some of his contemporaries made him the target of continual criticism because in their judgment he tended to be too inclusive in his human sympathies.

Why, then, did Jesus call attention to those extreme situations when severing close ties with natural affections becomes mandatory? Probably his own personal struggle with family pressures caused this emphasis. Jesus' first recorded words display friction with his parents. They "did not understand" their son's absorption in theological scholarship.[33] Also, Mark's Gospel indicates that Jesus was alienated from his frustrated Nazareth relatives. In an effort to protect him from increasing opposition, Jesus' family "set out to take charge of him; for people were saying that he was out of his mind."[34] However Jesus resolved to continue his hazardous mission and not return to the safe carpenter's shop even though his own family did not approve. In John the tension between Jesus and his family is also apparent. Mary is depicted as not comprehending her son. Rather curtly Jesus said to her, "O woman, what have you to do with me?"[35] And later in John Jesus' "brothers had no faith in him" and quarreled with him about the way he conducted himself.[36] Elsewhere he testified: "A man's foes will be those of his own household."[37] Jesus probably quoted these words from Heberw prophecy because he found them to be fulfilled in his own experience. For he said, "A prophet is not without honor, except in his own country, and among his own kin, and in his own house."[38] Jesus' tragic experience with his family and hometown paralleled that of Jeremiah.[39] In order to carry out the dictates of his conscience, Jesus found it necessary to replace some blood ties with the brotherhood of those who shared his interpretation of Scripture. He proclaimed his emancipation from kinship worship by asking when his natural family was at hand: "Who are my mother and my brother? . . . Whoever does the will of God is my brother, and sister, and mother."[40]

Jesus was not focusing on the renunciation of marriage but dealt with the expendability of the entire gamut of ordinary bonds. This is shown in Luke 18:29, which follows the episode of Jesus with the rich young ruler. A parallel is established between discarding material goods and leaving wife, home, children, parents, and brothers for the sake of God's rule.

In a treatise entitled "Who is the Rich Man that shall be Saved?" Clement discussed Jesus' teaching regarding forsaking possessions and loved ones. He perceptively rose above isolated sayings in the Gospel and recognized that what the Christian should abandon is not riches and family but attitudes toward them that are incompatible with the divine command of love.[41] It shows that at least one of the fathers had a clear notion of what Jesus meant in his teachings on "leaving" wife, family, and home.

Saint Anthony, a century after Clement, took literally Jesus' words to the rich young ruler.[42] Moreover, he and his followers made a universal rule from this exhortation to an individual: "If you would be perfect, go, sell what you possess and give to the poor."[43] The difference between Clement and Anthony is the difference between a rational and a fanatical Christian. Clement, faithful to the New Testament ethic, advocated a temperate use of wealth. It was not the *possession* of money but the *serving* of money that Jesus criticized.[44] Also, Paul stated that the root of evil is the *obsession* with money.[45] Both Clement and Anthony saw a parallel between the treatment of one's possessions and of one's physical desires. Anthony so renounced his natural impulses that even eating necessary food filled him with shame.[46] Clement, on the other hand, believed that the physical was a good creation of God and was to be so treated. Far from renouncing bodily functions, he claimed that Christians should marry even as all the apostles did. One of the greatest perversions of church history came when Anthony and the hermitic movement that he initiated took literally Jesus' words about hating one's own life, loved ones, and possessions.

JESUS ADVOCATED THE EUNUCH WAY OF LIFE

There are eunuchs who have been so from birth, and there are eunuchs who have been made eunuchs by men, and there are eunuchs who have made themselves eunuchs for the sake of the kingdom of heaven. He who is able to receive this, let him receive it (Matthew 19:12).

This verse has been paraded in orthodoxy from the third century onward as the cardinal authority for showing Jesus' advocacy of celibacy. According to the commonly held interpretation, the third usage of "eunuch" is not to be understood in the ordinary sense of a man who is congenitally impotent or castrated. Rather, it is assumed that Jesus gave the term an entirely new and glorious meaning: one who remains perpetually virginal for religious reasons, even though he is genitally sound. This interpretation holds that Jesus recommended such a life for those who have the temperamental capacity for receiving it. Although Jesus did not explicitly indicate that he was among those "eunuchs for the sake of the kingdom," it is generally assumed that he identified himself with those who had voluntarily renounced the sexual life.

This classic interpretation of the eunuch saying originated with Basilides, a Gnostic teacher who lived at Alexandria in the early second century.[47] He assumed that Jesus was speaking of those who abstain altogether from marriage.[48] Through a lengthy commentary on the Gospels he was able to disseminate his interpretations widely.[49] Basilides' judgment on this and other passages was dictated by his docetic conviction that Jesus did not get involved in the material realm. Indeed, he maintained that it was Simon of Cyrene who was nailed to Jesus' cross, while Jesus stood by laughing.[50] Although he was judged by later Christians to be an "arch-heretic,"[51] his perverse ideas nevertheless infected the mainstream of Christian tradition.

Some of the most eminent spokesmen of Catholic Christianity have championed an interpretation like that of Basilides'. Tertullian asserted: "The Lord himself opened the kingdom of heaven to eunuchs and he himself lived as a virgin. The apostle Paul also, following his example, made himself a eunuch."[52] In that same third century Cyprian assumed that Matthew 19:12 pertained to virginity and to the promise of higher heavenly reward to those who kept celibate vows in perpetuity.[53] In the next century Methodius,[54] Jerome,[55] and Augustine[56] adopted this position, thereby making it inflexible dogma. Jerome's comments on Matthew 19:12 have become especially significant due to a 1954 papal encyclical addressed to holy virgins. Pope Pius XII quoted this challenge of Jerome with approval: "The Lord's word is as it were an exhortation, stirring on his soldiers to the prize of purity. He that can take it, let him take it: let him who can, fight, conquer, and receive his reward."[57] Lest one think that Vatican II has caused some *aggiornamento* of this position, a document it approved in 1965 states: "Priests, through virginity or celibacy undertaken for the sake of the kingdom of heaven (Matthew 19:12) are consecrated to Christ in a new and exalted sense."[58] Moreover, Pope Paul VI, in his encyclical on priestly celibacy, uses Matthew 19:12 as his principal documentation for the pre-eminence of perpetual virginity.[59] Karl Rahner, although a bellwether of liberal Roman Catholicism, defends priestly celibacy by appealing exclusively to Matthew 19:12 in his recent open letter to a disturbed priest. Amid criticisms of those who distort scriptural texts, he declares that this particular text means that Jesus is ennobling the clerical renunciation of marriage.[60] Dogmatic interpretations of this verse similar to those of the celibates cited above are also usually given by Protestants. For example, Floyd V. Filson writes: "Undoubtedly Jesus meant . . . the deliberate decision to refrain from marriage to be free to devote one's entire time to the cause of the Kingdom. . . . Jesus . . . did not marry."[61] Dozens of similar interpretations by other outstanding scholars could be added.

The biblical exegete Bengel coined the profound epigram: a text without a context is no more than a pretext. This saying is well illustrated by the standard interpretation of Matthew 19:12. That obscure verse has been ripped from its context and made the vehicle for carrying ascetic freight through most of church history. This treatment has extensively damaged the image of a virile Jesus that is pictured in the Gospels. A careful restoration of the original context by literary and historical exegesis is needed. An analogy might be useful here. In Milan the figures of Jesus and his disciples as conceived by Leonardo da Vinci have in recent years been restored. Art technicians, working with delicate tools on the refectory wall where the Last Supper scene was painted, have been able to flake away the layers of pigment placed there by those who lacked the originator's genius. Only after restoration was completed did art lovers realize the loss of beauty that had resulted from centuries of glossing over by inferior painters. So, too, the exquisite Gospel portrait of Jesus has suffered from so many overlays by pallid ascetics that those looking for quality in religious life see little more in the popular image than a nonauthentic morose caricature. An excellent illustration of this is in the interpretations of Matthew 19:12 that we have examined. Like the art restorer with his painting, the theologian must recover the original meaning.

The eunuch saying is embedded in Matthew 19:3–15, a passage that emphasizes the positive values of marriage and children. Since Jesus offered an unprecedented use of the term "eunuch," its meaning can be extracted only in context. Yet the context, far from advocating vows of permanent virginity and thereby discrediting marriage, gives the strongest authority of the Christian religion for believing permanent marriage to be holy. One commentator refers to the passage as "the highest word ever uttered on marriage."[62]

In light of this main theme, would Jesus be likely to convert the meaning of "eunuch," a term associated with something horrible and despicable among Jews,[63] to a praiseworthy connotation? In his culture, to be a eunuch meant not only the loss of virility but also religious excommunication[64] because it contradicted God's will in creation. *Prima facie* it is unlikely that Jesus took what was associated with a detestable condition and made it a laudatory term referring to the spiritually self-castrated. Closely examined, the passage provides the clue to the real significance of the eunuch saying.

A question of the Pharisees in Matthew 19:3 sets the stage for the dialogue to follow: "Is it lawful to divorce one's wife for any cause?" The point of the inquiry is contained in the phrase "for

any cause." The legality of divorce per se was not an issue among
the Jews; the current concern was the *extent* of legitimate grounds
for divorce. The Mishnah indicates that beginning in the first
century B.C. divorce was disputed by prominent rabbis. According
to a Deuteronomic law a husband could divorce his wife if he
found "some indecency" in her.[65] At issue was the meaning of
those vague words. Shammai and his school contended that "a man
may not divorce his wife unless he has found unchastity in her,"
whereas Hillel affirmed that a man had the right to divorce his
wife for any cause—"even if she spoiled a dish for him."[66]

There is considerable evidence that Hillel's liberal position was
the prevailing one. The oldest extant Jewish marriage contract indicates that in the fifth century B.C. a husband could capriciously
divorce his wife without offering a reason, although reciprocal action by his wife was not sanctioned.[67] In the second century B.C.
divorce was advised on trivial grounds: "If your wife does not obey
you at a signal or a glance, separate from her."[68] Philo indicated
that divorce was easy to procure.[69] Josephus spoke dispassionately
of his many serial marriages and of divorcing those who "displeased him."[70] Rabbi Akiba believed that one should divorce and
remarry "if he finds another woman more beautiful."[71]

Gentile divorce mores at that time were quite similar. A Roman
consul inscribed upon his wife's tombstone: "Seldom do marriages last till death undivorced; but ours continued happily for
forty-one years."[72] Referring to the lax marital bond of his fellow
Romans in the first century A.D., Seneca quipped: "They divorce
in order to remarry; they marry in order to divorce."[73] When
Herod Antipas, a Palestinian tetrarch, was visiting Rome, he became enamored of his brother's wife Herodias. She agreed to separate from her husband and marry Antipas if he would divorce the
daughter of the Nabatean king, Aretas.[74] When Antipas agreed to
this scheme—irregular even by the tolerant mores of the time—
criticism arose in his home realm. John the Baptist was beheaded
because he condemned that scandal and thereby antagonized
Herodias.[75]

Jesus, evidently believing that the dignity and sanctity of marriage was being denigrated by the widespread flippant attitude toward divorce, resolutely proclaimed what he held to be the

Creator's reason for making two human sexes. Rather than citing the grounds for divorce championed by Shammai or by Moses, he directed his interlocutors to the view of marriage recorded in Genesis 2. Thus he avoided becoming involved in legalism while pointing to the ideal of permanent monogamy. It is significant that Jesus considered the last word on marriage to be the first word. He appealed to the Yahwist account, which stresses the companionship reason for marriage. His quotation, "The two shall become one flesh," is the climax of an episode in Genesis that begins with a criticism of celibacy (the term comes from *caelebs*, meaning "alone"). Would it have been possible for Jesus to exalt that primeval story and then conclude with an exhortation that it *is* good for man to be alone? Hardly.

There was no abrupt break between Jesus' ideal for marriage and the view expressed in Genesis 2. Max Thurian shows a better appreciation of his mentor, Karl Barth, than of the New Testament when he writes: "Christ did not experience marriage, physical love and sexual union. His life is therefore the valid foundation of the vocation of celibacy in the new era. Jesus Christ calls in question the system of creation and nature."[76] In light of Jesus' explicit endorsement of the "one flesh" theme of the Yahwist's story, the view that he challenged the creation order of marriage is not cogent.

Jesus found the highest standard of sex and marriage in the prelegal order of creation. A tacit assumption here is that marriage should not be considered principally a legal contract involving dowry payments, divorce certificates, and the like. Rather, the original and final norm for all men, Jew and Gentile alike, is that marriage is an unconditional interpersonal covenant witnessed by God.[77] Thus the nuptial bond is essentially not one the social order can give or take away. Omitted from Jesus' view was the magical presumption of a later time that no marriage could be "valid" and "indissoluble" unless a certified representative of God or the state performed the proper ritual. He did not consider the remedy for the frivolous attitude toward divorce to be new judicial enactment or priestly benedictions at weddings. For him the marriage bond occurred when two were joined by God, whose quintessence is love; they were thereby committed to one another for life.

Jesus appealed to what Moore calls the "utopian element" of Jewish ethical teaching.[78] In this and other situations he viewed the conduct of life not in terms of legal requirements, but in terms of fulfilling the categorical moral imperative of *agape*. For those who see the meaning of life from that vantage point, questions about grounds for divorce become trivial and banal. "What God has joined" was Jesus' way of referring to his marital idealism. Like some rabbis he endorsed the proverb: "Marriages are made in heaven." They believed that ever since creation "the Holy One has been sitting in heaven arranging marriages."[79] In Jewish tradition this providential claim is based on the statement in Genesis 24:50 concerning Isaac's marriage: "The thing proceeds from the Lord."[80] One quaint rabbi went so far as to say: "Forty days before the creation of a child, a proclamation is made in heaven: 'So-and-so's daughter is to marry so-and-so's son.' "[81]

Jesus followed his comments on the original purpose of marriage in Matthew 19:4–8 with an implication in 19:9 that his disciples found startling. This verse reads: "Whoever divorces his wife, except for unchastity, and marries another, commits adultery." "Except for unchastity" is probably an interpolation made after divorce for adultery became the practice in the early church. The judgment that the exception clause is not authentic is based on its being inconsistent with other New Testament treatments on marriage and inharmonious with the context of Matthew 19. Paul, Mark, and Luke dealt with Jesus' view of marriage and divorce but show no knowledge of this Matthean exception. Moreover, if this exception clause had been given by Jesus, it would make him a casuist, siding with Shammai's interpretation of the Mosaic code. Alan H. McNeile properly rejects the clause because it is "opposed to the spirit of the whole context."[82]

Matthew 19:9 is an implication drawn from the prophetic theology of the Hebrews. The covenant-making YHWH had an unconditional "for better, for worse" bond with his people, so a married couple should strive to imitate that relationship. From at least as far back as Hosea, the doctrine of divine forgiveness of the unworthy was a motif in Israel's religion. Hosea quite possibly understood the depth of both marital and divine love through a tragic personal experience. When his wife Gomer committed adultery, Hosea did not want to separate from her permanently.[83] He found in himself and in YHWH that infidelity of the loved one prompted the desire for reconciliation, not divorce. According to Hosea 2:13–14, Israel "went after her lovers and forget me says YHWH; therefore, behold, I will woo her." The response to adulterous behavior in both cases was not withdrawal of affection but more love. The same motif, which reversed the usual human response to infidelity, was developed by Ezekiel. He conceived of YHWH as a devoted husband who is brokenhearted when his bride Judah prostitutes herself to foreign lovers. Nevertheless, after disciplining his adulterous wife he forgives and restores the marriage covenant.[84]

"The ethic of Jesus is the perfect fruit of prophetic religion. Its ideal of love has the same relation to the facts and necessities of human experience as the God of prophetic faith has to the world."[85] This, Reinhold Niebuhr's astute judgment, is amply illustrated in Jesus' sayings and actions regarding marriage. He was chagrined that the prophetic doctrine of repentance and forgiveness was treated by many in his day as irrelevant to ordinary human problems. In the past, Manasseh, the most evil of Hebrew kings, committed many atrocities but was accepted by YHWH after repentance.[86] By contrast, Jesus saw wives unilaterally rejected for both petty and major offenses by men who believed this action to be part of their religious duty. Domestic forgiveness fell short of seven times, not to mention "seventy times seven." In Matthew 5:32, Jesus admonished that divorcing a wife often meant, in effect, casting her into a life of adultery. In the ancient Jewish culture homemaking was the only vocation open to a virtuous woman, so prostitution was the common means of support for a rejected wife. Jesus was convinced that self-righteous vindictiveness that scorns and abandons is a travesty of divine-human love. Consequently he unflaggingly emphasized divine forgiveness to the repentant.

Some Christians have fathomed Jesus' comprehension of true love in the marriage relation. In an exquisite manner Shakespeare intuited its nature:

> Love is not love
> Which alters when it alteration finds
> Or bends with the remover to remove.

> O no! It is an ever-fixed mark
> That looks on tempests and is never shaken. . . .
> Love's not Time's fool, though rosy lips and cheeks
> Within his bending sickle's compass come.[87]

In this ode to "the marriage of true minds" Shakespeare mirrored the love relation expressed in Ephesians 5:25–26. There Paul wrote: "Husbands love your wives as Christ loved the church and gave himself for her that he might make her holy." This injunction extols a self-giving quality of love that attempts to imitate in the marriage relation Jesus' gracious actions that fill the Gospel.

The earliest interpretation of Jesus' teaching on marriage apart from the New Testament is contained in the *Shepherd* by Hermas, which was composed about fifty years after the Gospel of Matthew. In the following dialogue Hermas questions an angel:

Q. If someone have a wife who believes in the Lord, and he finds her in adultery, does the husband sin if he continue to live with her?

A. . . . If the husband knows that his wife has gone astray, and if she does not repent but persists in her unchastity, and yet the husband continues to live with her, he also becomes guilty of her sin and shares in her adultery.

Q. What then shall the husband do if his wife continue to give way to her passions?

A. Let him dismiss her and remain by himself; if he remarries another he also commits adultery.

Q. What if the wife repents and wishes to return to her husband: shall she not be taken back?

A. Assuredly. If the husband does not take her back, he brings a great sin upon himself; for he ought to take back the sinner who has repented. . . . In this matter man and woman are to be treated exactly in the same way.[88]

Hermas believes that the only sanctioned options open for the Christian whose spouse is unfaithful are separation or reunion with the penitent. To marry someone else when no contrition is apparent closes the door to the future possibility of repentance and reconciliation, so this option is not permitted.

In his earlier years Tertullian interpreted Matthew 19:9 as Hermas did.[89] But after becoming a devotee of Monatist asceticism, he changed his perspective and lost the distinctive Christian approach to divorce. He came to abhor the idea of a husband pardoning his contrite wife after she committed a sexual sin and consequenty rejected the *Shepherd* as authoritative Christian literature. Consistent with this outlook, Tertullian also maintained that the parables of the lost sheep and the prodigal son are not applicable to Christians.[90] He not only rejected the *Shepherd* of apocryphal literature but, in effect, he also reversed the values of the "Good Shepherd" of the Gospel. Due in part to Tertullian it has often been thought that Jesus himself did not approve of forgiveness when a sexual sin was involved.

This exposition of Matthew 19:3–9 shows that Jesus was responding to a cultural situation in which there was considerable anxiety over the instability of the marriage bond. He focused on the Hebraic theology of marriage and shunned casuistry. Jesus believed that questions about grounds for divorce are irrelevant for couples who have an appreciation of the original intention of marriage and a prophetic understanding of the God who joins people together in love. Divorce arose because of a domestic disease that Jesus called "cardiosclerosis" (a transliteration from Matthew 19:8, meaning heart-hardening). The malady causes couples to become so calloused that divine love has no way of entering to transform hostility into harmony. Rather than adopting the pattern of interrelations between the compassionate father and the repentant prodigal, they act like the unforgiving elder brother. Jesus was pleading for open-minded empathy (or, to use a Hebrew idiom, "a circumcised heart") that values reconciliation rather than repudiation. Jesus thought that if separation did occur, the offended should display a measure of YHWH's steadfast love and be continually open to the renewal of the original covenant. This meant that one who was separated should not feel free to marry someone else while his first partner was still living.

The verses that follow can now be fitted into the movement of thought. In 19:10 the disciples articulate the customary marital outlook by saying, in effect, "If a husband is bound to his first wife so inextricably, it would be better not to marry at all." In a somewhat cynical manner they found marriage to be appealing only if easy divorce was sanctioned. Their rejection of the theological ethic of permanent marriage was totally unacceptable to Jesus. As

McNeile comments, "He cannot be supposed to agree with the disciples that 'it is not advantageous to marry,' after his solemn statement that marriage was a divine ordinance."[91]

The disciples' response functions here as elsewhere. For example, in Matthew 19:13–14, 23–26, the role of the disciples is to bring up a current point of view that shows a misunderstanding of Jesus' ethic. In each case Jesus corrected them by restating his point in a more forceful way. A recognition of the style of discourse is pertinent for grasping the thought flow in this passage. If there were the incongruity of Jesus approving the disciples' disapproval of his doctrine of permanent marriage, then Matthew 19:12 could easily be interpreted as a challenge to renounce marriage. Jesus would then be involved in double talk: lifelong marriage is the divine ideal but celibacy is better, and all who can avoid matrimony should. But both the theological context and the literary style of Matthew 19 make this impossible. So in Matthew 19:11, when Jesus said "Not all men can receive this precept," the antecedent of "this" is not the disciples' comment on the expediency of celibacy but his own teaching on no divorce and no remarriage. Recognizing human weakness, he was aware that only a portion of those involved in domestic alienation would be able to live up to the lofty ideal.[92]

This exposition of Matthew 19:3–11 provides a full background for interpreting verse 12. There we find the only reference to eunuchs in the Gospels; the eunuch saying is not alluded to in any of the three sources antecedent to Matthew: Paul's letters, Mark, and the common source "Q" used by Matthew and Luke. This raises the question of whether the saying is authentic.[93] However there is no textual evidence indicating that the saying is a later addition, and most of the scholarly commentators do consider it genuine.

Jesus first distinguished between eunuchs by nature and eunuchs by surgery, using a rabbinic classification.[94] To these Jesus added a type of "eunuchs who have made themselves eunuchs for the sake of the kingdom of heaven." Since the first two types exhaust the categories for physical eunuchs, it is agreed by virtually all biblical critics that the third usage is figurative.[95]

Several conjectures have been made about the meaning of the eunuch metaphor. The most popular one, which I have rejected, has been that Jesus was referring to the celibate life. A broader interpretation was offered by Chrysostom: "When Christ says, 'They made themselves eunuchs,' he is not speaking of the amputation of a member . . . but of the suppression of passionate thoughts."[96] However, the Matthew 19 context suggests not the suppression of passion so much as its expression when the two become "one flesh." Nor does the literal meaning of "eunuch" necessarily point to the suppression of sexual desire. As Chrysostom himself acknowledged, the physical castration of an adult often does not weaken passionate thoughts. It can destroy the ability but not the will to indulge in genital gratification. Few have found this interpretation plausible.

In 1 Corinthians 7, where the earliest recorded teachings of Jesus are found, Paul gave valuable clues for unraveling the eunuch metaphor:

To the married I give this charge, which is not mine but the Lord's: a wife should not leave her husband; if she does, she must either remain separated or be reconciled with him; and a husband must not, in similar circumstances, divorce his wife. . . . A wife is bound to her husband as long as he lives.[97]

Paul's counsel accords with my earlier exposition of Matthew 19:9. Regarding Matthew 19:12, Paul did not use the term "eunuch" in his writings, so there is no direct evidence of what meaning he would give it. However, he made one comment that indicates that either he was not aware of any saying about eunuchs by Jesus or that he did not think the saying pertained to those who had not married. At the beginning of a paragraph in which he advised some not to seek marriage, he admitted: "On the question of celibacy, I have no instructions from the Lord."[98] If Paul had any knowledge of a celibate Jesus or of his teaching recommending celibacy, he would probably have given some indication of this in 1 Corinthians 7.

Justin offered a further hint on the meaning of the eunuch saying. He quoted Matthew 19:12 and interpreted it as prohibiting "second marriages."[99] Although this ambiguous expression could possibly refer to remarriage after the death of the first partner, nothing in context indicates this. On the other hand, in the sentence immediately before the Matthew 19:12 citation, Justin quoted Jesus' saying, "Whoever marries a woman who has been put away from another man commits adultery." So it seems clear that Justin used the eunuch saying to witness that remarriage after divorce was not sanctioned by Jesus. He did not associate the eunuch metaphor with the virginal life but with the sacrificial demands of continence by those who have not been reunited after separation.

Clement of Alexandria explicitly interpreted the eunuch metaphor as referring to remarriage after separation. Concerning Matthew 19, he claimed that what the disciples wanted to know was whether it was permissible to marry again when a man's wife had been condemned for adultery. Clement counseled continence for such men. These "eunuchs" are compared to athletes who discipline themselves by abstaining from sexual intercourse.[100]

With the avalanche of sexual asceticism in the centuries immediately prior to the fall of the ancient Roman empire, this early interpretation of the eunuch saying—and probably the correct one—was disregarded. Only in recent years has it been dredged up and re-examined. Curiously enough, two celibates, Jacques Dupont,[101] a Benedictine, and Quentin Quesnell, a Jesuit, have shown unimpeachable evidence that the eunuch metaphor has no reference to Jesus advocating a lifelong virginal way of life. Quesnell not only discerns the way Matthew 19:10–12 fits into the immediate context but shows a depth of insight into the whole sweep of the prophetic ideal of steadfast love. He concludes his careful study with this summary:

"Then it is better not to marry at all." That is the unbeliever's foolish reaction. It is the choice of the safer way, the selfish way; it is attempting to "save one's life." Jesus does not accept this. He restates the doctrine, quite as strongly as before, and attaches to it the Christian challenge of faith; let him grasp it who can. Restating it, he admits that it is a frightening prospect. It can leave a man in a state comparable to that of those most pitiable of men—the eunuchs. . . . A man must in marriage take the risk of staking all he has and is on one person, becoming one flesh with her. And this means that in his fidelity and determination to continue to express that fidelity forever, he also takes the risk that if his wife and he have to separate, he will be left for the rest of his life pledged to loyalty to one who is not even there. To continue this loyal and perfect love, even when the love is not returned, is effectively to make oneself a eunuch, a person incapable of marriage for the rest of one's life. The world will not understand this. And it cannot make any sense except as a step toward inaugurating a world where all men will love perfectly and fully. It makes sense, that is, only as a contribution to the kingdom of heaven.[102]

Matthew 19:12 concludes with, "He who is able to receive this, let him receive it." In an understanding manner Jesus acknowledged that total adherence to his teaching is not anticipated. Some may not have the fortitude and patience needed to maintain continence until they can unite again with the one who has spurned their love. Others may not have the openness to engage in the therapy of mutual confession of sins. But some will persevere for the sake of expanding the sovereignty of God in domestic relations. They will allow the break in the "one flesh" to smart until a resetting can be made that will knit together into a stronger bond than before.

Those who have interpreted Matthew 19:12 as pertaining to perpetual virginity have violated the basic principle of literary interpretation, namely, to present the author's point of view. Within the context of Matthew 19 the eunuch saying refers to the till-death-do-us-part quality of true marriage. The thrust of the saying is that permanent marriage is sanctioned, not permanent virginity.

The contextual meaning of both Matthew 19:12 and of Luke 14:26 suggests that John Erskine's intuition of Jesus' personal life may have been accurate. Perhaps Jesus descended into the hell of having to endure—as did Socrates—a bitchy hussy. Or, like Hosea, he could have felt the pangs of separation from a prodigal spouse. Yet he was faithful to her, hoping that she would respond to his love. The evangelists, writing a half century later and coming from areas outside of Nazareth, may not even have been aware of these circumstances that could have been a part of Jesus' preitinerating life.

THE ANGELIC LIFE SHOULD NOW BE COPIED

Jesus said to the Sadducees, "The sons of this age marry and are given in marriage; but those who are accounted worthy to attain to that age and to the resurrection from the dead neither marry nor are given in marriage, for they cannot die any more, because they are equal to angels and are sons of God, being sons of the resurrection" (Luke 20: 34–36).

This reply of Jesus is commonly regarded as second only to Matthew 19:12 for providing authority from the Gospels for the Christian celibacy movement and for proving the hypothesis that Jesus never married. Otto Borchert shows how Luke 20:34–36 has been related to Jesus' outlook on marriage:

Jesus saw a great benefit in marriage. In some of his parables he depicted the joy of a wedding as the greatest there is. . . . Why did Jesus not have a wife if he believed that there is no higher or better state than that of marriage? . . . He was already living according to the laws of the fulfilled Kingdom of God, when there shall be no marriage, neither giving in marriage. He was already "the Son of man which is in heaven" (John 3:13).[103]

Marcion, a second-century heretic, was the first to give a celibate interpretation to this passage. He assumed that Jesus was depreciating those who marry by the clause, "the sons of this age marry," and was exalting the remainder who do not marry. Only the latter are Christians, and hence they are "those whom God accounts worthy of obtaining the resurrection of the dead."[104] A century after Marcion this interpretation affected orthodox Christianity. Cyprian did not hold that celibacy was prerequisite to salvation, but he did believe it was indispensable for all who wished to avoid worldly pollution. In an exhortation to virgins, which Pope Pius XII quoted with approval, Cyprian said: "That which we shall be, you have already begun to be. You already possess in this world the glory of the resurrection; you pass through the world without its contagion. In preserving virginal chastity you are the equals of the angels of God."[105] Jerome assumed that Jesus was teaching that human perfection consists of becoming like the sexless angels:

What others will hereafter be in heaven, that virgins begin to be on earth. If likeness to the angels is promised us, we shall either be of no sex as are the angels, or at all events, which clearly proved, though we rise from the dead in our own sex, we shall not perform the functions of sex.[106]

Augustine's view[107] was similar to the position of Ambrose, who interpreted Jesus' saying as: "Chastity has made even angels. He who has preserved it is an angel; he who has lost it a devil."[108]

Contemporary Roman Catholicism basically continues to champion the interpretation of the patristics. Vatican II recognized celibate priests as an eschatological vanguard, witnessing to this world of the resurrection life that is to come.[109] Likewise Pope Paul VI quotes Luke 20:35–36 and interprets it thus: "Perfect continence . . . anticipates the fulfillment of the kingdom as it sets forth its supreme values which will one day shine forth in all the children of God."[110] In concluding a clinical study Marc Oraison states: "The strongest motivation that gives the most complete meaning to celibacy is what we called the mystical motivation: the personal reference to the transsexual destiny of humanity in the world of the resurrection."[111]

Christians other than Roman Catholics have also been gripped by the fanciful notion of living the angelic life on earth. John of Damascus, the arch-dogmatist of the Greek church, equated the sinless life with the sexless angelic life: "Virginity is the rule of life among the angels, the property of all incorporeal nature. . . . Celibacy is an imitation of the angels. Wherefore virginity is as much more honorable than marriage as the angel is higher than man."[112] Thurian has also asserted on the basis of Luke 20:34–36 that celibacy is a living sign of the pure world to come: "Celibacy is related to the resurrection from the dead; it is a sign of eternity, of incorruptibility and of life."[113]

But is it legitimate to associate this saying of Jesus with celibacy? How strangely incongruous that those who profess to follow the Incarnate One should attempt to imitate angels, who by nature are not incarnate. It is only by spurious methods of textual interpretation that Luke 20:34–36 gives celibacy any support. As Tertullian long ago pointed out in criticizing Marcion, Jesus was arguing against Sadducees, who did not believe in the resurrection of the dead. Jesus' treatment of marriage was incidental to the affirmation of life after death. This being the case, Tertullian thought it was invalid to extract from Jesus' reply a standard regarding earthly marriage.[114] Clement, who also lived in the generation after Marcion (around A.D. 200), claimed that anyone examining the passage carefully would realize that Jesus was not being critical of marriage but of a carnal interpretation of human resurrection. The point was that corruptibility is not a quality of the immortal life, although it necessarily is intrinsic to all that is physically born.[115] By *reductio ad absurdum* logic, Clement argued that the ascetic who rejects marriage on the claim that he is now living the nonphysical life of the resurrection should also neither eat nor drink.[116] He showed that when the ascetic's reasoning is carried out consistently it leads to self-inflicted death.

If this resurrection saying of Jesus is not concerned with denigrating marriage and exalting celibacy, then what can its contextual meaning be? The members of the Jerusalem-based priestly party, called the Sadducees, were outraged by Jesus' action of the previous day. He had violently demonstrated against the priests, for he believed they were turning the temple into a commercial enterprise. The members of this religious establishment were determined to liquidate the outside agitator from the North as soon as possible. Realizing that it would be helpful to have some of his sayings to use against him, they grilled him with loaded questions. One thrust was probably their stock question for ridiculing the doctrine of the resurrection held by the rival Pharisaic party. The gist of the Sadducees' clever query was this: Assuming that there is a resurrection and that polyandry is not sanctioned, who would be married to a woman who survived seven husbands?

Given the materialistic concept of the resurrection popularly held by the Pharisees[117] and the Jewish doctrine of the sanctity of the marital relation, the Sadducees' question was a difficult one. Some rabbis in Jesus' day assumed that marriage and propagation would continue unchanged in the life after death.[118] Their belief in the reanimation of the corpse was quite similar to that of Christians who have accepted a doctrine of physical resurrection. Emanuel Swedenborg, for example, believed that the animal body of man is unchanged by death and that sexual desires and conjugal relations continue in heaven. He solved the Sadducees' riddle by saying that in heaven monogamy is the custom but that surplus husbands would wed spinsters who could not find a mate on earth.[119] This concept of a materialistic resurrection, common in most religions, was what Jesus was attempting to avoid in his cameo of the life after death.

Jesus alluded to the Jewish doctrine of angels in order to convey his incorporeal view of the resurrection in a current thought pattern. His era believed that angels did not eat or drink, marry or propagate.[120] Moreover, some Jews held that the righteous would become like angels in heaven.[121] Jesus believed that resurrected humans are like angels in that they do not die, and hence reproduction is unnecessary. Thus he indicated that the Sadducees' question could not be answered because it fallaciously assumed that the afterlife would be simply an extension of life as now experienced. Their question is similar to asking an atomic scientist to describe the colors of electrons, for the interrogator assumes that if there are such things as electrons, they must be colored.

Jesus could have replied to the Sadducees in the same manner that he answered another question raised that day in Jerusalem. Man should render unto earthly life the concepts and the physical practices that belong to the natural sphere but render to the resurrected life the radically different concepts that are appropriate to a fleshless existence. For Jesus, responsibility to civil government and to earthly marriage was important but not ultimate. Actually, Jesus' reply to the Sadducees can more properly be used to encourage marriage in this life than to authorize celibacy. D. H. Lawrence wrote with Christian insight: "We may well believe that in heaven there is no marrying or giving in marriage. All this has to be fulfilled here, and if it is not fulfilled here, it will never be fulfilled."[122]

Although Paul did not directly allude to the reply to the Sadducees, he does help to clarify Jesus' view of the relationship between marriage and the resurrection. Paul, like Jesus, opposed the Sadducees' disbelief in the resurrection and in angels.[123] Paul also rejected the metaphysical materialist's view that personal reality in the resurrection necessitates the physical body and metabolism.[124] He believed that natural desires and functions are metamorphosed by the resurrection in a way that mortals cannot fathom.[125]

He claimed: "Man's mind has not imagined what God has prepared for those who love him."[126]

The best clue to the nature of life after death comes from extrapolating on the nature of love as experienced in its greatest depth here and now. If love abides forever as an attribute of God,[127] then personal relationships in the deathless life cannot have less of it than at present. The quality of love that is essential for marriage will be intensified, even though its expression will inevitably be transformed as one moves from the provisional material to the permanent immaterial sphere. Maurice Wiles ably reasons that the marital relationship may become more inclusive:

Marriage represents the deepest form of personal relationship, the highest form of social experience which is open to us in this life. Within the limitations of our finite, human experience such a relationship can only be shared with one other person at one time. But need such a limitation apply to the life of heaven? Is it not more reasonable that the life of heaven should involve a going on from, rather than a drawing back from, the highest kind of personal relationship known to us? If this is so, the point of the saying of Jesus may be not that heaven involves a reversal of the words of God, "It is not good that man should be alone," but rather that a relationship which in this life necessarily involves exclusiveness finds in heaven an ultimate fulfillment in which the element of exclusiveness is done away. In epigrammatic form we might say that the real significance of the saying is not that in heaven we shall be married to nobody but rather that in heaven we shall be married to everybody.[129]

A characteristic of the life of the earliest Christian community may afford a clue to this more inclusive life. It was able, at least temporarily, to expand the communal bond of ideal family life with respect to sharing possessions and concerns. The transcending of a mine-thine dichotomy resulted in receiving from each community member according to his ability and in giving to each according to his needs. Perhaps marriage is not only the church in miniature but is, as Bishop Taylor suggested, the "nursery of heaven."[129]

Two Roman Catholics, Sidney Callahan and Ruud Bunnik, have recently shown how totally removed Jesus was from advocating virginity in his reply to the Sadducees. Since masculinity or femininity is an essential part of one's self-identity, Mrs. Callahan postulates that personal immortality cannot be characterized as a fellowship of neuter spirits. In the self that survives death, sexuality will probably be transfigured rather than suppressed or superseded. Callahan interprets Luke 20:34–36 in this suggestive manner:

Marriage and the exclusive relationship of the male-female couple can only be meaningful within the framework of limited time and space. Human procreation . . . depends upon the two-sexed couple for genetic variability, specialized reproduction, and efficient long-term nurturing. However, without time, death, or need of the sexual differences evolved in time for the service of procreation, the couple no longer need be exclusive. As Christ taught, the wife married to seven brothers sequentially in this life can hardly belong to one of them exclusively forever. . . . To say, however, that there is no marriage in heaven is not the same thing as saying that there is no sexuality. A withering of sexuality in the absorbing God-man relationship is not the only alternative to marriage. . . . In this life married people can experience through sexuality multidimensioned joy in knowing and loving another; perhaps this exclusive relationship prepares man for an inclusive love and joy of all in the new life. . . . Full communion with others would be possible. . . . The ecstasy of male-female coupling could be expanded to all human relationships.[130]

Bunnik indicates that the context of Jesus' reply to the Sadducees shows unmistakably that he rejects the absurd assumption of folk religion that social practices of the present life can be equated with the mode of living in the afterlife. Thus, when it is held that the virginal life is an anticipation of life in the "eschaton," the mistake is made of equating a category of earthly life with the resurrected existence. Bunnik also asserts:

When virginity is identified with the condition of life in the eschaton, it seems difficult to avoid the suggestion that in the eschaton the bond of marriage that has bound people on this earth is completely lost. This seems hardly possible: reborn man keeps his history and his personal solidarity. The eschatological realities transcend worldly realities, but they do not discard them as worthless. . . . If the strength of this eschatological argument is not very great with regard to virginity in general, it seems even weaker with respect to the ecclesiastical minister. . . . His ministry requires a maximum solidarity with his community.[131]

The celibate Bunnik offers both theoretical as well as textual reasons for rejecting the Roman Catholic interpretation of Luke 20:34–36. His judgment accords with the general New Testament doctrines of marriage and the resurrection.

The alleged evidence in the Gospels for Jesus' celibacy has been weighed and found wanting. The traditional "proof-texts" for his perpetual virginity, which have been ripped from their contexts by ascetically oriented interpreters, not only do not hint that he never married but can more properly be used to show that he endorsed permanent marriage as being of penultimate value. His use of the bridegroom metaphor proves no more than that he had a life-affirming general outlook and a positive view of weddings. His teaching about sexual desire means that the libido should not be adulterated by adulterous schemes. The hyperbolic saying about "hating" one's wife and family means that in cases of irreconcilable conflict domestic allegiance should be subordinated to commitment to God's cause. The eunuch saying, if authentic, pertains to Jesus' sanctioning fidelity to a wayward spouse in hope of eventual mutual reconciliation. His response to the Sadducees displays that the resurrected life will surpass but will not negate earthly love between spouses. Thus the five passages from the Gospels that are most frequently relied upon for justifying vows of celibacy and that at first glance may appear to condone or encourage such vows are legitimately open to quite different and even opposing interpretations.

Chapter V

PAUL AND SEXUAL
RELATIONS

Paul wrote more about sex and marriage than anyone else in first-century Christianity. What light do his writings cast, directly or indirectly, on the question: Was Jesus married?

THE MARITAL STATUS OF CHURCH LEADERS

In one of the earliest New Testament books Paul made an incidental comment that is of major importance for understanding the marital status of holy men in nascent Christianity. To defend his concept of freedom Paul raised the personal question: "Do we not have the right to be accompanied by *adelphēn gunaika* as the other apostles and the brothers of the Lord and Cephas?"[1] Scholars agree that *adelphē*, literally "sister," here means not a blood relation but a woman who belongs to the Christian community.[2] *Gunē* in an ambiguous term that can have either the general meaning "woman" or the more specific meaning "wife," depending upon the context. In English versions *gunē* is translated in about half of its New Testament occurrences as "woman" and half as "wife."[3]

There are several clues to the meaning of *gunē* in 1 Corinthians 9:5. First, it would be redundant if it meant "woman," following as it does a word meaning "Christian woman." Second, the verb and object in this verse form the idiom *gunaika periagein*, meaning in classical Greek "to have a wife."[4] Third, early Christian tradition recorded in the New Testament and in patristic literature claimed that Peter, who is included in 1 Corinthians 9:5 as one with a gunē, was married and had a mother-in-law.[5] Fourth, Clement of Alexandria, who knew Greek well, interpreted gunē in 1 Corinthians 9:5 to mean "wife."[6] Moreover, Basil, although an ascetic church father, accepted that all the apostles had once been married and put them forward as an example of the Christians of his time for whom celibacy was not attractive.[7]

In spite of solid evidence to support translating adelphēn gunaika as "a Christian wife,"[8] a consensus reading has long been delayed. Tertullian, who in his later years came to regard marriage as legalized fornication, asserted that in 1 Corinthians 9:5 Paul's connotation was "simply the unmarried women who used to minister to the apostles in the same way as they did when accompanying the Lord."[9] Jerome, assuming virginity to be prerequisite to the saintly life, injected his bias into the Vulgate. Avoiding the Latin term uxor (wife), he translated gunē as mulier (woman). Consequently, the standard Roman Catholic Douay version— which relies on the Vulgate—notes at 1 Corinthians 9:5 that "wife" is an erroneous translation. The proper translation of gunē has been widely accepted only in recent years. Today both Roman Catholic[10] and Protestant[11] exegetes agree that gunē in 1 Corinthians 9:5 definitely means "wife." Thus Paul affirms that he had not exercised his privilege of bringing along a wife on his journeys as the rest of the apostles had done.

The original Greek text of the Acts of the Apostles may have contained an explicit reference to apostles' wives. In the "Western" textual tradition it is stated that "wives and children" of the apostles were present in a Jerusalem "upper room" after Jesus' crucifixion.[12] Not only Erasmus and Calvin, but also major textual authorities today favor reading gunaikes in Acts 1:14 as "wives."[13] Thus it seems that the apostles lived with their wives at least from the time of Jesus' resurrection.

It is reasonable to assume that some wives were present in the band of Jesus from its inception, for there is no reason for postulating a basic change in attitude toward female companionship before and after witnessing the resurrection. As noted earlier, the indirect reference in the Gospels to Peter's marriage cannot be interpreted to mean that he was the only married disciple during the period of Jesus' public ministry. Since all of Jesus' disciples were subject to the traditional mores of their Jewish culture, it is most probable that those over twenty years of age when "called" were married. It is even possible that the wedding feast that Jesus attended in Cana was for one of them. Nathaniel was from Cana and the account of Jesus' visit with him comes immediately before the wedding episode.[14]

Luke 8:2–3 refers to many women or wives (*gunē*) who itinerated with Jesus and the "Twelve" and "provided for them." In light of the Palestinian custom of women being married at the age of puberty, and in view of the danger that a guardian would surely see in permitting a single daughter to live with men, it can be assumed that all of these women had married. Indeed, the very thought of a traveling ladies' aid society composed of virgins is so unfitting in first-century Judaism as to be ludicrous! Some of the women may have been widows. Perhaps Joanna's husband, Chuza, had died, leaving her free to travel. But some were probably also disciples' wives whose domestic obligations did not tie them down and who could cope with the rough life of travel. Frequently, due to various factors, Jesus' band did not even have the shelter customary for some animals.[15]

If Jesus married as hypothesized, then his wife, if still alive during his public ministry, may also have accompanied the group. Mary, called Magdalene, is the first named woman (*gunē*) in Luke 8:2 and she may have been his wife (also *gunē*). Jesus' several dozen followers traveled and lodged "two by two."[16] If Jesus and/or some of the disciples itinerated with their wives, it would be assumed that the married couples slept together in whatever accommodations they could find. The female companions continued in the band of Jesus after it left Galilee and went southward toward Jerusalem.[17]

Why would Jesus and his disciples travel with their wives? First, the wives could perform their customary role of providing for the needs and comforts of their husbands. Second, their presence could allay gossip. The suspicious outlook of Jews toward unattached men who traveled about is articulated in a book of wisdom from the second century B.C.:

He who acquires a wife gets his best possession, a helper fit for him and a pillar of support. Where there is no fence, the property will be plundered; and where there is no wife, a man will wander about and sigh. For who will trust a nimble robber that skips from city to city? So who will trust a man that has no home, and lodges wherever night finds him?[18]

Third, wives could function as evangelistic copartners. Clement stated that the apostles took their wives along "that they might be their fellow-ministers in dealing with housewives. It was through them that the Lord's teaching penetrated also the women's quarters without any scandal being aroused."[19]

There is evidence in Romans 16 of husband and wife teamwork in evangelism. Priscilla and Aquila were referred to by Paul as "fellow workers in Christ Jesus" and in charge of a church that met in their home.[20] It is also quite likely that a wife could even have been designated as "apostle." In spite of furtive attempts by some androcentric textual critics to convert a feminine name into a masculine name, it is probable that both Andronicus and Julia[21] were called "notable apostles" in Romans 16:7.[22] With respect to Julia one of the church fathers exclaimed: "How great was the devotion of this woman, that she should be counted worthy of the title apostle!"[23]

What bearing does the marital status of church leaders in the apostolic age have on the hypothesis that Jesus married? In Ephesians 2:20–21 Jesus is pictured as the standard-setting cornerstone for the apostolic foundation and for the entire structure of the Christian community. Since we know as a matter of fact that the apostles married and traveled with their wives on Christian missions, Jesus evidently did not object to that mode of living. Of course, all of the original twelve could, like Peter, have married before coming under Jesus' influence. If so, then the impact of Jesus' marital status could not be measured until the second-generation Christians came of age. Had Jesus been a lifelong celibate and advised the disciples to follow him, then they would be expected to enjoin future members of "the body of Christ" to emulate the "Head." On the other hand, if Jesus had married it would be expected that the apostles would advise the church leadership in subsequent generations to follow that pattern. The

latter situation seems to have been the case since church leaders
were generally married in the first centuries of Christianity. Indeed, historians have estimated that approximately forty of the
early popes were married.[24]

Paul's Pastoral Letters[25] show marriage to have been expected
of bishops, elders, and deacons. But there has been much controversy as to the type of marital experience expected. This is due
to the ambiguity of the phrase *mias gunaikos andra*, which is used
three times in the Pastorals to describe the prerequisites for different church offices.[26] A literal translation of the Greek is "husband
of one wife," but there are several possible meanings. It could
mean that an officer should not be a polygamist, but monogamy
was so completely accepted by Christians that such a stipulation
would have been needless. Interpreters have rightly preferred other
meanings. Some consider the phrase to be a prohibition of digamy,
that is, second marriage after the death of one's first partner.[27]
Although this interpretation does justice to the Greek, it should
be rejected because it is inconsistent wih the rest of the Pauline
corpus. Remarriage after the death of one's spouse is permitted
and in some cases recommended.[28] Also, would Paul encourage the
remarriage of widows who are not elderly[29] and in the same letter reject remarriage for widowers in similar circumstances?

There is a third interpretation that fits the context better: a
church officer should be one who is faithful to his wife. Jean P.
Audet adroitly comments:

If we follow the general trend of Paul's instruction, we soon realize
that he is not concerned here with an event in a man's past life which
suddenly appears in the present as an unexpected obstacle to the service of the assembly (as remarriage would be), but rather with a present
attitude which would naturally appear among the qualifications required for the pastoral service. . . . In short, what Paul is asking here
is that the servants of the assembly begin by giving all the signs of a
harmonious and stable marriage. Whether it be their first marriage or
their second does not matter.[30]

Audet's interpretation is in line with some of the best ancient
and modern biblical scholarship. Theodore of Mopsuestia has been
called with good reason "the greatest exegete of the ancient church
. . . emphasizing . . . the grammatical and historical method of

interpretation."[31] He held that Paul was excluding from ordination those unfaithful to marriage vows, but not the digamist.[32] Also, Walter Lock writes that it is unlikely that "husband of one wife" referred to anything except fidelity within monogamous marriage.[33]

The relevance of Paul's requirement of stable marriage for church officers is displayed in his question: "If a man does not know how to manage his own household, how can he care for God's church?"[34] Paul's use of imagery from parenthood shows that he believed there to be a close parallel between familial relationships and the wider relationships of the Christian community.[35] Since the local churches in which the officers served were house churches, the ability to govern one's own family had a direct bearing on the leadership in the "household of faith."[36]

Clement comprehended what Paul had in mind when he wrote:

The particular characteristic of the married state is that it gives the man who desires a perfect marriage an opportunity to take responsibility for everything in the home which he shares with his wife. The apostle says that one should appoint bishops who by their oversight over their own home have learned to be in charge of the whole church.[37]

Unfortunately, when the celibate wing of the church became powerful, this natural tie between household and church management was lost. Ironically, the church reversed Paul's position and codified it. In the Codex Justinian it is declared that a bishop is better equipped for responsibility in the extended church family if he does not have responsibility to a particular family of his own.[38]

THE DE-MARRIED APOSTLE

The earliest historical sources have disclosed that those who preceded Paul were married and those who followed him were expected to be married. Why then did Paul, by his own admission, deviate from the standard practice of being accompanied by a wife? Was it because he had been reared in a sexually ascetic milieu alien to Judaism? Or was it because of some nonascetic concerns that he became an exception to the norm?

In answering these questions we should consider Paul's social and religious development. Paul informed Christians in his autobiographical comments that he was Hebrew to the core.[39] He was raised a member of the Pharisaic party, which interpreted the requirement to marry and reproduce quite rigidly. Until recently it was assumed that Paul spent his prepuberty years away from Palestine in the Diaspora at Tarsus. As there was a Stoic school of philosophy in Tarsus, it has even been conjectured that Paul's Jewishness was greatly diluted by Hellenism at an early age.[40] However, this theory must be rejected on the basis of careful textual studies by W. C. van Unnik.[41] He has established that Tarsus-born Paul was reared at Jerusalem in his parental home by analyzing Acts 22:3 and 26:4–5. In contrast with a Diaspora Jew such as Philo of Alexandria, Paul was not exposed to the sexual asceticism that characterized much of the Gentile philosophy. Instead he was reared at the hub of Hebraic culture in the historic capital of Israel.

Paul did not think of himself as a Jewish renegade after his conversion to Christianity. Late in life he could in all honesty write of Jewish ethical requirements: "The law is holy, and the commandment is holy and just and good."[42] He did not substitute a Hellenistic ethic for a Hebraic one. What he rejected was not the traditional ethical imperatives of his culture but his attitude toward their fulfillment. He discarded as "refuse" his early ambition to get right with God by virtue of his own moral strivings.[43] Paul wrote: "Do we then overthrow the Torah by this trust? By no means! On the contrary, we uphold the law."[44] To illustrate that the Christain's godward trust is essentially Hebriac, he discussed the religious experience of the first Hebrew. Abraham, a married man, was praised as history's preeminent example that God declares righteous only those who renounce their self-sufficiency.[45]

Paul's writings evidence that he spurned the asceticism he encountered as a missionary to the Gentiles. He consistently embraced the Hebraic principle that the flesh was not intrinsically defiling, even though as an "ambassador of Christ" he diplomatically accommodated himself to the scruples of some Gentile converts. Responding to those who believed some physical indulgences to be tainted, he declared: "I am absolutely convinced, as a Christian, that nothing is impure in itself."[46] After reiterating the psalmist's testimony that "the earth is the Lord's and everything in it," Paul asserted that the physical should be received with thanksgiving.[47] He did not reject Hellenistic asceticism because he snobbishly believed that anything of pagan origin was necessarily inferior to what the Jewish culture had championed. For example, he introduced the Stoic concept of conscience into Christian thought. Although open to Hellenism in other ways, Paul believed that the acceptance of moral dualism would subvert the indispensable Hebraic concept of the psychosomatic unity of the personality.

In 1 Corinthians 7 Paul discussed his own marital status and the single life option. Those who assume that Jesus was a lifelong celibate often rely on parts of this chapter for their clinching documentation. They posit that Paul and Jesus both lived a virginal life because attending to concerns of the flesh would distract from devotion to spiritual matters. They also assume that Paul imitated Jesus, and that Paul articulated more fully than Jesus the reason why marriage should be renounced by those who could repress sexual desire.

In 1 Corinthians 7:8 the Greek text actually suggests that Paul had at one time married. However, due to faulty translations, this implication has been obscured. For example, the Revised Standard Version is doubly misleading when it renders verse 8 thus: "To the unmarried [agamoi] and the widows [chērai] I say that it is well for them to remain single as I do." "Single" is an interpretative addition that is not justified by the Greek text. Agamos in Pauline usage means "a de-married person," male or female, and it occurs in the New Testament only in verses 8, 11, 32, and 34 of 1 Corinthians 7. In verse 8 Paul included himself among the agamoi in a phrase coupled with chērai. There agamoi may mean widowers since the special word for widower, chēros, is not used in the New Testament or in the Septuagint and only rarely in classical Greek literature. In verse 11 agamos definitely refers to someone who is separated from a living spouse. To such a person Paul advised: "Let her remain unmarried [agamos] or else be reconciled to her husband." A male agamos is referred to in verse 32. The distinction between "the unmarried [agamos] woman and the virgin [parthenos]" in verse 24 confirms that agamos refers to someone who had at one time been married.

Among those interpreters who think Paul married, some have assumed that he was separated from a living spouse while others have considered him to have been a widower during his Christian career. Clement wrote around A.D. 200 that Paul as well as all the other apostles was married but that his wife did not accompany him on his journeys because of travel inconveniences.[48] Both Clement and Origen[49] believed that Paul's wife resided in Philippi and that he addressed her as a loyal "yoke-partner" (*suzugos,* Philippians 4:3). In classical and Hellenistic Greek the feminine noun *suzugos* can mean "wife" and those Greek fathers may well have had a more accurate insight into the contextual meaning of *suzugos* than modern exegetes. However, Ernest Renan cautiously endorsed the Alexandrian interpretation and speculated on who the Philippian wife might be. He thought she might have been Lydia, the wealthy businesswoman who opened up her home to Paul when he first visited Philippi.[50] Finding it remarkable that Paul did not explicitly mention this important convert in his letter to the Philippians, Renan believed that she might have been the unnamed yoke-partner.[51]

Other Roman Catholic and Protestant scholars have suggested that Paul's wife was living during his career as a Christian, but they do not tie him with a Philippian woman. Edward A. Schillebeeckx conjectures: "Paul's own life of abstinence was not the celibacy of an unmarried man, or of a widower. In all probability it was the celibacy of a man who had either left his wife or had been left by her on his conversion."[52] This conjecture fits nicely into the domestic reaction that might be anticipated when a son of orthodox Jews becomes a Christian. Paul's Pharisaic father[53] probably betrothed his son to a Pharisee's daughter. It is plausible that Paul's wife and parents severed connections with apostate Paul after his conversion, and because of this he did not refer to them in his letters. He did, however, express his "great sorrow and unceasing anguish" over the rejection of Christianity by his Jewish kinsmen.[54] Kenneth J. Foreman assumes that Paul wrote from personal experience when he dealt with the case of marital separation because of a non-Christian partner in 1 Corinthians 7:12–16. He suggests that Paul possibly had a wife who left him: "All that Paul says about marriage in this chapter suggests that he had been through a marriage that almost but never quite succeeded—a marriage which he felt interfered with his spiritual life, a marriage in which it had been impossible to be both a good husband and a good Christian missionary."[55]

From at least A.D. 300 on some interpreters have maintained that Paul was a widower. Even Methodius, who was passionately devoted to virginity, assumed that Paul married but was a widower when an apostle.[56] Luther states: "Paul counted himself among the unmarried and widowers, but it appears that he was married in his youth according to the custom of the Jews."[57] Modern scholars have followed up on Luther's conjecture and have pointed out that Paul could not have attained leadership as a Jewish rabbi in his pre-Christian years had he not been married.[58] According to the Mishnah, living without a spouse is forbidden unless one already had married and begotten children.[59] Also, ancient Jewish tradition states that "an unmarried man may not be a teacher of children."[60] Moreover, in the Talmud this custom is recorded: "A man shall first take unto himself a wife and then study Torah."[61] On the basis of rabbinic sources such as this and the New Testament evidence that Paul was a trained rabbi,[62] Johannes Jeremias concludes that Paul "must have been a widower rather than a bachelor."[63]

From this investigation it should be concluded that Paul married when young. However, there is no way of knowing whether his wife died before or during his career as a Christian apostle. She may have been alive throughout Paul's life, although 1 Corinthians 7:8 makes the widower status more probable. It may be translated: "To the widowers and widows I say that it is good for them to remain as I am." The marital circumstances of Jesus and Paul may have been parallel. As Jews both would have been betrothed by their fathers. Then, during their years of travel, they both could have been widowers or separated from their wives.

If Paul had married and had no ascetic prejudice against sexual relations, why was he reluctant to encourage those who had never married to do so, and those whose spouses had died to remarry? The apostle's preference for the unmarried state was on different grounds than those given by some of his Corinthian adversaries. Whereas they discouraged marriage for moral reasons, Paul's reasons were eschatological and practical. His advice was motivated not

by the belief that sex was bad but by the conviction that the end
was near. When Paul wrote the Thessalonian and Corinthian
letters he was convinced that human history would be completed
in his own lifetime.[64] The expectation of an imminent end of the
age is especially apparent in 1 Corinthians 7. The key to its interpretation is the recognition that Paul "thought of himself as living
not in the first century but in the last century."[65] He believed that
customary activities were shadowed by the "impending distress."
Consequently, in the brief span of time remaining, celebrating,
mourning, buying, and marrying were not the most urgent concerns.[66] As an interim measure slaves who had gained Christian
freedom were advised not to struggle for freedom within the social
order.[67] Similarly, the continuation of the status quo was advised
for the married and for the unmarried. The latter were advised to
remain unattached unless they lacked continence. Depending on
individual temperament, Paul thought it better for some to wed
and for others not to wed.[68] He clarified that in spite of the rapidly
approaching end of history "it is no sin" to marry if one feels im-
pelled by sexual passion to do so.[69] Yet, due to the emergency
situation, the Jewish requirement to marry was suspended.

A comparison of Paul's later letters with his earlier ones shows
that his eschatological fervor cooled considerably. Just as it is evident that other great intellects—such as Plato and Goethe—
changed their minds, it is equally apparent that Paul's theology
matured. He gradually shifted from a futurist apocalypticism to
an inaugurated eschatology, and in so doing came in line with the
outlook of Jesus himself.[70] Recognizing the fluidity of Paul's
theology, it is most unfair to attempt to extract from 1 Corinthians
7 his comprehensive and final position on marriage.

Partly separable from his eschatological reason for the single life,
Paul offered what he considered to be a practical reason. He
thought that the unmarried have fewer distractions and hence
more opportunities to "please the Lord."[71] There has been considerable disagreement over whether or not this contention is generally true. Francis Bacon agreed with Paul: "A single life doth
well with churchmen, for charity will hardly water the ground
when it must first fill a pool."[72] The Roman Catholic church has
also sided with him. Pope Pius XII, in an encyclical defending

ecclesiastical celibacy, quoted 1 Corinthians 7:32–35 and Aquinas. The "angelic doctor" had declared that marriage "keeps the soul from full abandon to the service of God."[73] Pius pontificated: "Virginity is more excellent than marriage chiefly because . . . it is a supremely effective means for devoting oneself wholly to the service of God, while the heart of married persons will always remain more or less divided."[74]

There are others who dissent from Paul's generalization about the incompatibility of pleasing one's spouse and one's Lord.[75] Indeed, it is just as easy to infer from particular cases that the opposite is true. For example, John Calvin testified prior to becoming married: "I whom you see so hostile to celibacy, have never taken a wife, and I know not if I shall ever marry. If I did so, it would be in order to devote my time to the Lord, by being more relieved from the worries of daily life."[76] Jeremy Taylor, an outstanding Anglican bishop, agreed: "Though marriage hath cares, yet the single life hath desires which are more troublesome and more dangerous." Taylor believed that "a married man may spend as much time in devotion as any virgins or widows do."[77] The life of Bach illustrates that marriage is not necessarily a distraction from a Christian vocation. He was married twice and had twenty children. Martin Luther King, Jr., by having a wife and children, was probably motivated to devote himself more unstintingly to his civil rights mission that was crowned by Christian martyrdom.

Some celibates think the married life would distract less from spiritual goals and some married people think the celibate life would be less distracting, so the glamorized conception of the single life in 1 Corinthians 7:32–35 does not prove anything about Paul's marital status or wisdom. Significantly he admitted that his opinions on the unmarried life were his own and were not derived from the teachings of Jesus.[78]

PAUL'S GENERAL SEXUAL OUTLOOK

Paul reveals his general attitude toward sex in his concept of sarx, in his outlook on kissing, in his theory of personality, and in his nuptial imagery. He frequently used the term sarx in ethical discussions. It is misleading to give the term the literal translation "flesh." For in our culture the use of "the flesh" in moral discourse refers exclusively to the physical appetites and to sexual desire. Thus when the King James version reads that Paul denounced the "lust of the flesh," it is assumed that he, like some Hellenists and Victorians, believed that sexual desire is the cause of evil. As a result of linking sin with sex, the righteous person becomes the one who denies sexual desire.

Paul's view of *sarx* is best comprehended by analyzing Galatians 5:16–24, where the *sarx* desires are contrasted with the Spirit desires. He catalogued some fifteen sins as belonging to the realm of *sarx*. Of these only two have a specific sexual connotation: *porneia* (unlawful sexual intercourse) and *aselgeia* (lewdness).[79] The Galatians 5 catalogue is similar to the one that Jesus gave. In Mark 7:21–23, out of a list of thirteen "evil things coming from within" only three are specifically sexual. In both passages the main source of the bad conduct is not the libido but the mind, which causes the evil thoughts and action. For Paul *sarx* is a generic term referring to all those natural impulses that are in conflict with the spiritual impulses.[80] "The fruit of the Spirit" is listed as "love, joy, peace, patience, kindness, goodness, faithfulness, gentleness and self-control."[81] *Sarx* pertains to those personality traits that block the expression of love to one's fellow man as delineated in 1 Corinthians 13.

There is nothing basically Hellenistic or ascetic in Paul's ethic.[82] Referring to Galatians 5:16–24, Raymond T. Stamm comments: "This is Paul's way of stating the Jewish doctrine of the 'two impulses' which are at war within the heart of man."[83] Paul's use of *sarx* is similar to the use of the Hebrew cognate term, *basar*, in the Qumran texts.[84] W. D. Davies discusses the parallel:

It is clear that existence in the flesh does not in itself, as in Hellenistic thought, suggest or signify perversion. . . . The flesh can be "cleansed" and "purified" (*Manual of Discipline* 3, 6; 4, 20). In Hellenistic thought it is not the purification of the flesh that is desired, but escape from it, because the "flesh" is conceived there not only as the sphere where evil dwells, but as itself constituting evil.[85]

Paul thought that modest physical expressions of affection were undefiling even between the unmarried. He promoted a custom that an ascetic would shun for fear of intemperate erotic displays. Several of his letters conclude with a request that Christians kiss one another.[86] Since Paul's customary term for referring to Christians is "saints" or "holy ones" (*hagioi*), the intimate exchange between them is called the "holy kiss." There is no indication that the kiss was restricted in the first centuries of Christianity to church assemblies or to members of one's own sex.[87] Thus Tertullian advised a woman against marrying a pagan because her husband might become suspicious when he sees her kissing a Christian brother.[88] K. M. Hofmann argues that the kissing custom advocated by Paul and Peter[89] was not adopted from antecedent religions but was a distinct symbol of the earliest Christians for expressing the *agape* fellowship.[90] Perhaps the fraternal kiss was an innovation of Jesus, for in some early traditions he is associated with this practice.[91]

In the early church kissing was a common practice,[92] but the erotic overtones soon became a source of embarrassment to those Christians who believed that physical contact tarnished chastity. Thus one church father warned: "The kiss, or rather the salutation, should be given with the greatest care; since, if there be mixed with it the slightest evil thought, it excludes us from eternal life."[93] Another patristic complained that the "resounding kisses" at church meetings were causing foul rumors. He declared that unless kisses are "mystic" they will "counterfeit sanctity." "Do you not know," he inquired, "that spiders, merely by touching the mouth, afflict men with pain? And often kisses inject the poison of licentiousness. It is then very manifest to us, that a kiss is not Christian love."[94] It was not long before the fleshly symbol of love endorsed by the apostles was banned between sexes. In the fifth century a general church regulation stated: "Let the men give the men, and the women give the women, the Lord's kiss."[95] It was perhaps this stultifying restriction that caused the custom's demise in the medieval era. In contrast to the apostles' advocacy of kissing to celebrate the warm fellowship of Christians, members of modern churches usually avoid any touch more sensual than a handshake.

Paul integrated sexuality into his concept of the whole self.[96] He saw the social as well as the physiological function of coitus and realized that, unlike the digestive function, it is interpersonal in nature.[97] In 1 Corinthians 6, after criticizing the dualism of some libertines, he asked: "Do you not know that your body is a temple of the Holy Spirit?" D. Sherwin Bailey finds Paul's insight into the psychological aspects of human sexuality to be profound. He points out that Paul rejected the concept that sexual intercourse is an act detached from the psyche, involving no more than an exercise of the genitals. "On the contrary, he insists that it is an act which, by reason of its very nature, engages and expresses the whole personality in such a way as to constitute an unique mode of self-disclosure and self-commitment."[98]

Paul believed that genuine sexuality as expressed in marital unity was so important that he drew from it a figure for picturing the intimate bond between Christ and the church. The apostle found the ideal of marriage in the Yahwist creation story and quoted it in his Ephesian letter.[99] He then asserted that the deeper significance of Genesis 2:24 was hidden until the coming of Christ and the church.[100] One of the pranks in the history of biblical interpretation has been the sterilization of Paul's concept of marriage in this Ephesian passage. For example, Pope Paul VI used this passage to document his assertion that clerical celibacy is a sign of "the virginal love of Christ for the church."[101] Yet, as the Dutch Catholic Ruud Bunnik recognizes, it is the married state that the apostle has in mind. "The biblical image of the church as Christ's bride does not refer to virginity at all. The church is not a virgin; her chastity and flawlessness are those of marital faithfulness."[102]

Paul employed a daring analogy: "Husbands, love your wives, as Christ loved the church and gave himself up for her." Dorothea Krook suggests that the marital act can be viewed as symbolizing the essential features of Paul's theology:

Where more intimately, more intensely, more spontaneously, and more universally than in the act of sexual union between a husband and a wife is this experience relived and re-enacted—the "dying' to the world by a complete giving up of each self to the other, and the "rising" again into life, new-born, replenished, full of life and joy drawn from the divine plenitude itself.[103]

A devoted couple blending together in fleshly communion

parallels in some ways the grace-ful "Word made flesh" that "we have looked upon and touched with our hands" (1 John 1:1). In 1 Peter 3:7 husbands are advised to "dwell according to knowledge"—that is, have marital sexuality—with their wives and share with them the "grace of life."[105]

Ephesians 5:21–33 exposes Paul's ambivalence toward the opposite sex that he was never able to fully resolve. As a product of the ancient Mediterranean world he held that the wife's role should be subordinate to that of her husband. Yet, as one who attempted to imitate Jesus, he believed that men and women should have equal status. Thus within the same paragraph Paul can admonish wives to "be subject in everything to their husbands" and instruct the husband to "love his wife as himself." In 1 Corinthians there is the same ambivalence: he tells women to keep silent in churches but shows that he expects them to speak there; or again, he finds in the Hebraic doctrine of creation a basis for claiming both man's superiority to woman and man's equality with woman.[104] Paul was unable to extricate himself completely from the pervasive androcentricity of his culture. What is surprising is the extent to which he internalized the outlook of Jesus and accepted women as persons of importance. It was no misogynist who wrote Romans 16 or conducted the mission in Philippi. In Romans 16 Paul warmly greeted Christians, about one-third of whom were women. According to Acts 16 he spoke with women, lived with Lydia, his first European convert, and assisted a slave girl at Philippi.

RESPONSE TO SEXUAL ASCETICISM AT CORINTH

1 Corinthians 7 is often examined in isolation from the rest of the Pauline corpus by critics of Paul's view of sex and marriage. Thus interpreters frequently find just what they are searching for: an apostle abysmally warped in sexual outlook and in personal practices. Edvard Westermarck, for example, writes of Paul's "horror of sexuality as the worst sin of the flesh."[106]

Further, 1 Corinthians 7 is often interpreted without an examination of the Corinthian situation that he addressed. What was the general outlook on sex and marriage in the tiny Christian community within the large Greek city of Corinth? Paul's letters show that the Judaeo-Christian concept of the sanctity of the flesh was not well received by many. At Corinth there was a strong current of asceticism that originated in schools of Greek philosophy and religion.[107] This background of the fresh Corinthian converts made it difficult for them to assimilate a radically different ethic. Several passages indicate that the Corinthian Christians had been affected by the Gnostic movement.[108] Although it was characterized by a wide latitude of beliefs, most of the Gnostic sects were pessimistic in their view of the physical. Some Gnostics thought that promiscuous intercourse could be condoned because the flesh was insignificant.[109] Others condemned all sexual expression among both the married and the unmarried.[110]

Paul wished to demonstrate to Gnostic-prone Corinthian Christians that their philosophy of speculative knowledge that failed to dignify sexuality was inferior to the *agape* mode of life. Hence he combated both a promiscuous group of Gnostics in 1 Corinthians 6 and an ascetic group in 1 Corinthians 7.[111] But he knew that considerable diplomacy was needed in order to convince both groups that the flesh has an important role for the Christian.[112]

In 1 Corinthians 6:12–13 Paul quoted the position of the promiscuous and then responded. Did he do the same in 1 Corinthians 7:1 for the ascetics? Chapter 7 begins: "Now concerning the matters about which you wrote. It is good for a man not to touch a woman." The latter sentence has usually been interpreted as Paul's own position. Tertullian and Jerome believed it to be the apostle's judgment and so they drew the implication that it is bad to have marital relations.[113] But if verse 1b states Paul's position then the following verses make little sense. Because of this there is a growing consensus that 1b was a Corinthian slogan that Paul quoted for the purpose of rebuttal.[114] Moreover, he could well be accused of being mildly demented if in the same correspondence he advised the same men not to touch a woman but to kiss fellow Christians and in another letter he criticized those who have a self-abasing "Do not touch" prohibition.[115]

In 1 Corinthians 7:2–4 Paul defended marital intercourse as both a right and a duty. More explicitly than anywhere else in the Bible it is affirmed that partners are equally obligated to surrender their bodies to one another for mutual enjoyment. In connection with this passage Emil Brunner has written: "To the scandal of all ascetics, the New Testament nowhere explicitly bases sexual intercourse upon procreation, but always upon the natural impulse. . . . The Christian ethic must stand for the independent meaning of the erotic and sex element within marriage as an expression of love."[116] An ascetic scribe, evidently finding Paul's position embarrassing, doctored the text of 1 Corinthians 7:3 so that it read: "The husband should give to his wife the *good will (eunoia)* she is due." The King James version perpetuated that erroneous addition of *eunoia*.

Paul stated the traditional Jewish position in 1 Corinthians 7:5: "Do not withhold sexual intercourse from one another unless it is only temporary and by mutual agreement in order that you may devote yourselves to prayer; but afterwards resume relations, lest Satan tempt you through lack of self-control." Exodus 21:10 declares that a husband owes his wife her conjugal rights as a divine command. In the Mishnah the concession is given that a man preoccupied with religious matters could, with his wife's consent, abstain for one or two weeks from intercourse.[117]

After Paul presented his view on conjugal duties and temporary continence he made the ambiguous comment: "I say this by way of concession." What is the antecedent of "this"—marital intercourse or temporary continence? Celibate interpreters from the patristic era onward have usually maintained that Paul permitted sexual relations in marriage only because of the weakness of human nature. Augustine even argued on the basis of 1 Corinthians 7:6 that marital intercourse when pregnancy was not desired is a "venial sin."[118] However, since Paul was reared as an ultraorthodox Jew[119] and since the verses preceding this comment are fully in accord with practices sanctioned in Judaism, he certainly did not think of conjugal relations as a mere concession for those temperamentally unfit to cohabit in a nonphysical manner. Rather, like the rabbis Paul believed that short periods of abstinence from intercourse were a concession to the special dispositions of some. In order to avoid antagonizing the ascetically prone Corinthian Christians too much, Paul made some allowance for their scruples.

A close examination of the opening paragraph of 1 Corinthians 7 has disclosed that Paul's outlook on sex and marriage has often been twisted beyond recognition in the course of church history. J.-J. von Allmen observes: "Many warped interpretations of this chapter come from the fact that for centuries it has been scrutinized by celibates for whom marriage, not being their vocation, appears as a temptation and a fall."[120] The warning to be wary of ascetic exegetes is also apropos of other paragraphs of this chapter.

Due to the ambiguities in the Greek text of 1 Corinthians 7:36–38, it is sometimes assumed that Paul favored continent cohabitation.[121] Although "spiritual" marriage was occasionally found in the postapostolic church, the inspiration for it did not come from Paul. Indeed, it would be more legitimate to fault Paul for neglecting in 1 Corinthians 7 the spiritual aspects of marriage.[122] In 1 Corinthians 7:2–5, 9 marriage is regarded as a relief for those "aflame with passion." Werner G. Kümmel has persuasively demonstrated that verses 36–38 refer neither to a "spiritual" marriage nor to a father betrothing his daughter but to an engaged couple appehensive about consummating marriage due to the influence of ascetic Corinthians.[123] Henry Chadwick considers Paul's advice to the betrothed an excellent illustration of his way of delicately moderating some Corinthian fanaticism.[124] Those having a strong sexual desire for their fiancées were encouraged by the apostle to marry; correlatively they were advised that it is better to remain unmarried if such desire is absent.

REVIEW AND PREVIEW

This exploration of Paul's views of sex and marriage shows that, for the most part, he had a positive outlook.[125] Unless one resorts to the cunning method of citing isolated texts and overlooking the full context of Pauline thought, there is no basis for the claim sometimes made that he believed the virginal state to be intrinsically more holy or perfect. The fact that Paul had eschatological views when he wrote the Corinthians, which he later modified, and the fact that he was responding to specific needs of different factions of the Corinthian church should cause interpreters to exercise caution in extracting from 1 Corinthians 7 general norms regarding Christian sexual relations. Paul's most mature thought is in Ephesians, where there is no hint of preference for the unmarried state. In that letter, written toward the end of his life, Paul stated the Judaeo-Christian theology of marriage at its best. He took the old Levitical injunction regarding neighbor-love and applied it to the marital bond: "Husbands should love their wives as their own bodies. He who loves his wife loves himself. For no man ever hates his own flesh, but nourishes and cherishes it, as Christ does the church, because we are members of his body."[126]

What progress has been made toward proving the hypothesis that Jesus married? In previous chapters the absence of lifelong celibacy in ancient Judaism and the Jewishness of Jesus' ethic have been demonstrated. From the evidence of the Gospels it appears most likely that Jesus married. In this chapter we have seen that the earliest interpreter of Jesus in the New Testament had an attitude toward marriage basically in harmony with what the Gospels later recorded of Jesus. Paul steered between the Scylla of sexual asceticism and the Charybdis of sexual anarchy as he piloted Christianity westward into the perilous Greco-Roman culture.

If there were no celibates among the prominent founders of the church in the New Testament era, what accounts for the assumption that came to prevail in the postapostolic church that Jesus and many other biblical figures were celibates? In the next chapters this complex question will be the central one which we shall attempt to answer. Suffice it here to introduce that subject by discussing a heresy first condemned in Paul's Pastoral Letters. According to 1 Timothy 4:1–5, those "who forbid marriage and enjoin abstinence from foods" are judged to have a demonic outlook that contradicts the Hebraic doctrine of the goodness of God's creation. Who were Paul's opponents in those letters? As we have seen, it was a Gnostic group within the Corinthian church that believed that whatever is associated with the flesh is polluted. In the Pastorals Paul considered his adversaries to have the same basic outlook, and specifically warned Timothy against what is "falsely named Gnosis."[127] This is probably the same "philosophy and empty deceit" that had ascetic proscriptions that Paul asked the Colossians to shun.[128]

Gentile asceticism, the earliest cause of Christian heresy, left a profound impact on church history. In the early second century followers of a Syrian named Saturninus had an outlook that corresponds closely to the Gnostics denounced by Paul. They declared that "marriage and begetting children are from Satan." Also, Irenaeus tells us that "many of those who belong to this school abstain from animal food." Their Gnostic theology as well as their practices was completely contrary to that which Paul defended. Rejecting the reverence that Jesus and Paul had for the God of the Hebrews, Saturninus believed that "Christ came to destroy the God of the Jews." He implied that sexuality was absent from Jesus inasmuch as he "was without birth, incorporeal, and without real matter."[129]

The virus carried by Saturninus and other heretics infected the main arteries of the church and caused religious expressions that an ancient Jew would have regarded as sick. Although the mainstream of the church never prohibited marriages for all Christians as some of the heretics attempted to do, nevertheless the institutional church through most of its history has manifested some similarity of outlook to those condemned in 1 Timothy 4:1–5. In the Reformation era the Catholic church attempted to reject the Protestant charge that it was like the heresy that Paul denounced by pointing out that its celibacy law did not prohibit marriage for *all* Christians. John Calvin contemptuously dismissed this defense as "childish quibble" and drew this keen analogy: "It is as if a tyrant should contend that a law is not unjust when only a part of a city is oppressed with its injustice!"[130] Ironically, it is not Protestants so much as celibate priests who now carry on Calvin's crusade against that unbiblical and inhumane papal law.

The Pauline letters, far from affording a genuine basis for sexual asceticism, affirm the goodness of the physical body at least as strongly as other portions of biblical literature. Von Allmen's conclusion is sound: "The New Testament knows nothing of the very considerable depreciation of marriage which the influence of an ascetic dualism is to introduce into the church; it affirms, on the contrary, that those who wish to forbid marriage spread abroad the doctrines of the devil."[131]

Chapter VI

SEXUAL ATTITUDES IN SECOND-CENTURY CHRISTIANITY

During the seventh decade of the first Christian century two major events transpired that were to reorient the moral perspective of the church. First, the beginning of the Roman persecutions and the martyrdoms of Peter and Paul resulted in Gentiles replacing the initial Jewish leadership. Second, the destruction of the Jewish state meant that the Hebraic mores had much less influence upon the church. After the first focus of Christianity, Jerusalem, was razed, the largest Roman cities—Rome, Alexandria, Ephesus, and Antioch—became the main centers of Christianity. As the Judaeo-Christian element in the church dwindled, and as the proportion of church members with a pagan background rapidly increased, there was a significant change in ethical outlook. In the post-apostolic church, moral standards began coming more from Hellenistic customs and philosophies fashionable in the Roman cities than from Hebraic tradition. Second-generation Christians were predominantly Gentiles who had little historical knowledge of the Old Testament or appreciation of the Jewish way of life.

In no area was there a more striking cultural difference than in the outlook on sexuality. Michael Novak describes the situation:

Compared with Greco-Roman culture, it appears that Jewish culture at the time of Christ had a far more sensible attitude toward sexuality. The flesh is good; a good wife is a man's most precious treasure; salvation is in pairs. The Greeks and Romans, on the other hand, alternately tried to live superior to the flesh and then, weakly, brutally indulged in it. It appears that their womenfolk were treated as less than equals in the sexual act. It is no wonder that sects and movements which denounced sexuality and even marriage as abominable evils would find responsive hearts in the Greco-Roman world for generations to come.[1]

It might be said that the infant Christianity was orphaned prior to coming of age sexually. Consequently, as Paul Ricoeur has pointed out, it became vulnerable to pagan views of the body before it could create a culture for itself. When the spirit-flesh dichotomy dominant in the Gentile Mediterranean world infiltrated into Christianity, it broke down the psychosomatic unity characteristic of the biblical view of man. This dualistic contamination of Christianity "sterilized its sense of creation, perverted its confession of evil, and limited its hopes of total reconciliation to the horizon of a narrowed and bloodless spiritualism."[2] How did this dualism develop into such a pervasive influence?

GRECO-ROMAN MORAL DUALISM

Greek dualism can be historically traced to the Orphic cult. Plato used a pun in describing it: "Some say that the body (*soma*) is the tomb (*sēma*) of the soul. It is the followers of Orpheus who . . . were under the impression that the soul is undergoing punishment for sin and that the body is an enclosure or prison in which the soul is incarcerated."[3] Pythagoras, the first Greek to call himself a philosopher, adopted this moral dualism in the sixth century B.C. and the fraternity that he founded extrapolated from it a metaphysical dualism. Females were associated with qualities such as dark, evil, odd, and crooked, which compose one of the substances.[4] Pythagoras was reported to have said: "Keep to the winter for sexual pleasures, in summer abstain; they are less harmful in autumn and spring, but they are always harmful and not conducive to health." Asked once when a man should consort with a woman, he replied, "When you want to lose what strength you have."[5] Empedocles, a pupil of Pythagoras,[6] denounced all forms of sexual intercourse. Eric R. Dodds, in discussing Empedocles, observes that sexual asceticism not only originated in Greece but "was carried by a Greek mind to its extreme theoretical limit."[7]

Democritus, an admirer of Pythagoras, did not approve of sexual activity.[8] In turn, his most famous disciple, Epicurus, maintained that "sexual intercourse never benefited any man." Far from advocating unrestrained hedonism, as often connoted by the term "epicurean," he stated: "The pleasant life is not the product of . . . sexual intercourse with women."[9] Lucretius, who popularized Epicurus' philosophy in the Latin culture, asserted that sexual desire was a sickness that could not be cured by intercourse. A wise man should avoid that "madness" altogether, for it cannot be used as a means of reaching the ideal unruffled life.[10]

Plato, the most influential of all philosophers, was indebted to Pythagoras for a number of his doctrines, not the least being that the body is a tomb from which one is emancipated by death. In the *Phaedrus*, Plato gave his fullest treatment of *eros* working between individuals. "Platonic love" is shown to be the mutual attainment of self-mastery that cures the disease of physical craving.[11] Although Plato was referring to abstinence from homosexual activity, "there is little in his writings to suggest that his revulsion from heterosexual intercourse was not equally strong."[12] Plato thought that copulation lowered a man to frenzied passions characteristic of beasts. He relegated sexual desire to the lowest element of the tripartite psyche and vented his antipathy toward it by comparing it with an ignoble hot-blooded horse.[13]

In the Hellenistic era, Diogenes, the most picturesque member of the Cynic school, "praised those who were about to marry and refrained."[14] When asked when was the right time to marry, he quipped: "For young men, not yet; for old men, never."[15] Zeno, the founder of Stoicism, patterned his life after the Cynics.[16] Epictetus, the most outstanding Stoic during the period of the early development of the church, admired Diogenes' ascetic values.[17]

At Alexandria there was a revival of Greek philosophy in the first century B.C. It was eclectic, the principal ingredients being Pythagoreanism, Platonism, and Stoicism. Knowledge of this eclecticism comes mainly from Philo, inasmuch as most of his writings have survived. Although he was a Jew, he was more influenced by Hellenistic culture than by rabbinic Judaism.[18] Eusebius stated: "It is on record that in his enthusiasm for the systems of Plato and Pythagoras he surpassed all his contemporaries."[19]

That Philo shared the moral dualism of those Greeks can be seen in this exhortation: "Depart out of the earthly matter that encompasses you: escape, man, from the foul prison-house, your body, with all your might and main, and from the pleasures and lusts that act as its jailers."[20] Stoic thought also contributed to Philo's doctrine that pleasure is the source of all sin.[21] Consequently, the serpent and the woman in the Garden of Eden symbolize lust while the man symbolizes intellect.[22] Philo seems to have been the first to associate the sin of Adam and Eve with sexual relations: "Love gave to both of them the desire for intercourse with a view to reproduction. And this desire engendered likewise bodily pleasure which is the source of all wickedness."[23] Due to the influence of Hellenic culture Philo had "a superstitious reverence for virginity." "The words virgin, virginity, ever-virginal, occur on every other page of Philo."[24] There is no indication that the sexual outlook of Philo, which he probably shared with some of his fellow Diaspora Jews, affected Palestinian Judaism, and there is no allusion to Philo in rabbinic or New Testament literature.

The eclectic philosophy at Alexandria and elsewhere, which is adequately labeled Neoplatonism, came to its full flowering during the patristic era of the church. Sexual asceticism was one of its dominant motifs. In the second century a pagan philosopher, Numenius, expressed many of the same ideas as Philo.[25] He also employed the allegorical method devised by the Stoics and injected Greek philosophy into Hebrew Scripture. When performing that intellectual sleight of hand, Numenius asked, "What else is Plato than a Moses who reveals Greek tendencies?"[26] He claimed that Pythagoras rightly believed that the physical stuff from which the world is created is evil and opposed to God.[27] For Numenius individual salvation consisted of abandoning sexual activity so as to liberate the soul from passion and gain mystical ecstasy.[28] Plutarch, writing in the era when Neoplatonism was the dominant Roman philosophy, applauded certain philosophers who abstained from wine and women in order "to honor God by their continence."[29] Also, Strabo described a community at Thrace where men aspiring to perfection lived apart from women.[30]

It is no accident that most of the outstanding philosophers who stem from Greek culture have been bachelors and/or celibates.[31]

Nietzsche, who was himself unmarried, points out that the tradition has been continued to the modern era: "What great philosopher hitherto has been married? Heraclitus, Plato, Descartes, Spinoza, Leibniz, Kant, Schopenhauer—these were not."[32] Some unmarried philosophers that Nietzsche neglects to mention are Epicurus, Epictetus, Plotinus, all the medieval scholastics, Hobbes, Locke, Hume, and Kierkegaard. Like those who conversed about wisdom in the Athenian agora, philosophers through the ages have usually been men; there has never been a widely acclaimed woman philosopher. Prejudice against the flesh and the female sex has probably had much to do with this characteristic style of philosophic life.

SEXUAL ASCETICISM IN GENTILE CHRISTIANITY

This brief review of Greco-Roman philosophical asceticism should let us dispense with a fantasy that some Christians have had regarding the original motivation for Christian celibacy. It has been seriously maintained that celibacy was begun in the ancient world by the founders of Christianity as a reaction against the prevailing licentious practices of the heathen. For example, Roman Catholic scholar R. J. Devine asserts that celibacy was "practically unknown in ancient Greece." He holds, quite unhistorically, that it was Jesus and Paul who initiated celibacy into the ancient world and that Christians valiantly used this superlatively pure mode of living to combat the prevailing sexual degradation of secular society.[33] Likewise, Max Thurian claims that lifelong virginity as a Christian ideal was strongly influenced by a revulsion toward depraved pagan morals and a longing for the vocation of celibacy that Jesus innovated.[34]

There is abundant evidence for rejecting this assumption. A recent study by Johannes Leipoldt demonstrates decisively that early Christian celibacy sprang not from the nonascetic Gospel but from the impact of Greek philosophy.[35] Emil Brunner also correctly assesses the cause-and-effect relationship between ancient asceticism and early Christianity:

The argument for virginity which forced its way into the Christian church at a very early stage must be described as a serious distortion of the biblical idea of marriage. Through Platonic Hellenistic mysticism the idea penetrated into the early church that the sex element, as such, is something low, and unworthy of intelligent man, an idea which . . . is in absolute opposition to the biblical idea of creation. This idea, actualized in monasticism, erected into a standard in the Catholic ideal of virginity, was not wholly overcome by the Reformation.[36]

Thus the growing preoccupation with celibacy and other forms of asceticism within the early church was due to its assimilation of an originally Greek assumption that gratification of the passions was impure per se. Morton S. Enslin succinctly describes the situation: "Christianity did not make the world ascetic; rather the world in which Christianity found itself strove to make Christianity ascetic."[37] The cultic and philosophical streams that flowed into Mediteranean culture were flooded with self-mortifying sentiments in the second century. As Christianity embarked from the Middle Eastern culture and navigated westward it was struck by the currents of Hellenistic moral dualism. Joseph W. Swain states: "Beginning in the first century B.C., a wave of asceticism swept over the whole Greek world, which became more and more powerful as time went on. World-flight and other-worldliness were the characteristic features of the thought of decaying Greece; they were one of the important contributions of Hellas to Christianity."[38]

A shift in the theological outlook of postapostolic Christianity left its ethic vulnerable to the impact of pagan asceticism. As we have seen, Paul believed early in his Christian career that he was living on a temporal isthmus between Jesus' resurrection and his coming at the end of history. Consequently there was little point in buying a home, marrying, and planning a family. However, the exclamation of the earliest Christians, "Lord, come!"[39] was converted into a question as the first century continued without the "Second Coming." With the fading of that eschatological expectation many Gentile interpreters of Paul assumed that he, like the ascetics of their contemporary culture, favored the unattached life because it had permanent and intrinsic moral worth. But Paul had a quite different frame of reference and thought of celibacy as a temporary expedient. Roland H. Bainton writes:

Paul's discouragement of new marriages because of the Lord's imminent return early lost its relevance since the Lord did not return. . . . But other reasons for disparagement crept in and replaced the eschatological. The second century was marked by an increasing prevalence of the Gnostic disparagement of life in the flesh and specifically of marriage.[40]

In the early centuries of Gentile Christianity, sexual asceticism was applied with varying degrees of rigor. Just as there had been ascetic practices in paganism ranging from mild to wild, so in Christianity some leaders sanctioned copulation if motivated exclusively by desire for children, while others demanded celibacy of all church members. Since Christianity was competing with other salvation cults, the degree of sexual repression in a particular area was somewhat determined by the practice of its leading local rival. Christians sometimes tried to gain status by outdoing pagans at asceticism. Galen, a pagan physician of the late second century, stated that the Christian community in Rome included men and women "who refrain from cohabiting all through their lives." What is interesting is his observation that the sexual restraint of Christians is equal to that of philosophers.[41]

An examination of second-century expressions of Christianity displays the impact of pagan asceticism and the way in which this moral dualism was projected back upon the literature and the personalities of the New Testament. The *Teaching of the Twelve Apostles*, commonly called the *Didache* and dating from the second century, is a good point of departure. Since it is a Judaeo-Christian document,[42] it is understandable that Gnostic themes and sexual asceticism are absent.

In the earliest Christian letters apart from the New Testament there is a trace of sexual asceticism. At the turn of the second century Clement of Rome wrote: "He who is pure (*hagnos*) in the flesh must not boast."[43] A similar comment was made by Ignatius, a Syrian convert from paganism, in a letter written at about the same time: "If any one can continue in a state of purity (*hagnos*) in honor of him who is Lord of the flesh, let him do so without boasting."[44] This injunction from his letter to Polycarp occurs in a context pertaining to duties of husbands and wives, so the *hagnos* endorsed has reference to continence, not virginity.[45]

HERMAS AND "SPIRITUAL" MARRIAGE

The *Shepherd*, written by Hermas around A.D. 130, was the first Christian document in which sexual asceticism is prominent. The book opens with a vision of Hermas, a Roman convert to Christianity. He sees a beautiful lady bathing in the Tiber and desires her for his wife. But then, by a dream, he learns that his desire is sinful.[46] Later there is a reference to "your wife who is also to be your sister."[47] This may refer to a continent or "spiritual" marriage.

One tale in the *Shepherd* was motivated by a heroic asceticism. A dozen virgins invite Hermas to spend the night with them while he is waiting for the master of the house to return. Although he is reluctant to stay, they insist that he sleep with them "as a brother and not as a husband." The virgins say they love him greatly and proceed to hug, kiss, and dance with him. Then they spread out their undergarments on the ground and make him lie down in the midst of them. While in that posture they pray together until the master returns in the early morning. His interrogation evokes evasive responses.

" 'Have you molested him?'

" 'Ask him yourself,' the virgins said.

" 'Sir, I was delighted to remain with them,' Hermas said.

" 'What did you eat?'

" 'I partook of the words of the Lord the whole night.' "[48]

Although a modern reader might be tempted to read naughtiness into these oblique replies, the story was originally designed to show how an impeccable spiritual athlete could spend the night amid nude virgins without becoming sexually excited or involved.

The *Shepherd* became the *Pilgrim's Progress* of the early church, and some fathers accepted it as canonical Scripture.[49] It inspired some to test their self-control by placing themselves in seductive situations and praying to remain chaste as Hermas did. Later in the second century beatitudes are placed on Paul's lips commending "spiritual" marriage. In the apocryphal *Acts of Paul* the apostle is said to have proclaimed: "Blessed are they that possess their wives as though they had them not, for they shall inherit God. . . . Blessed are the bodies of the virgins, for they shall be well-pleasing unto God."[50] In the next century Tertullian advised Christians to live with one or more widows "as spritual spouses." They were encouraged to share married life in all aspects except the sexual. "It is pleasing to God," he assured, "to have several such wives."[51]

Human nature proved too weak to withstand the exposures to strenuous temptation that Tertullian and others recommended. Irenaeus was the first to express suspicion of Christians who "pretend at first to live in all modesty with women as with sisters."[52] Cyprian admitted that his credulity could not be stretched to believe that girls who sleep with men are telling the truth when they declare that they have maintained their vows to remain chaste. He exclaimed: "What a multitude of virgins we behold corrupted by unlawful and dangerous conjunctions of this kind!"[53] In the fourth century Jerome was also not so naïve as to believe that spiritual marriage could occur without scandalous conduct. He testifies:

I blush to speak of it, it is so shocking: yet, though sad it is true. How comes this plague of "dearly beloved sisters" (agapetae) to be in the church? Whence come these unwedded wives, these novel concubines, these harlots, so I will call them, though they are one-man women? One house holds them and one chamber. They often occupy the same bed, and yet they call us suspicious if we fancy anything wrong. . . . Both alike profess to have but one object, to find spiritual consolation . . . but their real aim is to indulge in carnal intercourse. It is on such that Solomon in the book of Proverbs heaps his scorn. "Can a man take fire in his bosom," he says, "and his clothes not be burned?"[54]

How did the custom of spiritual marriage begin? Nonsensual marriages were found in Hellenistic culture before the advent of Christianity.[55] In the first century the Neopythagorean Sextus advised the married to abandon conjugal intercourse in order to glorify God.[56] Porphyry, a Neoplatonist, entered into a Platonic marriage with Marcella.[57]

MARCION AND CASSIANUS

The most notorious figure in second-century Christianity was Marcion, whose teachings permeated Roman civilization.[58] In capsule form Clement of Alexandria related the theology of Marcion and his followers to their ascetic practices: "Nature is regarded by the Marcionites as evil because it was created out of evil matter. . . . On this ground, that they do not wish to fill the world made by the Creator-God, they decide to abstain from marriage."[59] Tertullian elaborated on the way Marcion's major writing was aimed at severing Christianity from its Hebraic roots:

His *Antitheses* centers in this: the establishment of a diversity between the Old and New Testaments so that his own Christ may be separate from the Creator, as belonging to this rival god, and as alien from the law and the prophets. . . . He had erased everything that was contrary to his own opinion and made for the Creator.[60]

Marcion discarded the Old Testament and "circumcised the Gospel according to Luke, taking out everything written about the generation of the Lord."[61] His intention is clarified by Tertullian: "In order that he might not admit the flesh of Christ he denied his very birth."[62] Marcion found the flesh repulsive, along with its reproduction and growth. By cutting out the birth, boyhood, and temptation narratives in Luke, Marcion's Christ descends from heaven as an adult man.[63] Marcion not only personally refrained from sexual relations with women but also prohibited marriage for all Christians.[64] The sacraments of baptism and the eucharist were limited to virgins, widows, and married couples "who agree together to repudiate marital consummation."[65]

Had orthodox Christianity adopted Marcion's asceticism, the church could not have been self-perpetuating. Recognizing the dire consequences of making virginity an absolute requirement for all future Christians, even later church leaders with ascetic practices found it necessary to combat Marcion. Tertullian expressed hostility toward Marcionites "who are for destroying the God of marriage."[66] Marcion's doctrine that only those uncontaminated by sex could be moral was shown by Clement to be self-incriminating: "If it is the view of those people who themselves owe their existence to sexual relations that such relations are impure, must not they be impure?"[67] In later centuries orthodox Christianity settled for a semi-Marcionite asceticism, permitting marriage for the rank and file but advocating celibacy for the holier Christian.

Where did Marcion's sexual asceticism originate? Evidently he followed the eclectic approach then fashionable in philosophy. Heresiologists associated him with a variety of schools. Irenaeus maintained that Marcion's basic theology was of Gnostic origin, for the Gnostic influence in the Mediterranean world was at its height during his lifetime. Irenaeus claimed that Marcion's teacher was the Gnostic Cerdo, who had a doctrine of two gods—an inferior Creator-god and a good God of the New Testament.[68] Tertullian, while admitting the influence of Cerdo, pointed out that Marcion was a "zealous student of Stoicism."[69] Perhaps he was especially influenced by the most ascetic of the great Stoics, Epictetus, who lived in the previous generation near Marcion's birthplace in Asia Minor. Hippolytus accused Marcion of emulating not Christ but the pre-Socratic Empedocles, who taught his disciples "to refrain from intercourse with women."[70] Clement sagaciously traced Marcion's position on the evil of generation to the Orphics, the Pythagoreans, and to Plato. He wrote: "That sexual intercourse as the cause of birth was rejected long before Marcion by Plato is clear from the first book of the *Republic:* . . . 'It is with greatest joy that I escaped from it—as if I had escaped from a wild and raging tyrant.' "[71] Marcion's view of the evil material creation was similar to that of his Neoplatonic contemporary, Numenius.[72]

Julius Cassianus shared the ascetic outlook of his contemporary, Marcion. Both said that "man became like the beasts when he came to practice sexual intercourse."[73] Therefore Jesus' mission in this world was to save man from copulating. In *Concerning Celibacy,* Cassianus wrote:

Let no one say that because we have these members, that the female body is shaped to receive and the male to sow seed, sexual intercourse is allowed by God. For if this arrangement had been made by God, whom we seek to attain, he would not have praised the eunuchs (Matthew 19:12); nor would the prophet have said that they "were not a fruitless tree" (Isaiah 56:3).[74]

A favorite text for Cassianus and other ascetics was a counterfeit saying of Jesus. Clement commented:

Those who are opposed to God's creation, disparaging it under the fair name of continence, also quote the words addressed to Salome . . . in the Gospel of the Egyptians. They say that the Savior himself said, "I am come to destroy the works of the female" meaning by "female" sexual desire, and by "works" birth and corruption.[75]

JUSTIN AND TATIAN

In the mid-second century Justin Martyr and his pupil Tatian absorbed ascetic notions from pagan Hellenism. After studying under Pythagorean and Platonist teachers Justin claimed that "philosophy is the greatest possession and most honorable before God to whom it leads us"[76] and that "the teachings of Plato are not alien to those of Christ."[77] Arthur C. McGiffert perceptively noted: "Christianity he [Justin] insists is the supreme and the one true philosophy, but upon examining his interpretation of it we find that it is in substance simply the common moral philosophy of the day."[78] Justin described approvingly a Christian youth who asked surgeons to emasculate him as a protection for bodily purity. Realizing that celibacy was widely admired in pagan culture, Justin pointed with pride to some Christians who renounced marriage and lived in perfect continence.[79] A similar view was expressed by Minucius Felix, a contemporary of Justin and, like him, well read in the classics of pagan culture. Felix presented the ascetic view that was dominant in the patristic era:

We gladly abide by the bond of a single marriage; in our desire for off-spring we have only one wife, or none at all. . . . Chaste in conversation and even more chaste in body, very many enjoy the perpetual virginity of a body undefiled. . . . Even the thought of sexual intercourse causes them to blush.[80]

Justin borrowed the allegorical methodology of Philo as well as some of his ascetic interpretations of the Old Testament. Both associated the serpent in Eden with sexual intercourse. The disobedience and death brought by "virgin Eve" was caused by her intercourse with "the logos of the serpent." Postulating that Eve's antitype was the "virgin Mary," Justin told of her becoming impregnated by the overpowering logos of God.[81] In devotion to the Neoplatonic ethic that associated virtue with sexual abstinence, Justin labored hard to convince Trypho the Jew that the Isaiah 7:14 prophecy referred to a virgin conceiving and that Mary was its fulfillment.[82] Justin also deduced from the Old Testament that "Christ derives blood not from the seed of man, but from the power of God" and that "Christ is not man of men, begotten in the ordinary course of humanity."[83] Since Justin considered Jesus to be even holier than Mary, if Mary did not have sexual relations then certainly Jesus did not either. However, Justin did not discuss Jesus' marital status, as did his disciple Tatian.

Tatian, from Eastern Syria, was noted for his *Harmony of the Four Gospels*, commonly called the *Diatessaron*, and for the prohibitions of sexual intercourse, intoxicants, and meats in the Encratite school he founded.[84] The tenets of the Encratites are summed up by Irenaeus and related to other ascetics:

Those who are called Encratites ("the self-controlled") preached against marriage, thus setting aside the original creation of God, indirectly blaming him who made male and female for the generation of human beings. They also introduced abstention from animal food, showing ingratitude to God who made all things. Also, they deny the salvation of the first created man. This notion they adopted quite recently: Tatian was the first to introduce this blasphemy. He had been a pupil of Justin, and as long as he continued with him he expressed no such views, but after Justin's martyrdom he separated from the church . . . and repudiated marriage as being depravity and fornication, just as Marcion and Saturninus had done.[85]

The Greco-Roman philosophies made at least as deep an impact on Tatian and the Encratites as they had on Justin. Martin Elze shows Tatian's heavy indebtedness to Platonism and Stoicism for ascetic doctrine.[86] Like a Platonist he cast vitriol on those who "wallow in matter and mud."[87] Pythagorean influence is also manifested in Tatian and the Encratites. Around the same time that Tatian lived Philostratus wrote a biography of Apollonius, a Pythagorean who allegedly lived in the first century A.D. and who refused to touch wine, meat, or women.[88] So permeated were the Encratites with Hellenistic flesh-hatred that Hippolytus called them Cynics rather than Christians.[89] He could not believe that any sect could be Christian that professed what Paul denounced in 1 Timothy 4:1–5. Paul also recommended moderate wine drinking,[90] although imbibing was strictly forbidden by the Encratites. Later Epiphanius recorded their teaching that woman was entirely a creation of the Devil, but man was only halfway so; above the waist he is a creation of God, but his belly and below is made by the Devil.[91] According to Tatian, sexual intercourse was invented by the Devil, and consequently anyone who attempted to be married and be Christian was attempting to serve two masters.[92]

In a pernicious manner Tatian slightly altered the text of New Testament writings and bent the meaning of Scripture so that it appeared that "the price of eternal life is virginity."[93] By a gloss on Matthew 19:5 in the *Diatessaron* he made it appear that Adam rather than God established marriage. He believed that action of Adam was iniquitous and as a punishment he was deprived of the opportunity for redemption. Tatian showed his bias again in his treatment of Galatians 6:8. He interpreted Paul's words in an ascetic manner: "He sows to the flesh who is joined to a woman; therefore he who takes a wife and sows in the flesh, of the flesh he shall reap corruption."[94] Also, in *On Perfection According to the Savior*, Tatian took a passage from 1 Corinthians 7 that dealt with the duty of conjugal relations in marriage and made it appear that Paul prohibited such relations.[95]

Tatian was especially eager to sever Jesus' connections with the flesh. Clement indicates that Tatian and his followers "proudly say that they are imitating the Lord who neither married nor had any possession in this world, boasting that they understand the Gospel better than anyone else."[96] In the fifth century Bishop Theodoret recorded this regarding Tatian:

He composed the *Diatessaron* by cutting out the genealogies and such other passages as show the Lord to have been born of the seed of David according to the flesh. This work was in use not only among members of his own sect but also among those who follow the apostolic doctrine, who naïvely used it as a summary of the Gospels without recognizing the craftiness of its composition. I myself found more than 200 copies in reverential use in the churches of my diocese, all of which I removed, replacing them by the Gospels of the Four Evangelists.[97]

It seems that Tatian deliberately perverted the New Testament so that Christians would worship a figure who was separated from a Jewish heritage and from the institution of marriage. He effectively propagandized his sexual asceticism, for the *Diatessaron* was one of the most widely used books in the early church.

Armed with Jesus as the paradigm of virginity, the celibate movement had the emotional thrust it needed to spread widely.

Encratism permeated deeply, especially in Tatian's home area. Although Clement of Alexandria judged Tatian's views on marriage "blasphemous,"[98] he was not considered a heretic in Syria.[99] The Encratites produced apocryphal books[100] in which marital relations were treated as sordid and abominable. In one wedlock is referred to as "a polluted and foul way of life."[101] In another, those being wed are counseled to "abandon this filthy intercourse."[102] In still another the apostle John at his hour of death offers a prayer of thanks to Jesus. John is grateful that Jesus had thwarted his youthful desire to marry and had thereby saved him from "carnal madness." As for Jesus, he not only had no physical relations with a woman but he also had no corporeal substance. When he moved about he never made a footprint![103] Regarding third-century Syrian Christianity Vööbus says: "All the available sources are unanimous in their testimony that the fundamental conception around which the Christian belief centered was the doctrine that the Christian life is unthinkable outside the bounds of virginity."[104]

Mani, who was born in the same area in which Tatian lived a half century later, carried forward Encratism in a movement that was to threaten Christianity for the next millennium. The Manichean ethic is summed up in the three Encratite prohibitions already cited.[105] The long survival of Manicheism is displayed by the Cathars ("the pure") of Southern Europe who were prominent in the twelfth century.[106] Having the dualistic premise that flesh and generation are inherently evil, the Cathars were opposed even to touching meat, eggs, or the opposite sex.[107] Denis de Rougemont has traced the root of European poetry to Cathar-inspired troubadour songs that usually have the theme of unfulfilled sexual desires.[108] The chaste virgin was idolized and marriage was correspondingly denigrated.

Hellenistic asceticism, covered by a veneer of Christianity, left an impressive legacy in sexually inhibiting movements of later Western civilization. Jesus and Mary became the virginal models for all who aspired to immaculate purity. Although the notion that Jesus was unmarried originated with second-century heretics such as Basilides and Tatian, their dogma of the perpetual virginity of Jesus soon became accepted as axiomatic throughout Catholic Christianity.

THE VALENTINIANS' MARRIED JESUS

In the second century there was another Christian sect that stood in bold relief to the Encratites. It was founded by Valentine, a leader who almost succeeded in becoming the bishop of Rome.[109] He and his followers considered the unmarried to be on a lower level than the married. According to Clement, the Valentinians found earthly marriage of special significance because it was thought to be modeled after heavenly unions.[110] Tertullian elaborated on this:

It is held amongst them that, for the purpose of honoring the celestial marriages, it is necessary to contemplate and celebrate the mystery always by cleaving to a companion, that is, to a woman; otherwise they account any man degenerate, and a bastard to the truth, who spends his life in the world without loving a woman or uniting himself to her.[111]

This sect was also influenced by the pervasive Gnostic ideas of that era,[112] but it was not overcome by the sexual asceticism usually characteristic of Gnostic philosophy. Henry Chadwick points out: "The Valentinians were distinguished from other Gnostics by their warm approval of monogamous marriage. For Valentine there was no question of any licentiousness, nor any frowning disapproval, much less outright rejection, of the married state."[113]

Until recently there were virtually no primary sources for probing the Valentinian doctrine of marriage. In 1945 some fragmentary Coptic manuscripts were discovered in Egypt that have cast much more light on the Valentinians. One of those manuscripts, the *Gospel of Philip*, is of special significance. Johannes Leipoldt and H. M. Schenke have demonstrated beyond reasonable doubt that the Gospel is Valentinian.[114] The Coptic text is based on a Greek original that dates from the second century.[115] It is a tantalizing document because it presents an outlook on physical substance that is quite atypical of the general Gnostic view. Robert M. Wilson comments: "The document is certainly Gnostic, although it does not altogether fit into the standard pattern of Gnostic theory. . . . The author of this text was not a docetist but the exponent of an inverted docetism. It is our flesh which is phantasmal, and the flesh of Jesus which is the true."[116]

What reason can be given for the *Gospel of Philip*'s assertions that "Jesus is the true flesh"; "The holy man is altogether holy, even his body"[117]; and for its general positive view of the material creation? It is likely that the writer had appreciation for the Hebraic world-view. In saying 6 of *Philip*, reference is made to "when we were Hebrews" prior to becoming Christians. It is interpreted by Jack Finegan: "This seems to say that the author, and perhaps his readers, had come out of a Jewish background."[118]

The Jewish influence on the *Gospel of Philip* is shown in its treatment of Jesus' conception. Its author believed that a human was responsible for the impregnation of Mary, whereas God was responsible for Jesus' divine qualities. The Lord's Prayer is treated thus: "The Lord would not have said 'My Father in heaven' unless he had another father; he would have simply said, 'My Father.' "[119] Elsewhere the Gospel clarifies the nature of Jesus' dual paternity by declaring that he was the "seed" of Joseph the carpenter; yet "the Father of the All united with the virgin."[120] As noted in chapter three, it accords with the Hebraic outlook to assert that both divine and human fathers participate in the production of a child. The Hellenistic-inspired doctrine of the virginal conception of Jesus was not accepted as a matter of course by Christians in the time of Valentine (around A.D. 130–50). Ignatius was an exception among the apostolic fathers in mentioning that Jesus was born of a virgin.[121] Some Jewish Christians maintained that Jesus was a "man born of men."[122] They denied his virginal conception and held that he was a "child of normal union between a man and Mary."[123] Thus the explicit reference in the *Gospel of Philip* to its author's association with Jewish culture and his Hebraic interpretation of the birth of Jesus dovetail to show that the ancient Jewish doctrine of man is responsible for its optimistic view of the flesh.

The *Gospel of Philip* also contains an intriguing treatment of Jesus' marriage. C. J. DeCatanzaro[124] translates saying 32 as: "There were three who walked with the Lord at all times, Mary his mother, and her sister, and Magdalene, this one who is called his partner (Greek, *koinōnos*)."[125] In the next sentence Mary Magdalene is referred to as Jesus' "spouse" (Coptic, *hōtre*).[126]

Saying 55, which also refers to that woman as Jesus' *koinōnos*, says that he kisses her often and asks others, "Why do I not love you as I do her?" The fact that these Coptic sayings leave *koinōnos* untranslated indicates that they have a Greek original behind them. Assuming that the author of the Gospel had a Hebraic background, it may well be that these sayings go back in oral tradition to first-century Palestine. If so, this authentic tradition would outweigh the late speculation and dogma in Gentile Christianity that Jesus was unmarried. It would afford documentary validation of the hypothesis that Jesus married, and marriage to Mary Magdalene is one possible option that could fit into the New Testament portrayal of Jesus.

Some other ancient manuscripts support the assertion in the *Gospel of Philip* that Mary Magdalene was Jesus' wife. The second-century *Gospel of Mary*, which was discovered in Egypt in 1896, contains a conversation between Mary and the disciples. Peter said to Mary: "Sister, we know that the Savior loved you more than other women. Tell us his words which you have in mind." Mary then related to Peter what Jesus had told her. On realizing that Jesus had given a woman more intimate revelations than he himself had received, Peter became upset. Then Matthew said: "Peter, you are always irate. Now I see that you are contending against the woman like the adversaries. But if the Savior made her worthy, who are you to reject her? Surely the Savior knew her very well. For this reason he loved her more than us."[127] In *Pistis Sophia*, a third-century document, Mary Magdalene dominates the discussion throughout the book. Peter vented his frustration over this by complaining: "My Lord, we shall not be able to endure this woman, for she takes our opportunity and has not let any of us speak, but talks all the time herself."[128] And Jesus informed Mary that she was closer to understanding him than the others.[129] As in the *Gospel of Philip*, she kissed him frequently.

With the passage of time embellishment was probably added to the tradition of Jesus' erotic interest in some woman named Mary. But is this association altogether fictional or is it an elaboration of a tradition from nascent Christianity? The latter seems more likely because it harmonizes with the Gospel of John, which has more themes championed by the Valentinians than any other New

Testament book.[130] In John and in *Philip* Jesus is referred to as Joseph's son and a virgin birth is not suggested.[131] Also in John the mother of Jesus is with her son at the beginning and at the ending of his ministry,[132] so it is understandable that the author of *Philip* assumed that she accompained Jesus throughout his ministry. If Mary Magdalene is identified with Mary the sister of Martha, then John does show that she was more devoted to Jesus than the other women and, in turn, more loved by him.[133] Therefore the assumption held by the Valentinians that Jesus married has considerably more basis for acceptance than the opposite contention of their Encratitic rivals.

However, the Valentinian presentation of married Jesus and hence their extolling the purity of marital sexuality had no permanent effect on the church. It is reasonable to posit that the sect's demise and the destruction of its literature was due in large part to the fact that it so strongly rejected virginity as a crowning virtue. Consequently Tatian's sect influenced subsequent ascetic movements for many centuries but Valentine's sect lasted only about one century.

ATHENAGORAS AND IRENAEUS

Toward the end of the second century Athenagoras, a Christian philosopher of Athens who was influenced by Platonism, Pythagoreanism, and Stoicism, carried forward the ascetic ethic.[134] In two particular ways he showed that the ethic had become commonplace in mainline Christianity. First, he claimed that Christians approved of sexual intercourse only when there was hope of begetting legitimate offspring.

We despise the enjoyments of the present even the pleasures of the soul. According to our laws, each of us thinks of the woman he has married as his wife only for the purpose of bearing children. For as the farmer casts his seed on the soil and awaits the harvest without sowing over it, so we limit the pleasure of intercourse to bearing children.[135]

Athenagoras was indebted to Plato and the Pythagoreans for this standard of abstinence.[136] Also, Philo had earlier expressed the same outlook: "They are pleasure lovers when they mate with their wives, not to procreate children and perpetuate the race, but like pigs or goats in quest of the enjoyment which such intercourse gives."[137]

Second, Athenagoras condemned digamy: "He who severs himself from his first wife, even if she is dead, is an adulterer in disguise. He resists the hand of God, for in the beginning God created one man and one woman."[138] He rejected the Hebaric custom of digamy that was practiced by Abraham and accepted by his descendants, including Paul.[139] It seems that the denigration of digamy in the late patristic era was mainly motivated by a concern that the surviving spouse mortify the flesh and not by sentiment that the spouse should continue to adore the deceased partner.

The rejection of digamy proved to be too strenuous to become church law for all Christians. Henry C. Lea states: "Although the church forbore to prohibit absolutely the repetition of matrimony among the laity, it yet, at an early though uncertain period, imitated the rule enforced on the Flamen Dialis, and rendered it obligatory on the priesthood."[140] The Flamen Dialis was the Jupiter priest order that was highly honored in Rome. Tertullian[141] and Jerome[142] implored Christians who had survived their first partners to emulate the Flamen who married only once. At the Council of Elvira it was admitted that in extreme cases baptism could be administered by a layman but not by a digamist priest.[143]

Irenaeus, the Bishop of Lyons, was the most formidable defender of the faith in the second century and did much to entrench the dogma that Jesus and Mary were virgins. By deft allegorical manipulation of Scripture he was able to feature virginity at the start and at the climax of the biblical revelation. He started his theological construction with the typology of Paul, for he had referred to Adam as "a type of the one who was to come" and to Christ as "the last Adam."[144] Irenaeus elaborated on the Pauline doctrine of recapitulation that maintained that Christ Jesus summed up in himself all that belongs to human nature, thereby restoring humanity to its original purpose.[145] The last Adam underwent experiences parallel to those of the first Adam and embodied the way of life that would have been present from the beginning had sin not entered.[146] But Irenaeus misunderstood Paul's generic usage and treated Adam as a male vis-à-vis Eve. In a bizarre fashion the Adam-Jesus type is mixed with the Eve-Mary type that Justin had introduced into theology. In Irenaeus' dual typology, Jesus and Mary are Adam and Eve in reverse. To avoid mother and son incest as well as to inject a presupposition regarding the perfect sexual state, the original state of Adam and Eve and the permanent state of their antitypes is virginal. Adam is made from "untilled and yet virgin soil."[147] Irenaeus believed that Adam and Eve were created as young children, although from the outset they were married.

Eve indeed had a husband, Adam, but was nevertheless still a virgin— for in Paradise "they were both naked, and were not ashamed." Having been created a short time previously, they had no understanding of the procreation of children; for it was necessary that they should first come to adult age, and then multiply from that time onward.[148]

As children Adam and Eve had no sexual desire: "Their thoughts were innocent and childlike, and they had no conception or imagination of the sort that is engendered in the soul by evil, through pleasurable and shameful desires."[149]

According to Irenaeus Jesus' birth was parallel to that of Adam: "While it was still virgin God took dust of the earth and fashioned the man, the beginning of humanity. So the Lord, summing up afresh this man, reproduced the scheme of Adam's incarnation, being born of a virgin by the will and the wisdom of God."[150] The crucial contrast between Adam and Jesus is then given:

As the human race fell into bondage to death by means of a virgin, so it is rescued by a virgin; virginal disobedience having been balanced in the opposite scale by virginal obedience. For the same way the sin of the first created man receives amendment by the correction of the First-begotten.[151]

There is a similar contrast between Eve and Mary: "Eve became disobedient and was made the cause of death both to herself and to the entire race. So also did Mary, having a man betrothed to her and being nevertheless a virgin, by yielding obedience, became the cause of salvation, both to herself and the whole human race."[152]

Hence the resolves of Mary and Jesus to remain virginal became the most significant decisions in world history. Also, had Adam and Eve chosen to live together without marital sexuality, they would have been obedient and Paradise would not have been lost for them and their posterity. Most people who are not obsessed about sex would assume that the human species would have been liquidated had the hypothetical first human pair renounced the libidinous impulse, but Irenaeus seemed to think that the salvation of man would have resulted. Fittingly, this description of second-century Christian asceticism ends on a note of incongruous fanaticism.

Chapter VII

SEXUAL ATTITUDES IN EARLY ORTHODOXY

Out of the wide latitude of second-century beliefs and practices a normative Christianity jelled in subsequent centuries. The most influential leaders of third-century Christianity were North Africans. Their differing views with regard to sexual asceticism had enormous impact on Christian thought in general, and on the orthodox view of Jesus' sexuality in particular.

TERTULLIAN'S SEXUAL ASCETICISM

Tertullian, the founding father of Latin orthodoxy, was ambivalent toward the connubial bond. On the one hand he rejected Marcion's requirement of celibacy for church membership. He echoed the dominant Christian ethic when he wrote: "We vindicate marriage against those who disparage the Creator. We do not give up marriage because of the possibility of lust any more than we give up clothes because of the possibility of luxury."[1] On the other hand he was as frigid toward marital coitus as he was fervent in his defense of the Christian's right to marry. In a letter to his wife he manifested a loathing of sexual intercourse and a longing for the afterlife when it would no longer be possible. Even though he was outspoken in his belief in a carnal resurrection, he nevertheless expressed this hope to his spouse: "There will at that day be no resumption of voluptuous disgrace between us."[2] He exhorted Christians to "slay sexual desire" and to "cease from that way of life which is not found in Paradise."³ Also, he spoke of having children as "a most bitter pleasure."⁴

Tertullian had accurately charged Marcion with being intoxicated by Greek attitudes toward sex, yet he himself was also influenced by them, especially in later life. To stimulate Christians to outdo the pagans he reviewed some prominent Mediterranean practices of celibacy:

> We know about the Vestal Virgins, the virgins of Juno in a city of Achaia, those of Apollo at Delphi, of Athena and Artemis in certain other places. We know about others, also, who live a celibate life: the priests of that famous Egyptian bull, for example, and those women who of their own accord, leave their husbands and grow old in the service of the African Ceres, renouncing forever all contact with men, even the kisses of their own sons.⁵

Tertullian was embarrassed that pagans often did a better job of mortifying the flesh than Christians.⁶ His enthusiasm for Greek asceticism demonstrates that he incriminated himself in his famous rhetoric: "Heresies are themselves instigated by philosophy. . . . What indeed has Athens to do with Jerusalem? What has the Academy to do with the Church? . . . Away with all attempts to produce a Stoic, Platonic, and dialectic Christianity!"⁷

Tertullian's scale of sexual values, ranging from the highest good to the lowest evil, looks like this: (1) perpetual virginity; (2) continent marriage; (3) sexual intercourse in marriage exclusively for procreating children; (4) marital intercourse for pleasure; (5) intercourse by digamists and extramarital sexual relations.⁸ This gradation of values was widely adopted by the church in subsequent centuries.⁹

In order to justify making virginity the acme of virtues, Tertullian attempted to deduce the lifelong virginity of the principal biblical characters. Starting with the presupposition that Mary was a virgin mother, he offered this *non sequitur:* "Christ was himself a virgin even in the flesh, in that he was born of a virgin's flesh."¹⁰ Moreover, since the apostles followed Jesus' example, all of them except Peter were celibate.¹¹ In Tertullian's time a similar position was advanced in a pseudo-Clementine letter. It contained this admonition: "Do you wish to be Christian? Imitate Christ in everything." There follows the affirmation that Elijah, Elisha, John the Baptist, John the apostle, Paul, Barnabas, and Timothy were all virgins.[12] This spurious appeal to Jesus as the model virgin has been virtually unchallenged from the third century to the present day.

Tertullian also introduced into orthodoxy an appeal to Revelation 14:4 to buttress arguments for celibacy.[13] It reads: "It is these who have not defiled themselves with women, for they are virgins; it is these who follow the Lamb wherever he goes." Cyprian, who followed Tertullian's positions closely, and Jerome employed that verse as one of their favorite proof-texts for showing the excellence of virginity.[14] Augustine believed it affirmed the perpetual virginity of Jesus: "Virgins follow the Lamb, because the flesh of the Lamb is also virginal. For he preserved it himself in his manhood what he did not take away from his mother in his conception and birth."[15] Aquinas also interpreted Revelation 14:4 as referring to those who imitate Jesus the virginal "Lamb." He claimed that "the new hymn (Revelation 14:3) which virgins alone sing, is their joy at having preserved the flesh."[16] To magnify the status of consecrated virgins, Pope Pius XII has quoted Augustine's appeal to Revelation 14:4.[17]

At first glance it does look as though Revelation 14:4 associates sin with sexual intercourse, and, as a corollary, holiness with virginity. Yet biblical scholars today recognize that virtually all of Revelation is symbolic; hence they reject the literal interpretation of Tertullian and others. Indeed, if that verse is taken literally, the contextual meaning would be that the "redeemed" will consist exclusively of 144,000 male virgins. What then might be its meaning?

Interpretations in recent Protestant and Roman Catholic commentaries are clarifying. G. B. Caird writes on the treatment of "virgins" by the author of Revelation: "He is not disclosing in an unguarded moment his personal predilection for asceticism. . . . This is a symbol . . . for moral purity from the seductions of the great whore of Babylon and from that fornication which is idolatry."[18] In a similar manner the Jesuit Jean L. D'Aragon notes: "The 144,000 whose foreheads bear the seal constitute the totality of the Christian people. . . . Virginity is a metaphor for fidelity to God."[19] Also, Hans von Campenhausen maintains that the "virgins" of Revelation 14:4 symbolize those who are determined not to worship false gods at the risk of martyrdom and who confess Christ as Lord.[20] Thus the untarnished sexual virtue of youth who have not married is a fitting metaphor for picturing Christians who are innocent of worship at the pagan altars of Rome ("Babylon").

Tertullian also displayed his sexual asceticism in his acid denunciation of women. It would have been difficult for him to have opposed Jesus' female sympathies more if he had deliberately tried. One of his diatribes reads:

Do you not know that each of you is also an Eve? . . . You are the devil's door; you are the unsealer of that forbidden tree, you are the first deserter of the divine law, you are the one who persuaded him whom the devil was too weak to attack. How easily you destroyed man, the image of God! Because of the death which you brought upon us, even the Son of God had to die.[21]

Tertullian's meticulous description of feminine grooming and his fascination with the way women dress and undress expose his own sexual anxieties. Not only should cosmetics be shunned but also "natural grace must be obliterated by concealment and negligence, since it is dangerous to those who glance at it."[22] In another essay he described the fair sex thus:

They consult the looking-glass to aid their beauty, and thin down their over-exacting face with washing, perhaps withal vamp it up with cosmetics, toss their mantle about them with an air, fit tightly the multiform shoe, carry down more ample appliances to the baths. Why should I pursue particulars?[23]

An appropriate answer to his rhetorical question might be: because obsession with these details affords compensation for what you have fenced off as "forbidden fruit."

CLEMENT'S BIBLICAL PERSPECTIVE

The ethic of Clement of Alexandria is an oasis amid the barren asceticism of North African Christianity. It is paradoxical that he accepted less of Hellenistic asceticism than his contemporary Tertullian, for Clement did not assume that there was a radical discontinuity between classical and Christian culture.[24] Whereas Tertullian had asserted that marriage was appropriate for the Old

Testament era but that continence was better for the Christian dispensation,[25] Clement maintained that Jesus came to fulfill Hebraic marital mores.[26] Over against Tertullian's caustic comments on women, Clement declared that she was man's equal in knowledge and character[27] and was endowed with the same potential for perfection.[28]

A difference in the educational background of Tertullian and Clement helps to explain why Clement's outlook was unusual in Gentile Christianity. While both had been schooled in the pagan classics, Clement had also studied under a Palestinian Jew.[29] This may have caused him to understand the Hebraic outlook on sex and marriage. Thus he held that marriage was holy and that a couple cooperates in the work of creation when they obey God, who said, "Be fruitful."[30] In accord with the biblical outlook, Clement maintained that celibacy was an unmanly evasion of responsibility.[31] He stated: "Eating and drinking and marrying are not the main objects of life, though they are its necessary conditions."[32] Far from the Christian revelation detracting from those aspects of human life that pertain to the flesh, Clement believed they had been enhanced by it. If Jesus lived a pure life as God's enfleshment, he reasoned, this implied that the physical was not intrinsically corrupting.[33]

Clement applied the biblical doctrine of the goodness of creation to the human organism. "It is not the sex organs, or marital coitus, which is obscene. . . . The sexual parts of man's body deserve not to be treated with prudery but with privacy. It is only the immoral use of sex which is obscene."[34] Clement's position stands out when compared with that of Arnobius, who referred to the genitals as "hideous," to intercourse as "obscene," and to the body as "a filthy bag of urine and excrement."[35] Clement's wholesome outlook can also be contrasted to that of his prudish Victorian editors, who left untranslated the most balanced treatment of marriage by any church father. They thought that Book Three of Clement's major work, *Miscellanies*, was "necessarily offensive to our Christian tastes."[36]

There Clement used the differing attitudes of various groups toward sex as a criterion for distinguishing acceptable from unacceptable interpretations of Christianity.[37] The heretical sects are those that do not afford the flesh the dignity that it had in biblical culture. He divided the sects that fail to hallow sexuality into two major subcategories—the licentious and the ascetic. The former category—the Nicolaitans and the Carpocratians—advocated unrestrained sexual activity.[38] Some of them converted the *agape* feast into a promiscuous orgy. Clement believed that the licentious, in abusing the flesh, were manifesting contempt for its Creator.

The other category expressed their emotional antipathy for the goodness of creation by celibate practices. Marcion and Tatian were the prominent leaders of ascetic sects that Clement criticized. He did not mince words: "Those who from a hatred for the flesh ungratefully long to have nothing to do with the marriage union and the eating of reasonable food, are both blockheads and atheists, and exercise an irrational chastity like other heathen."[39] To those attracted by Marcion he asked:

How . . . can marriage be a state only intended for ancient times as an invention of the law, and marriage on Christian principles of a different nature, if we hold that the Old and the New Testaments proclaim the same God? "For what God has joined together no man may ever put asunder" for any good reason; if the Father commanded this, so much the more also will the Son keep it.[40]

And regarding the Encratites he said: "Fornication and marriage are . . . far apart as God is from the devil."[41]

It is unfortunate that Clement's presentation of Christian sexual ethics had so little effect on subsequent generations, for he was a levelheaded scholar who was so well grounded in the biblical outlook that he could, without fear of becoming overwhelmed, study and borrow the treasures of pagan philosophy. Although he lived in the citadel of Hellenism, he had the wisdom to steer a middle path between extreme hedonism and asceticism. In an article entitled "A Gentleman Among the Fathers," Morton S. Enslin contrasts the winsome temperament of Clement with the relentlessness of Tertullian and the stringency of Origen, Clement's student.[42]

ORIGEN THE EUNUCH

Origen, the most influential theologian between Paul and Augustine, drank deeply from the sources of pagan literature. His younger contemporary Porphyry reported that Origen was "always reading Plato" and Neoplatonic writings.[43] Plotinus, who became the preeminent Neoplatonist, shared with Origen the same Neoplatonic teacher, Ammonius.

Origen responded not only to the intellectual challenge of Platonism but also to the ascetic practices that it enjoined. Eusebius provided this information about Origen's self-punishment:

> He went to the limit in living like a philosopher; sometimes he trained himself by periods of fasting, sometimes by restricting the hours of sleep, which he insisted on taking never in bed, but always on the floor. . . . For several years he went about barefooted, and for a much longer period he abstained from wine and all else beyond the minimum of food, so that he ran the risk of upsetting and even ruining his health.[44]

Origen, like many teetotalers of later times, assumed that he was imitating the way in which Jesus mortified the flesh. He was convinced that the road to salvation that Jesus delineated was paved with abstinences from sensual pleasure. Henry Chadwick comments: "The entire tendency of Origen's ethic is to build on the antithesis of spirit and matter and to think of the way of moral and spiritual advance as a progressive suppression of the mind's responsiveness to the pull of the flesh."[45]

Eric Dodds points out that in the third century it would have been difficult to distinguish Origen's ethic from that of the Neoplatonists.[46] Celsus, a Jewish critic of Origen, asserted that the ethic of his opponent was not different from what was expressed in the current philosophies. Rather than deny this, Origen replied that God had impressed all with sound ideas of morality.[47] The sexual ethic of Origen is so different in tone from the biblical outlook that one can presume that he was more impressed by his pagan teachers than by the instruction he received from Clement. Origen thought it was better for Christians to remain celibate even though Clement believed the opposite. Both looked on the life of Adam and Eve in Eden as ideal, but Origen believed they had no sexual intercourse while living there.[48] Yet Clement had regarded it a "blasphemy against the creation" to believe that Adam and Eve did not have sexual union until persuaded by the serpent.[49]

Origen's self-castration displays the extent to which he rejected Clement's teaching of moderation. As described by Eusebius: "Origen did a thing that provided the fullest proof of a mind youthful and immature, but at the same time of faith and self-mastery. The saying 'there are eunuchs who made themselves eunuchs for the kingdom of heaven's sake' he took in an absurdly literal sense."[50] He also records that Origen was then teaching a class that included females. Evidently his mutilation was an attempt to eliminate the troublesome excitement caused by some girls in the mixed group. Later Origen deplored his act, perhaps because he realized that the removal of testicles after puberty does not take away sexual desire. The ineffectiveness of such surgery is displayed in a conversation in which Luther participated. He was told of a clergyman who "had had himself castrated in his youth and confessed that in his old age he regretted it, for he burned more with desire then than before." Luther replied, "Eunuchs are more ardent than anybody else, for the passion doesn't disappear but only the power."[51]

Origen came to realize that his true motivation for becoming a eunuch was not the ethic of Jesus. He referred to particular maxims of Sextus and Philo that had influenced him.[52] Sextus, who compiled aphorisms that were principally of Pythagorean origin[53] had recommended cutting off the genitals as a protection against fornication.[54] Philo had also advised: "It is better to be castrated than to be mad after illicit unions."[55] They were alluding to a practice found in several contemporary pagan cults. Priests of Cybele, the mythical Great Virgin Mother of Attis, emasculated themselves at the climax of a frenzied ritual.[56] At Ephesus there were eunuch priests of Artemis and in Syria there were eunuchs devoted to Astarte.[57]

Even though Origen condemned the scalpel technique for suppressing passion that he and some pagans had employed, he never rejected his pagan aim to cut out all libidinous craving. He thought that it should be renounced because it originated when spirits created by God rebelled against him. Origen wrote as a good Neoplatonist when he gave his version of creation: "God made the present world and bound the soul to the body as a punishment."[58] Since birth in the material world is a lamentable pollution, Origen recommended that birthdays should not be occasions for merriment. "You will never find any of the saints celebrating his birthday," he confided, "or holding a birthday party."[59] His fellow student Plotinus was also ashamed of having a body and rejected birthday parties.[60] Origen believed that moral contamination is inherent in all that has to do with the physical from the process of birth onward.[61] He stated: "Flesh does not contain beauty in the true sense of the word, seeing that all of it is shameful."[62] It is small wonder then that he was relatively unconcerned with Jesus in "the days of his flesh."[63]

While admitting that Christians could marry, Origen believed that participating in marital intercourse could be justified only as a means of producing children.[64] Those who copulate during pregnancy were worse than beasts, for even beasts abstained after insemination.[65] Origen also introduced cultic taboos to stifle the joy of conjugal relations, and advised that religious and sexual activities be separated as far as possible. Praying is not efficacious in the marital bed, for the Holy Spirit will not be given where there has been sexual preying.[66] Origen also admonished: "Whoever, after the conjugal act and the stain contracted by it, approaches boldly to receive the eucharistic bread, dishonors and profanes what is holy."[67] He chided Christians by appealing to pagan practice: since some pagans abstained from sexual intercourse in order to worship idols, how much more should worshipers of the supreme God abstain.[68]

Origen contended that no Christian who wanted to remain perpetually virginal lacked the disposition to do so. Since Jesus had promised his followers, "Ask, and it will be given you," all who ask will receive the gift of absolute celibacy.[69] Sexual abstinence is the foremost of living sacrifices which are pleasing to God.[70]

According to Origen the excellence of virginity is depicted in both the Old and New Testaments. The virginal conception of Jesus is prefigured in the prophecy of the suffering servant. "Like a root out of dry ground" (Isaiah 53:2) was interpreted to refer to Mary's virginal womb that was not moistened with semen.[71] The two pristine pure figures of the Bible and the reason for their superlative characters is given: "Jesus was the firstfruit among men of the purity which consists in virginity, and Mary among women."[72]

Pursuant to his concern that cultic functionaries be separated from sexual defilement, Origen borrowed from paganism the concept of an ascetic priesthood. The history of religions shows that from primitive times onward ascetic practices have been one of the main ways that priests have distinguished themselves from ordinary men.[73] In Inca, Aztec, and Hindu civilizations sexual abstinence was expected of the religious mystic.[74] This pattern of behavior was also found in Greek culture. Joseph W. Swain writes: "The Greeks were particularly insistent upon the sexual purity of priests. There were innumerable cults which demanded the absolute chastity of the priest or priestess."[75] Also Albrecht Oepke, with full documentation, states: "In early Greek thinking a certain antithesis was found between sexual intercourse and cultic approach to the godhead. Continence was demanded of the Eleusian hierophants before and during the fasts, and of some other priests more generally."[76]

In view of the prevailing pagan ideal of absolute continence, it is surprising that nascent Christianity withstood the sacerdotal system as long as it did. There were no Christian priests in the apostolic and early postapostolic church, indicating that the early Christians believed in the priesthood of all believers[77] and did not endorse the common pagan idea of a dual standard of moral holiness in the community. Church fathers did not use the term for priest (Greek: *hiereus*, Latin: *sacerdos*) in connection with the Christian ministry until the time of Origen.[78] But from the third century on celibacy became more and more associated with a sacred class set apart to emulate Jesus and Mary. Origen significantly contributed to this pagan infiltration, for he believed that continence was incumbent upon priests inasmuch as they serve the holy altar.[79] He spoke of "perfect priests" who "keep themselves in act and in thought in a state of virgin purity."[80]

JESUS THE BRIDEGROOM

Origen allegorized the Song of Songs to convey his Neoplatonic gospel of "pure spirituality."[81] By substituting Jesus for Plato's heavenly eros,[82] Origen located an ethereal partner for the pure Christian.[83] At the beginning he clarified his moral dualism: "There is a love of the flesh which comes from Satan, and there is also another love, belonging to the Spirit, which has its origin in God; and nobody can be possessed by the two loves. . . . If you have despised all bodily things . . . then you can acquire spiritual love."[84] Origen then warned those who were tempted to read the Song of Songs as an expression of physical love: "We earnestly beg the hearers of these things to mortify their carnal senses. They must not take anything of what has been said with reference to bodily functions, but rather employ them for grasping those divine senses of the inner man."[85] Origen treated the Song of Songs as a mystic cryptogram to be deciphered. Thus, for example, he claimed that the opening line of the poem, "May he smother me with kisses," meant that Jesus satisfied the church's craving for union with him.[86]

The Song of Songs allegory became the most popular of Origen's voluminous biblical interpretations. Although he was not the first to refer to celibates as spouses of Christ[87] or to convert the Song of Songs into a Christian allegory,[88] he was the first to give an extended and attractive treatment to a book that had heretofore embarrassed ascetics. Ingeniously he took the Scripture that was the greatest liability to sexual asceticism and converted it into an asset for disincarnate spirituality.

The analogy of Jesus as the bridegroom of the pious Christian has been expressed throughout church history. Origen's contemporary Cyprian wrote to warn some fallen virgins of their Spouse's displeasure:

If a husband come upon his wife and see her lying with another man, is he not angry and raging, and in his passion does he not perhaps take his sword into his hand? And what shall Christ our Lord and Judge think when he sees his virgin, dedicated to him, and destined for his holiness, lying with another?[89]

Although Jerome deplored the puerile way some of his adversaries read their own pet ideas into Scripture,[90] he had no reservation about making the Song of Songs a vehicle for Jesus' passion play with virgins. So he exhorted maidens:

Ever let the Bridegroom sport with you. . . . When sleep falls upon you he will come behind and will put his hand[91] through the opening and will touch your body. And you will arise trembling and cry, "I am lovesick." And you will hear him answer: "A garden enclosed is my sister, my spouse; a spring shut up, a fountain sealed" (Song of Songs 4:12). . . . Jesus is jealous. He does not wish your face to be seen by others.[92]

In the same letter a woman whose daughter was a "bride of Christ" was greeted by Jerome as the "mother-in-law of God"![93]

Ambrose told of St. Agnes, who preferred martyrdom to marriage with a man. As she was being executed she explained that she would have been unfaithful to her heavenly Spouse if she consented to an earthly marriage. Ambrose asserted that the consecrated virgin was "married to God."[94] That same figure is appealed to by Pope Pius XII.[95] The divine-human connubial theme was also displayed in the patristic era by an episode involving fellow seminarians Chrysostom and Theodore of Mopsuestia. When Theodore fell in love with a woman, Chrysostom sent him this embittered letter: "If he who has been attached to a heavenly Bridegroom deserts him, and joins himself to a wife the act is adultery, even if you call it marriage ten thousand times over; or rather it is worse than adultery in proportion as God is greater than man."[96]

The religious experiences of Jan van Ruysbroek in the fourteenth century (beatified in 1908), St. Teresa of Avila in the sixteenth century, and St. Mary Alacoque in the seventeenth century exemplify mystical marriages with the eligible heavenly God-man. Ruysbroek described the individual's rapture when the divine Bridegroom expresses his fervent love: "There flow rivers honey-sweet with all delights. . . . The more he touches us, the more we hunger and strive." Overtly carnal imagery abounded as he spoke of the climactic "sinking down into the essential nakedness" and the delectable love hugs. He concluded: "This is the dark silence in which all lovers lose themselves."[97] Ruysbroek showed that if sexual intercourse is repudiated in the natural sphere, a simulated experience tends to occur in the supernatural sphere. This experience for a male celibate symbolizes a homosexual liaison.

In her allegory on the Song of Songs, Teresa, a favorite Spanish saint, told of her thrill when the Bridegroom inebriated her with kisses.[98] She experienced excruciatingly delightful pain when ravished by her lover:

I saw in the angel's hand a long golden dart with a fiery tip. Several times he thrust it into my deepest self in such a manner that it pierced my bowels. When he drew it out it seemed as if my bowels came with it, leaving me all on fire with a great love of God. The pain was so intense that it made me moan; and yet so surpassing was the sweetness thereof that I could not wish to be rid of it.[99]

Mary Alacoque, the French nun who initiated the Sacred Heart of Jesus devotional practice, related how Jesus wooed her: "Let me do my pleasure. There is time for everything. Now I want you to be the plaything of my love, and you must live thus without resistance, surrendered to my desires, allowing me to gratify myself at your expense."[100]

These examples show the erotomania that can occur when sexual desires are denied normal satisfactions. William James, while judiciously rejecting the thesis that all piety is perverted sexuality, commented: "For the hysterical nun, starving for natural life, Christ is but an imaginary substitute for a more earthly object of affection."[101]

From the third century on it has been a boon to sexual asceticism to interpret the bridegroom of the Song of Songs as Jesus and the male or female celibate as his spouse. This nuptial mysticism continues to be a favorite theme of contemporary Catholic celibates. Bernhard Häring, the eminent moral theologian, asserts that the essential feature of Christian virginity is being seized and aroused in love by the divine Bridegroom.[102] Lucien Legrand, drawing on Origen and others, interprets the Song of Songs as the fiery love that virgins exchange with the heavenly Spouse.[103]

In the fifth century, Theodore of Mopsuestia made a valiant attempt to reject the allegorical interpretation of the Song of Songs and to return to the ancient interpretation of the poem as a mutual exchange of human passion and devotion. His view was condemned by the Council of Constantinople in 553.[104] However, Roman Catholic exegetes are now beginning to acknowledge that the Song of Songs was originally interpreted and should now be interpreted as a description of human love.[105]

VIRGINITY THE CHIEF VIRTUE

A generation after Origen, Methodius, the Bishop of Olympus, made virginity the *summum bonum* of Christianity. He claimed that those virgins who "have detached themselves from the absurdities of the flesh" receive "the pure and fertile seed of doctrine" from Jesus, to whom they are wedded.[106] "Archvirgin" was Methodius' favorite title for Jesus. He reviewed biblical history to justify his claim that Jesus was the first and foremost virgin:

Let us inquire for what reason it was that no one of the many patriarchs and prophets and righteous men, who taught and did many noble things, either praised or chose the state of virginity. Because it was reserved for the Lord alone to be the first to teach this doctrine, since he alone, coming down to us, taught man to draw near to God; for it was fitting that he who was first and chief of priests, of prophets, and of angels, should also be saluted as first and chief of virgins. For in old times man was not yet perfect, and for this reason was unable to receive perfection, which is virginity.[107]

The *Symposium*, Methodius' only extant work, copies Plato's dialogue style and articulates Neoplatonic asceticism. Ten virgins inveigh against sexual intercourse and advocate the complete suppression of all sensual appetites. James Mackinnon offers a penetrating evaluation:

[The *Symposium*] is a striking example of the tendency of these virgin panegyrists of virginity to indulge in prurient and morbid descriptions of the sex relation and function. In spite of their striving to repress the sex instinct, and to a certain extent because of it, their imagination is haunted by gross pictures of the sex function in both men and women. In this respect many of them were evidently not the virgins they professed to be in deed. At all events they show a strange predilection for imagining and describing the very thing that they profess to abhor and abjure. In this subtle fashion, nature has a way of avenging herself.[108]

Methodius followed Origen in lauding celibacy as the highest expression of self-renunciation. He made this appraisal: "Of all the means offered to men to guide us to eternal life, nothing is superior to chastity in its power to restore mankind to Paradise, reconcile them with God and transform them into a state of incorruptibility." "Whoever strives to keep his flesh undefiled from childhood by the practice of virginity is the one who offers himself perfectly to God."[109] The cardinal "love your neighbor" injunction of the biblical ethic is, in effect, changed by Methodius to "keep your virginity"; a passionless self-centeredness is substituted for a compassionate concern for others.

In Methodius' day Christian martyrdom belonged to a past epoch and hence the virgin was beginning to replace the martyr as the supreme expression of sacrifice. This transition can be detected by comparinng Methodius' position with both his predecessors and his successors. Paul had maintained that martyrdom had no intrinsic merit.[110] Since *agape* is the sine qua non of Christian virtue, unless the persecuted one has been witnessing to neighbor-love as defined in 1 Corinthians 13, his execution may be no more than a display of mad egotism and masochism. Paul's profound statement about the ethic of martyrdom was overlooked in the patristic age.

Cyprian, who became a martyr, determined before his death what his heavenly reward should be. He took Jesus' interpretation of the parable of the soils to refer to rewards in the life after death. Fruitful hearers of the word of God have thirtyfold, sixtyfold, and a hundredfold yields.[111] Cyprian believed that virgins and martyrs were much alike because both had "no thought of the flesh"; however, he differentiated between the virgin's sixtyfold and the martyr's hundredfold reward.[112]

A half-century later Methodius pronounced that virgins, because they imitate Jesus better than Christian martyrs, would be honored more.

For they are martyrs, not bearing the pains of the body for a little moment of time, but enduring them through all their life. . . . Resisting the fierce torments of pleasures and fears and griefs, and the other evils of the iniquity of men, they first of all carry off the prize, taking their place in the higher rank of those who receive the promise. Undoubtedly they are the souls whom the Word calls alone his chosen spouse and his sister.[113]

Methodius' conviction was accepted by Athanasius, causing him to alter Cyprian's account of heavenly rewards. Athanasius, in a letter to Amun, explained:

There are two ways of life: . . . marriage is the more moderate and ordinary; virginity is angelic and unsurpassed. Now if a man choose the way of the world, namely marriage, he is not indeed to blame; yet he will not receive such great gifts as the other. For he will receive, since he too brings forth fruit, namely thirtyfold. But if a man embrace the holy and unearthly way . . . he grows the perfect fruit, namely a hundredfold.[114]

Jerome, in the generation after Athanasius, agreed that marriage is less than a third as meritorious as virginity. The sixtyfold reward goes to widows "since it is extremely trying when one has once tasted pleasure to abstain from its enticements."[115] Jerome's contemporary, Chrysostom, gave the highest tribute possible to celibacy. He wrote: "The root, and the flower, too, of virginity is a crucified life."[116] Robert Briffault observes with respect to Christianity in this era:

The sexual aspect of holiness came to eclipse all other issues, and morality came to mean, what it has ever since connoted in European tradition, sexual purity. . . . Sexual continence was not only regarded as of the same importance as the most essential doctrines of the Christian faith and the principles of Christian ethics, but it was proclaimed to be the chief of all virtues, and the first and indispensable condition of righteousness and of faith itself.[117]

After Christianity became the established Roman religion, Gregory the Great indicated how virginity came to supersede martyrdom as the crowning Christian virtue: "Now, though the era of persecution is gone, yet our peace has its martyrdom, because though we bend not the neck to the sword, yet with a spiritual weapon we slay fleshly desires in our hearts."[118] Pope Pius XII, in an address to consecrated virgins, approved of this value structure of Methodius and Gregory.[119] Today the celibate Legrand shows a similar admiration for Methodius and indirectly for his own condition. He brazenly claims: "Undoubtedly virginity, implying perfect self-control, brings along with it all the other virtues."[120]

To hold that virginity is the superlative virtue is, in effect, to admit that the religion of the Bible is expendable. Other religions in the Mediterranean and elsewhere did much better at focusing on its excellence. The Athenians crowned their city with the Parthenon (virgin-temple) in which the gold and ivory statue of the virgin Athena was the center of adoration. In Asia Minor there was the well-organized cult of Artemis, who was called " the virgin goddess and the immaculate one." G. J. Laing argues that the worship of Artemis (or Diana) at the grand Ephesian temple has contributed to the veneration of Mary. It is significant that both were called the "Queen of Heaven," and that it was at an ecumenical council held in 431 at Ephesus, the historic headquarters of that pagan religion, that Mary was first designated "mother of God."[121]

The veneration of virginity was at least as prominent in Roman as in Greek civilization. For the thousand years of Roman history the "most sacred of priestly offices," according to Cicero, was that of the Vestal Virgins.[122] The women selected for office were regarded as personifications of the virgin goddess Vesta. This cult exemplified that in Rome ideal purity was inseparable from sexual continence. Also Mythraism, the popular mystery religion of the Roman empire and the chief rival of early Christianity, had virgins and celibates associated with it.[123]

Gerhard Delling explains the widespread esteem for virginity in pagan cults:

The lifelong sexual abstinence demanded of priests and priestesses by certain duties carries with it in the first instance the thought that virginity conveys a special religious power. But in the case of a priestess the main idea in chastity may be simply that she lives in marital relation to the god. . . . It is conceivable that the idea of demonic infection through sexual intercourse also played some part.[124]

For similar reasons, all of which are unbiblical, virginity became the prerequisite of absolute purity in Catholicism.

Later in the fourth century Gregory of Nyssa adopted Methodius' thesis that virginity was the quintessence of the Christian virtues. He was significantly influenced by Neoplatonism.[125] In a eulogy on virginity Gregory lamented that it was his misfortune to be married. To express his longing for the virginal condition, he compared himself to a parched man gazing at a stream of which he can never drink.[126] Gregory, who at the ecumenical council of 787 was given the title "Father of the Fathers," found fatherhood to be a miserable experience. He reflected:

Everything wrong in life has its beginning in marriage which distracts one from the true life. . . . Think of the types of misfortunes which come to men from marriage. . . . Can anyone lament widowhood, orphanhood, calamities concerning children, if he does not marry? The longed for delights and joys and pleasures and whatever else is hoped for in marriage come to an end with these pains. . . . Giving up marriage means being exempt from participation in all these evil experiences and this is not at all unreasonable.[127]

But Bishop Gregory's preference for the virginal life was not merely to avoid hardships. To prevent the invasion of forces that would soil virtue, "a safe protective wall is the complete estrangement from everything involving passion."[128]

It was Gregory's position that Mary and Jesus had to avoid sexual intercourse in order to be completely pure. He referred to the pleasurable sensations afforded by marital generation as "the impulse to vice in all living men" and as "a disease of our nature."[129] Neither the conception of Jesus nor the entire life of Jesus had any connection with sensual pleasure. Gregory seemed to think that Jesus and Mary were somewhat like Adam and Eve, who were originally sexless. Since the first human creations were in God's true image, they did not have such animal functions as sexual intercourse, growth, and excretion.[130] Those inferior functions were created in a second stage of creation.[131]

According to Gregory, the holy person followed Hebrews who allegedly inaugurated the virginal life. He thought that Miriam was the archetype of the virgin mother of Jesus and all others who pommel and subdue their sexual desire. In a quirky way he found evidence of Miriam's sexual restraint in the description of a dance celebration after her brother led the Israelites across the exodus sea. He took the Exodus 15:20 comment that she played on her tambourine to mean allegorically that she beat down her body and became sensually dead.[132] Elijah was Miriam's male counterpart in the Jewish Scripture. Gregory inferred that Elijah was a virgin because he wore a hairy garment. Had he married, he would have worn less austere clothing due to having "grown soft because of the pleasures of the body."[133] Here we see one of the most learned of the church fathers ferreting out alleged virgins from Scripture by ridiculous means. Utilizing Gregory's hunting technique, John of Damascus later found another Old Testament celibate. Daniel's body could not be penetrated by the wild beasts because his flesh had been hardened by virginity.[134] Although it is easy to recognize that these patristic judgments are ill founded, it is apparently more difficult for Christians to reject similar unsubstantial arguments advanced by theologians for Jesus' lifelong virginity.

PAGAN ROOTS OF MONASTICISM

The ascetic presuppositions and biblical interpretations of Gregory and other patristics laid an adequate theoretical basis for the rise of the Christian monastic movement. Prior to the fourth century celibates had not deliberately separated themselves from their communities. But now some of these ascetics believed that it was defiling not only to live with a spouse in marriage, but also to live amid other married Christians.

The first outbreak of hermitic and monastic life was in Egypt. In the early fourth century Anthony inaugurated a movement toward hermitic life. Shortly afterward the monastic life was introduced by Pachomius. If reports of their endeavors can be believed, withdrawal from conventional society quickly reached epidemic proportions. For example, at Oxyrhynchos in Egypt there were more monks than laity, and accommodations for 30,000 celibates were constructed outside the city wall.[135]

A story about Ammoun, who lived at Alexandria around A.D. 300, is a good illustration of the motivations that stimulated Christians to separate from ordinary life. On his wedding night Ammoun convinced his bride that both should become celibates and engage only in spiritual marriage. An early church historian reported that he discussed

the inconveniences and discomforts attending matrimonial intercourse, the pangs of child bearing, and the trouble and anxiety connected with rearing a family. He contrasted with all this the advantages of chastity, described the liberty and immaculate purity of a life of continence; and affirmed that virginity places a person in the nearest relation to the Deity. By these and other arguments of a similar kind, he persuaded his virgin bride to renounce with him a secular life, prior to their having any conjugal knowledge of each other. Having taken this resolution, they retired together to the mountain of Nitria and in a hut there inhabited for a short time one common ascetic apartment.[136]

Finding that continent cohabitation did not quench sexual desire, Ammoun and his wife agreed to separate.

This new manifestation of Christian asceticism in Egypt was soon duplicated elsewhere as the monastic movement swept through Eastern and Western Catholicism. Its widespread popularity in the fourth and fifth centuries no doubt caused a decline in population. This in turn was a factor that hastened the decline of the Western Roman Empire. There had been for centuries a problem of underpopulation, which Augustus and his successors had tried to eliminate through legal sanctions. Yet the first impact of Christianity on Roman law came in 320 when Constantine responded to monastic pressure and terminated the Augustan legislation.[137] These circumstances caused Richard Lewinsohn to conclude that "sexual abstinence did more than excess to bring the downfall of Rome."[138] It is ironical that the Catholic church favored population diminution when Western civilization needed more offspring and now, in effect, it favors large families when the social problem is reversed.

What caused the rise of Christian monastic communities in Egypt? Some pagan religious practices show the social environment to have been ripe for this development. At the beginning of the Hellenistic era, Ptolemy I established the cult of Sarapis to unify his empire. Porphyry described the priests of that cult as recluses who devoted themselves to sexual and dietary abstinences.[139] The pagan practices that he detailed are remarkably like those of the cloistered Christian of a later date.

At the same time that the Sarapis cult was developing, the Pythagorean school was being revived at Alexandria.[140] The Neopythagoreans claimed to have learned from the Egyptian priests, and in imitation of them they observed silence and a life of solitude.[141] Porphyry[142] and Jerome[143] indicate that the Pythagoreans dwelt in solitary places in the Egyptian desert. William Lecky writes: "The whole school of Pythagoras made chastity one of its leading virtues, and even labored for the creation of a monastic system."[144] Dodds points out that Athanasius' biography of Anthony is similar to hagiographic treatments of Pythagoras.[145]

Philo told of a monastic community of the first century B.C. that was basically Neopythagorean in cultic rites and ascetic practices.[146] It was located near Alexandria and was called the Therapeutae. Perpetual virginity was a central principle of the sect and was regarded as a means to perfection.[147] However, the Therapeutae also included those who had left spouses and children. Women as well as men were admitted to the celibate life.[148]

The Cynic-Stoic philosophy was also a causative force in the rise of Christian monasticism. Sages of that school aimed at absolute passionlessness (apathia) by extinguishing sensual desires. Herbert Workman claims that the ideal of apathy was a "powerful factor" in the evolution of Christian monasteries.[149] The monks, like the Stoics, tried to go beyond moderating their passions, aiming at the liquidation of natural impulses.[150]

The practices of the Christian ascetics were so similar to the Sarapis priests, the Therapeutae monks, and the Cynic-Stoic philosophers that identity confusion resulted. In the second century Emperor Hadrian described the religious situation in Egypt: "There are Christians who adore Sarapis; and there are people who, having consecrated themselves to Sarapis, call themselves bishops of Christ."[151] In the fourth century Eusebius mistakenly regarded the Therapeutae as Christian monks of the apostolic age.[152] Evidently he anachronistically assumed that Jesus was the first monk. Also, later in the fourth century, Maximus, a Cynic of Alexandria, wore the distinctive white robe and long hair of his brotherhood when he was consecrated as Bishop of Constantinople.[153] Because he accepted the Nicene Creed he was admired by Christians.[154] Basil, the father of Greek monasticism, praised the Cynic Diogenes and considered his ascetic life style a model for monks.[155] In the thirteenth century the Dominican friars punned on their name and called themselves "Domini canes," meaning "the Lord's Cynics."[156]

Christian monks agreed that the elimination of sexual activity was prerequisite to purity, even though the more realistic ones admitted that humans could not jettison all physical satisfactions. Nemesius, a Syrian bishop of the fourth century, made this analysis:

Of the pleasures called bodily, some are both necessary and natural, and without them life would not be possible; for example, the pleasures of the table. . . . On the other hand, there are pleasures that are natural but not necessary, such as normal and legitimate marital intercourse. . . . Therefore a true man of God must pursue only the pleasures that are both necessary and natural.[157]

As Nemesius acknowledged, Plato was the source of this ethical theory. He held that nature does not compel man to satisfy his sexual appetite and hence its gratification is unnecessary. By contrast, the appetite for food cannot be diverted or suppressed.[158] Plato's distinction between necessary and unnecessary sensual activity had a profound impact on later philosophy and religion.

During the patristic era Plato's perspective was used to give a rationale for Jesus' alleged celibacy. An unknown third-century Christian thought that Jesus, like a good Platonist, participated in only those practices of the flesh necessary to stay alive. His assumed perpetual virginity was explained:

Christ did not submit to discharging the sexual function, for regarding the desires of the flesh, he accepted some as necessary, while others, which were unnecessary, he did not submit to. For if the flesh were deprived of food, drink, and clothing, it would be destroyed; but being deprived of lawless desire, it suffers no harm.[159]

Chapter VIII

SEXUAL ATTITUDES IN ROMAN CATHOLICISM

The belief that the sexual impulse is bad and that Jesus could not have had any contact with it came to a full flowering in the late patristic era. The influential Jerome and Augustine played a major role in establishing the sin-sex syndrome as a dominant motif in the Christian tradition. Eight centuries later Thomas Aquinas endorsed the Augustinian sex ethic and thereby insured its influence on subsequent Christian thought.

JEROME'S HORROR OF SEX

Jerome was well trained in the philosophers who championed moral dualism. He acknowledged having studied Pythagoras, Empedocles, and Plato; he admitted feeling guilt over his excessive devotion to Cicero.[1] He was especially delighted by the recurring theme of sexual asceticism in the philosophical classics. In one treatise Jerome prefaced a six-chapter survey of pagan writers with this comment: "I will quickly run through Greek and Roman and foreign history, and will show that virginity ever took the lead."[2] He quoted at length from Theophrastus, an Aristotelian, who went about as far as possible in disparaging wives and marriage. Several samples of his cynical outlook follow:

A wise man must not take a wife. . . . To support a poor wife is hard: to put up with a rich one is torture. . . . Horses, asses, cattle, even slaves of the smallest worth, clothes and kettles . . . are first tried and then bought: a wife is the only thing that is not shown before she is married, for fear she may not give satisfaction. . . . A faithful slave is a far better manager, more submissive to the master, more observant of his ways, than a wife.[3]

Theophrastus' biting satire is appraised by Jerome as "worth its weight in gold."

As an adult Jerome admired virginity not only because of the philosophy he had read and accepted but also because it was a quality he personally lacked. He testified: "I extol virginity to the skies, not because I possess it, but because, not possessing it, I admire it all the more."[4] In order to punish himself for youthful fornication, the future saint left Rome and went to the East to live as a hermit. Jerome related this in an autobiographical letter: "Many years ago I renounced home, parents, my sister and my relatives and, what is much more difficult, the familiar good kitchen too; for I had made myself 'a eunuch for the sake of the kingdom of heaven' and I wanted to move to Jerusalem."[5]

After living in Palestine for some years he returned to Italy and promoted the movement of monasticism from the Eastern to the Western Mediterranean. Throughout his career as a recluse he wrote fervent letters and polemics that were aimed mainly at extolling his way of life and castigating those with lesser holiness. Sometimes he pleaded for Christians to "cut down the tree of marriage with the ax of virginity."[6] At other times his rhetoric was more restrained, since he realized that "virginity is to marriage what fruit is to the tree."[7] He knew that the survival of a celibate system was dependent upon noncelibates supplying fresh generations of virgins.[8] Even so he occasionally unleashed his verbal ferocity and damned "the swelling womb and wailing infancy, the fruit as well as the work of marriage."[9] By chipping away at marriage, Jerome thwarted its future health in Christendom.

Jerome's bitter diatribes drew the opposition of Jovinian and Helvidian. Although he was a monk, Jovinian believed that virgins were no better than the married in the sight of God.[10] In a treatise published in Rome, he supported his position by pointing out that 1 Corinthians 9:5 states that the apostles were married. Jerome countered Jovinian's scholarship by personal invective and by strained biblical interpretations. He claimed that John the apostle "was a virgin when he embraced Christianity, remained a virgin, and on that account was more beloved by our Lord and lay upon the breast of Jesus." Moreover, it was because of his pure body that at the crucifixion "the Virgin Mother was entrusted by the virgin Lord to the virgin disciple."[11] According to Jerome, John was more virtuous than the married Peter and it was only because of deference to age that John was not made the head of the church. Peter had the misfortune to marry before he came under the sway of the Gospel, but "when he forsook his boat and nets he forsook his wife also."[12] Jerome also maintained that John the Baptist was a celibate "so that by a virgin prophet the virgin Lord might be both announced and baptized."[13] Concerning Jesus, Jerome cited the biblical account of his circumcision to show that he had genitals. The question is them raised: "What necessity was there for him to be born with members which he was not going to use?" This was because Jesus wanted to set an example of sexual abstinence for Christians.[14] Jerome also argued that in the Old Testament "chastity was always preferred to the condition of marriage."[15] Thus he attempted to show that Joshua was a virgin because God was not displeased with him as he had been with Moses, his married predecessor.[16]

Since Jerome was an acknowledged genius in understanding and translating Scripture, his "proofs" for the superiority of virginity carried weight. Consequently Jovinian was condemned for "heresy" and "blasphemy" at councils called by Pope Siricius in Rome and Bishop Ambrose in Milian.[17] However, Jovinian's view that fleshly abstinences are not necessarily indicative of a holier life was more biblical than the outlook of his adversaries. Jerome's shrill criticism of sex and marriage in his tract Against Jovinian had much influence in the Middle Ages.[18] Not long ago the Jesuit Gerald J. Campbell, after probing that tract and some of Jerome's letters, concluded that although the saint was "somewhat harsh" in his attitude toward women, he stated what has traditionally been Roman Catholic doctrine.[19]

Helvidian, like Jovinian, attempted to counter the virginal obsession of his fellow Christians. Hoping that he might persuade the church to return to the outlook of earlier Christianity, he focused attention on the New Testament statements about Jesus' family. While holding that Jesus was miraculously conceived by Mary, he denied her perpetual virginity. He argued, as Tertullian had done two centuries earlier,[20] that verses such as Matthew 1:18, Luke 2:7, and Luke 8:20 implied that Mary conceived children in a normal manner after delivering her "first-born." Helvidian favored this interpretation because he believed that it was historically accurate and that there was nothing intrinsically evil about marital intercourse.[21] He argued that male contact with feminine sexual organs could not be sinful per se, because the sinless Jesus was born through a vagina.[22]

In response to Helvidian's position, Jerome offered an entirely new concept of Joseph's life. He wrote: "You say that Mary did not continue a virgin: I claim still more, that Joseph himself on account of Mary was a virgin."[23] In earlier ascetic literature Mary had been pictured as a virgin for life and married to Joseph, an aged widower who had fathered Jesus' stepbrothers.[24] But that apocryphal tale was not enough for Jerome, so he invented the notion of Joseph's perpetual virginity. He also rejected the positions of Helvidian and Tertullian[25] that Jesus had uterine brothers. Jerome held not only that Mary had no carnal relations either before or after the birth of Jesus, but also that her hymen was unruptured by the delivery of Jesus. He believed that a miracle occurred at that occasion similar to Jesus' going through closed doors after his resurrection.[26]

The Roman Catholic church has approved Jerome's doctrine of the perpetual virginity of Joseph and Mary as articulated in *Against Helvidian*, the first Mariology treatise. During the past century the papacy has repeatedly affirmed that Joseph as well as Mary was a virgin through life.[27] Simultaneously biblical scholars have endorsed Helvidian's position and have rejected Jerome's fabrication.[28]

AUGUSTINE'S ANTISEXUAL ETHIC

Augustine continued Jerome's crusade and fought against Jovinian and others who attempted to exercise a moderating influence on sexual ethics. The time in which Augustine lived and his early life both led to his antipathy toward sex and marriage. Augustine's life span (354–430) coincided with a precipitous decline in the power of ancient Rome. Recognizing that the fall of the empire was imminent, Augustine assumed that this last worldly culture would soon be replaced by the eternal "City of God." That he had less hope in the future of secular society than Jerome can be seen by comparing their responses to a dilemma posed by Jovinian: "If everyone were a virgin, what would become of the human race?" Jerome dismissed the question by saying there was little reason to fear that there would be no future generations because the majority of people would not accept virginity.[29] By contrast, Augustine faced the prospect of human extinction cheerfully, asserting that the sooner this happened the sooner God's triumphant reign would come at the end of time.[30] He interpreted Ecclesiastes 3:5 to mean that the era before Christ was the time for marriage, but since Christ it had been "a time to refrain from embracing." Christians could best leave the dirty work of generation up to others and work toward effecting pagan "spiritual regeneration."[31]

The ascetic currents of thought that swept through the youthful Augustine in successive waves helped to shape his later writings as the Bishop of Hippo. He was infatuated for a decade with Manicheism, which was then popular in his native area of North Africa. During that period, between the ages of 18 and 29, he lived with a mistress who bore him a child. Since Manichean doctrine prohibited procreation, Augustine lived for years with a festering guilt complex. He was faithful to his mistress and claimed that the relation lacked only "the honorable name of marriage."[32] But due to pressure from his dominating mother, Augustine dismissed his common-law wife and became engaged to someone his mother deemed socially acceptable. He expressed poignantly his affection for the mother of his son: "My heart which clung to her was torn and wounded till it bled."[33] In defiance of his mother and as a concession to his libido, which was "a slave of lust," he took another mistress as a temporary relief until he was legitimately married. All of this gave him a tumultuous conscience that prayed pathetically: "Give me chastity and continence but not just yet."[34]

Then followed Augustine's famous "conversion" in Milan when he committed himself to a life of sexual abstinence. He stated: "Thou didst so convert me unto Thyself that I sought neither a wife, nor any other of this world's hopes."[35] He thought of that experience as a conversion to Christianity, but by rejecting marriage for himself he was actually a better Manichean afterward than before. His contemporaries Jovinian and Julian charged that Augustine was never able to discard his Manichean outlook.[36] Some modern scholars also maintain that Augustine, in spite of his verbal opposition to Manicheism, often endorsed exactly what Mani would have favored.[37] In his scholarly biography of Augustine, Peter Brown asserts that "Augustine found himself agreeing wholeheartedly with Mani."[38]

Augustine's fabric of mature thought also had woven into it other strands of Greco-Roman ascetic philosophy. He endorsed Cicero's sentiments:

Should one seek the pleasures of the body, which, as Plato said truly and earnestly, are the enticements and baits of evil? What injury to health, what deformity of character and body, what wretched loss, what dishonor is not evoked and elicited by pleasure? Where its action is the most intense, it is the most inimical to philosophy. . . . What fine mind would not prefer that nature had given us no pleasures at all?[39]

Augustine went on to say that Cicero should cause Christians to blush because he had the wisdom to condemn sexual desire even though he lived before Christ.

Of all philosophies, Augustine was most fascinated with Neoplatonism as articulated by Porphyry, the popularizer of Plotinus. Porphyry, whom Augustine called "the noble philosopher," despised sexual intercourse.[40] Plotinus had also preached, "To lapse into carnal love is a sin,"[41] and accordingly practiced strict coital abstinence.

Due to his personal illicit sexual pleasures, and due to the influence of various Hellenistic philosophies during his formative years, Augustine came to assume that shame was normative even in marital expressions of sex, and discussed it in several ways. Augustine's terminology conveys that he thought the sexual urge was evil in itself. One of his favorite terms was *concupiscentia*, which was a neutral term in classical Latin meaning strong desire. Augustine is largely responsible for the term coming to mean tainted sexual desire in the Middle Ages. The Jesuit John P. Kenny writes that Augustine appears

to identify concupiscence with fleshly desire in general and with lust in particular. He seems to regard it as evil and nothing but evil. . . . He seems to undermine the dignity of Christian wedlock, because, while on the one hand marriage (in his theory) cloaks concupiscence with respectability, it is itself degraded by its traffic with what he continues to castigate as evil.[42]

To prove that sexual impulse even in marriage is sinful, Augustine drew on human experiences from Adam onward: "The first human pair, on experiencing in the flesh that motion which was indecent because disobedient, and on feeling the shame of their nakedness, covered these offending members with fig-leaves."[43] Augustine was considerably embarrassed to realize that man's conscious will could not control sexual activity. He regarded involuntary penis erections, spontaneous ejaculations, and the intensity of venereal pleasures as proof that human nature had fallen. Augustine found it significant that except for his penis every other part of his body was subordinate to his will power. In the marital act, he lamented that "sometimes it refuses to act when the mind wills, while often it acts against its will!"[44] Augustine thus considered it quite proper to call the sexual organs indecent and dishonorable.[45] He admonished: "Detest these members as adultery is detested."[46] To prove that the sexual impulse was evil Augustine also appealed to what he thought was a common experience in marital sexuality. He believed that the shamefulness of the sexual impulse is manifested in conjugal partners who desire privacy while engaged in intercourse[47] and who blush at what they have done together.[48]

Augustine understood the biblical creation account to mean that there would have been human procreation even if there had been no sexual desire, so he speculated on how the process of conception could have occurred in Paradise. In a whimsical way he argued that the genitals were under complete rational control before human corruption came. Just as now some deliberately "make their ears move, either one at a time or both together," and others "can make musical notes issue from the rear of their anatomy, so that you would think they were singing," in like manner "our organs without the excitement of sexual desire, could have obeyed human will for all the purposes of parenthood."[49] In his *magnum opus, City of God,* Augustine went on to suggest a superior way in which the passionless husband could have transmitted seminal fluid without breaking his wife's hymen and without having vaginal contact. Unwittingly he pictured a Stoic utopia of ataraxia:

Without the seductive stimulus of passion, with calmness of the mind and with no corrupting of the integrity of the body, the husband would lie upon the bosom of his wife. . . . No wild heat of passion would arouse those parts of the body. . . . The male semen could have been introduced into the womb of the wife with the integrity of the female genital organ being preserved, just as now, with that same integrity being safe, the menstrual flow of blood can be emitted from the womb of a virgin. To be sure, the seed could be introduced in the same way through which the menses can be emitted. . . . Thus not the eager desire of lust, but the normal exercise of the will should join the male and female for breeding and conception.[50]

Hence, had Adam not fallen there could have been virginal insemination by the force of gravity. Physical conception of a baby would have been as unemotional as the routine intellectual conception of a mathematical formula.

Augustine was among the first to equate sexual desires with "original sin."[51] He stated quite bluntly that "everyone who is born of sexual intercourse is in fact sinful flesh."[52] The evil sexual impulse inherent in parents is transmitted to offspring in the same physiological way as children inherit the skin pigmentation of their parents.[53]

This theory of the transmission of sin through the genes had monumental implications for Augustine's doctrine of salvation. It necessitated that a perfectly pure man could only be conceived in an unnatural manner. Augustine held that Jesus had the prerequisite of perfection in being virginally conceived, and that "except for him no man is without sin at the beginning of infancy."[54] The damnation of unbaptized infants was another gruesome implication of Augustine's theory of sex.[55] He maintained that apart from sacraments of the church there was no salvation. By tying his ascetic ideas of sex to his ecclesiastical mechanics of salvation, he thereby made the institutional church essential for all who accepted his doctrine.

Baptismal water, although prerequisite to salvation, does not at all guarantee that the church member is accepted by God. Rigorous ascetic discipline is also prescribed for those who desire to live a godly life. Augustine advised those who planned to marry that they live together but dispense with physical consummation. He cited the example of Joseph and Mary to justify his position that carnal relations are not integral to married life.[56] Augustine had the notion that sexual intercourse is a dispensable accessory to married life and held that truly holy wedlock is uncontaminated by conjugal pleasures.[57] He solemnly confessed: "I feel that nothing so casts down the manly mind from its heights as the fondling of women and those bodily contacts which belong to the married state."[58] The safest way of keeping morally clean was to avoid even "spiritual" marriage. Augustine pronounced: "Holy virginity is a better thing than conjugal chastity. . . . A mother will hold a lesser place in the kingdom of heaven, because she has married, than the daughter, seeing that she is a virgin."[59]

Augustine warned men to beware of all women. He advised them that women made poor work partners and were not nearly as consoling for loneliness and pleasant for conversation as male companions.[60] Job's wife was called by Augustine the "devil's advocate"[61] even though she did not forsake her husband in joy or in sorrow. Men should never forget that it was woman who brought on the fall of man and the loss of Paradise. The devil did not attack man directly because he knew that man was too smart to yield to straightforward temptation. Rather woman, because of her lower intelligence, became the devil's prey. Mary Daly points out that Augustine was so neurotic in projecting guilt upon women that he did not recognize his inconsistency. Regarding Eve she says: "This dull-witted creature . . . was clever enough to seduce man, which the ingenious devil could not do. Why did that paragon of intelligence and virtue succumb so easily?"[62] According to Augustine the Genesis flood as well as the fall was occasioned by woman. Horrified by women as incarnations of sensuality, he claimed that they seduced the sons of God. It was their "corrupt manners" and "bodily beauty" that brought on that second calamity.[63] Assertions like this show how Augustine was able to "canonize, on paper, the fears and prejudices that the common man accepts unconsciously."[64]

How could the theologian who made the love ethic central have such a cynical outlook on the opposite sex? He maintained that sex was no more intrinsic to human nature than hatred is to one's adversary. A Christian "loves his enemy not in so far as he is an enemy, but in so far as he is a human being." Likewise, "it is characteristic of a good Christian to love in a woman the creature of God whom he desires to be transformed and renewed, but to hate corruptible and mortal intimacy and sexual intercourse—that is, to love the human being in her but to hate what belongs to her as a wife."[65]

Near the end of his life Augustine had a controversy with Julian of Eclanum over sex and its relation to Christian doctrine. Julian, a married bishop, argued that sexual desire was a neutral energy that became sinful only when the individual chose to express it in illicit extramarital behavior.[66] Augustine's doctrine that the guilt that originated in Adam was transmitted to each infant by means of his physical inheritance was, in Julian's opinion, uncivilized and a slander against God.[67] He also found it repugnant because it destroyed the sanctity of marriage. Julian held that within marriage the sexual impulse could perform the work of God, and therefore intense passion for one's own wife was commendable.[68] Sexual desire should no more be condemned because of obscene excesses, he maintained, than hunger because of gluttony.[69] Julian daringly asserted that Jesus had sexual desires and yet his nature was not sinful.[70] Norman P. Williams, in his study of the patristic doctrine of sin, makes this significant judgment: "Julian may thus claim the credit of having been the first Christian writer to grasp with absolute clearness the crucial idea of the moral neutrality of bodily appetite."[71]

Julian's theology and ethic vis-à-vis Augustine is profoundly biblical. That Julian's outlook is commensurate with that of ancient Jewish thought is displayed in this comment by Moore:

There is no notion that the original constitution of Adam underwent any change in consequence of the fall, so that he transmitted to his descendants a vitiated nature in which the appetites and passions necessarily prevail over reason and virtue, while the will to good is enfeebled or wholly impotent.[72]

Moreover, Julian's Christology is in line with the affirmation about Jesus in Hebrews 2:18: "Because he himself has suffered and been tempted, he is able to help those who are tempted." But Augustine reversed New Testament doctrine in his response to Julian: "If Christ had had in his nature sexual desire which is not good, he would not have healed it in ours."[73]

Julian, whom Augustine regarded as an intelligent but detestable heretic, was deposed and exiled as a reward for his audacious challenge to the sexual asceticism of his day. After being ousted from Italy, he went to live in Syria with Theodore of Mopsuestia, who shared his Christology. As a result, the Council of Constantinople in 553 condemned Theodore's teaching. He was charged with the "blasphemous" view that Christ was "vexed by the sufferings of the soul and the desires of the flesh."[74] It is unfortunate that the works of Julian, a rational and balanced Christian, are no longer extant, and that his ideas can only be known through the writings of his opponents. In spite of the overwhelming historical impact of Augustine, most humane Christians today would probably prefer Julian's sexual ethic and judge Augustine's to be immoral. But history is often unkind to those who challenge contemporary authority. There is, for instance, no entry for Julian in the *Encyclopaedia Britannica*, and he is not even mentioned in the columns devoted to Augustine.

What legacy has Augustine's antisexual ethic had in history? Coming as it did at the beginning of Western monasticism, it appealed to those celibates who would provide future ecclesiastical leadership. Paul Lehmann comments on Augustine's treatise *On Marriage and Concupiscence:*

It is at once the basis for and the most succinct statement of the ethical teachings of the Roman Catholic church concerning sex. If one wants to know why the Roman Catholic church holds that the chief and decisive end of marriage is procreation, that divorce and birth control are inadmissible, and that continence is the ideal of sexual self-discipline, the reasons are all given by the bishop of Hippo in his discussion of marriage.[75]

Father John A. O'Brien agrees basically with the judgment of the Protestant ethicist Lehmann.[76] But Augustine's impact has been felt beyond the Roman Catholic church. D. Sherwin Bailey writes: "Augustine must bear no small measure of responsibility for the insinuation into our culture of the idea, still widely current, that Christianity regards sexuality as something peculiarly tainted with evil."[77]

The common identification today of the sexual ethic of Jesus and Augustine is tragic, because the latter came from nonbiblical sources. Augustine played a part in turning Christianity into what Nietzsche contemptuously termed "Platonism for the people."[78] Paul Tillich accurately perceived that Augustine "never overcame the Hellenistic and especially the Neoplatonic devaluation of sex."[79] Another irony is that Augustine, who wanted to diminish sex in life, actually caused more emphasis to be placed on it through his fanaticism. Those who identify becoming Christian with suppressing sexuality, and who assume one is moral if he has no sexual irregularities, are indebted to Augustine. Moreover, those who separate sex from love in contemporary culture are following an Augustinian outlook. Thus contemporary hedonism and classic asceticism both tend to depersonalize sexual intercourse. Nicholas Berdyaev remarks that Augustine's treatises on sex "remind one of treatises on cattle breeding."[80] Likewise Waldemar Molinski asserts that "Augustine assigns sexuality to the animal domain, seeing no specifically human aspect in it at all."[81] Sexual relations at their best were for him little more than the shameful means for female insemination.

AQUINAS' BLOCK AGAINST SEXUALITY

Thomas Aquinas' views on sex and marriage distinctly echo the views of Augustine, even though he lived over eight centuries later. And because of this, the Augustinian doctrine of sex survived the medieval era basically unchanged and was accepted as completely authoritative. Both Augustine and Aquinas maintained that there was no sexual intercourse before the fall of man. However, if disobedience had not come so quickly, intercourse would have transpired in Paradise. The participants would have functioned like Aristotle's ideal philosophers, under complete rational control, and hence without sin. In that state of innocence there would have been no genital turpitude, according to Aquinas, and no loss of physical virginity during conception. Heterosexual procreation was intended from the beginning, for God would obviously have given man another man for a partner had there been any other purpose in mind.[82]

Aquinas had no difficulty matching Augustine's misogyny. Males are naturally superior to females in mind, body, and will.[83] In woman the sexual appetite predominated, while in man more stable rational qualities are found. Woman was invented to play a passive role in generation.[84] Because of her nature and purpose "man is the beginning and end of woman, just as God is the beginning and end of every creature."[85] In some ways a woman is inferior to a slave: "Woman is in subjection according to the law of nature, but a slave is not."[86] Aquinas borrowed Aristotle's definition of a woman: "The female is a defective male." He also believed that nature always wanted to produce a male, so a woman is a man gone wrong.[87]

Aquinas followed the Augustinian dogma that the virginal conception of Jesus was essential, because "it would not have been possible for his flesh to have been born in a nature already corrupted by matrimonial intercourse, without thereby becoming infected by original sin."[88] Jesus "chose a virgin mother" to demonstrate that virginity is of higher merit than the married state.[89] Virginity was better because it is "unseared by the heat of sexual desire which is experienced in achieving the greatest bodily pleasure which is that of conjugal intercourse."[90]

"A woman's sole purpose in marrying," according to Aquinas, "should be motherhood."[91] Also, a man committed a mortal sin if he was attracted to marital intercourse by purposes other than procreation.[92] C. S. Lewis presents the outlook of Aquinas and his fellow scholastics when he writes: "According to the medieval view passionate love itself was wicked, and did not case to be wicked if the object of it were your wife."[93] Aquinas, like Augustine, believed that "matrimony is holier without carnal intercourse."[94] The sexless relation of Joseph and Mary was appealed to in order to show that those who mutually vowed to abstain from coitus were truly wed.[95]

Augustine and Aquinas, although geniuses, both had a mental block against sexuality and failed to treat it wisely. Indeed, they remind one of a comic-tragic scene of "the blind leading the blind," resulting in both falling from the biblical way into the pit of Hellenistic asceticism.

EFFECTS OF MEDIEVAL CELIBACY

As we have seen, beginning in the late second century church fathers advocated that Christians emulate Jesus, the paragon of purity because of his assumed perpetual virginity. Since only a minority of Christians voluntarily refrained from marital relations, those who did abstain began to have a reputation for special sanctity. Out of this developed a split between the sacred and the secular vocations, an endemic tendency in the history of religions. Writing in the fourth century, Eusebius explained this dichotomy well, and projected back onto the teachings of Jesus the dual life styles:

Two ways of life were . . . given by the law of Christ to his church. The one is above nature, and beyond common human living; it admits not marriage, childbearing, property nor the possession of wealth, but wholly and permanently separate from the common customary life of mankind, it devotes itself to the service of God alone in its wealth of heavenly love! And they who enter on this course, appear to die to the life of mortals, to bear with them nothing earthly but their body, and in mind and spirit to have passed to heaven. . . . Such then is the perfect form of the Christian life. . . . It is fitting that those in the priesthood and occupied in the service of God should abstain from the intercourse of marriage.[96]

Eusebius called the marital way a "secondary grade of piety" and considered it fit only for the profane Christian.[97]

While Eusebius was flourishing in the East, the first celibacy legislation was enacted in the Western extremity of Christianity. The earliest recorded attempt to imitate the sexual abstinence regulation of pagan sacerdotal offices for Christian leadership was around A.D. 305 at the Council of Elvira in Spain.[98] Canon 33, which was approved at that council, displays the belief that the sexual and the sacred are incompatible: "All clerics who have a place in the ministry shall abstain from their wives and shall not beget children—this is a total prohibition: whoever does so, let him forfeit his rank among the clergy." Two decades later, at the Ecumenical Council at Nicea, an effort was made to extend the Elvira regional council decision to apply to the whole Christian church. However, Bishop Paphnutius urged that the proposed celibacy law for the clergy be rejected because it was contrary to the biblical ethic.[99] He called sexual intercourse within marriage chastity, and quoted Hebrews 13:14: "Let marriage be held in honor among all." Paphnutius' view prevailed, perhaps because many of the bishops present were married.[100]

Later in the fourth century two bishops of Rome, in the earliest papal decrees on record, attempted to impose on the whole Western church the Elvira regulation. In a letter that Pope Damascus wrote to some Gallican bishops, sexual intercourse was called a pollution, and Christian priests were advised to abstain from it as pagan priests did. Since Jerome was the papal secretary at that time, he may have ghostwritten the letter. Damascus' successor, Siricius, in a letter to a Spanish Bishop Himerius, referred to the conjugal acts of married priests as a crime and their desire for it an "obscene cupidity." Their way of life was condemned on the grounds that it was irreconcilable with biblical teaching. In the following year a council meeting at Rome commanded "that priests and deacons not live with their wives."[101] The influential Bishop of Milan, Ambrose, was in hearty agreement with this ban. He declared that married priests are "foul in heart and body" and that "the ministerial office must be kept pure and unspotted, and must not be defiled by coitus."[102]

Although the bishops and councils of the fourth century made explicit demands for clerical celibacy, the church lacked the power of enforcement. Consequently, married priests were common in the following centuries, and as late as the ninth century Pope Adrian II was a married man.[103]

As the church's temporal authority grew stronger in the latter part of the Middle Ages, the enforcement of priestly celibacy became more evident. In 1049 Pope Leo IX made slaves at his Lateran palace of wives taken from priests.[104] Later in that century Pope Urban II offered such women as slaves to any noble who wanted them.[105] The drive to stiffen the celibacy requirement did not proceed without resistance. In 1060 some Lombard bishops, who claimed that it was no sin for priests to marry, captured Rome and set up their own pope. However, the revolt failed two years later and the imposition of celibacy continued.[106] In 1139 the Lateran Council played the final trump in the legislation against clerical marriage by declaring that it was not only illicit but also invalid.[107] Since the church was now in control of civil law, it was able to rule that all priestly marriages were null and void.

The ban against marriage was not motivated mainly by concern for moral reform. Eager to increase church control of property, the pontiffs shrewdly counted the families of priests as economic liabilities. Father Joseph Blenkinsopp points out that offspring, if pronounced legitimate, would be entitled to inherit property and hence the church holdings would diminish.[108] The Jesuit sociologist Joseph H. Fichter has shown the main reason for continuing celibacy in our time is also economic.[109] It is much cheaper to house, feed, and move an unmarried priest or nun. As would be expected, this motivation is not admitted publicly by the prelates.

In 1563 the Council of Trent, in protest against the Protestant challenge to the celibacy doctrine, reinforced the earlier ecclesiastical legislation. Canons 9 and 10 harshly assert:

If anyone says that clerics . . . who have made solemn profession of chastity can contract marriage, and that the contract is valid . . . : let him be anathema. . . . If anyone says that the married state is to be preferred to the state or virginity or celibacy, and that it is not a better and more blessed thing to abide in virginity or celibacy than to be bound by marriage, let him be anathema.

In Eastern Catholicism clerical celibacy developed in a less extreme manner. In 435 Emperor Theodosius II outlawed clergy separating from their wives under pretext of piety. He made this humane ruling: "Women who obtained lawful marriage before their husbands assumed the priesthood should not be deserted."[110] In 692 the Council of Trullo adopted positions that have continued virtually unaltered in the Eastern church. Canon 96 states that priests are not permitted to marry after ordination and that bishops are required to be continent.

The movement toward more sexual repression in the medieval

church brought with it more unconscious fascination with sex, and in some instances the blocking of erotic satisfactions brought noxious results. Jerome expressed these prurient thoughts in writing a young woman: "Your vest is purposely slit to show what is beneath. . . . You wear stays to keep your breasts in place, and a tight girdle closely confines your chest. . . . Your shawl sometimes drops so as to leave your white shoulders bare; and then it hastily hides what it intentionally revealed."[111] Just as a man on an austere diet may focus more on tempting cuisine than a man who is regularly satisfied with modest and wholesome meals, so sex-starved Jerome was an obsessive girl-watcher.

That abstinence often makes the heart grow more desirous is also portrayed in a sixth-century deathbed scene. Gregory the Great told of a priest who left his wife in obedience to papal injunction. Forty years later when he had a severe illness his old wife visited him, and bent over his bed to discover if he was still breathing. Her close presence caused erotic inflammation and "in great fervor of spirit he burst out saying, 'Get thee away, woman, a little fire is yet left; take away the straw!' "[112]

The lives of some of the popes also illustrate the crass compensatory expressions that frequently ensue when marriage is not sanctioned. Pope Sixtus III, who became a saint, was accused of seducing a nun. In his trial he defended his indiscretion by quoting to his accusers Jesus' words to the adulterous woman: "He who is without sin cast the first stone." The holy father was acquitted by the clerical court and later his bastard son became pope.[113] Also, Pope John XII was a notorious lecher and participated in orgies of debauchery at the Lateran palace.[114]

The Lateran Council's nullification of priestly marriage did little more than change the nomenclature of sexual liaisons. Consorts were henceforth called something other than wives. A citizen of Constance in the fifteenth century recorded that when it was announced that a church council would meet in his city, some 700 prostitutes visited to provide clerical entertainment.[115] The confessional system was used by some priests to solicit women for seduction. So extensive was this scandalous conduct that in 1561 Pope Paul IV called for an investigation.[116]

In addition to the illicit expressions of heterosexuality, there were medieval perversions that read like a casebook in abnormal psychology. Horace's words aptly describe the result of those attempts to lock out sex: "If you drive nature out with a pitchfork she will find a way back."[117] James Cleugh has shown that unmarried clergy frequently obtained their sexual pleasure by masochism and sadism. The thesis of his lengthy disclosures is that "the remarkable proliferation of sexual perversions among the clergy of the Christian Middle Ages, especially the monks, from flagellation and sodomy to bestiality, was directly due to the senseless enforcement of celibacy."[118] Pathological sexuality was also associated with the belief in and persecution of witches.[119] Gordon R. Taylor, after presenting numerous pathetic cases of sexual aberrations in medieval cloisters, concludes:

The Church's code of repression produced, throughout Western Europe, over a period of four or five centuries, an outbreak of mass psychosis for which there are few parallels in history. . . . While the Church claims that repressive measures were required because of the immorality of the times, it seems more probable that, in reality, the immorality of the times was a result of the pressures.[120]

Generally speaking, the nadir of wholesome sexuality in church history came in the late Middle Ages. And it was caused in no small way by those theologians who posited that Jesus had no sexual desire and was perpetually virginal.

SEX AND SIN IN MODERN HISTORY

If there has been any movement in Catholic doctrine pertaining to sexuality since the counterreformation, it has been toward adding even more luster to the hypothetical human who has no sexual desire. In modern history a pronouncement by Pope Pius IX has insinuated that the libidinous impulse was absent in Jesus' mother.[121] In 1854 he declared that Mary had been "immaculately" conceived and implied that she was generated by her parents, but that she was from that moment onward preserved "from all stain of original sin."

The Immaculate Conception dogma expresses the logical outcome of Augustine's antisexual ethic. If sexual desire is evil and is always transmitted physically from parents to child, then Jesus would have been contaminated even if his contact with the primeval first parents was only through his mother. Hence Augustine said that Mary "undoubtedly had no sin" and was thus an exception among humans.[122] A *deus ex machina* is necessary according to the Augustinian scheme to get a morally untainted man into the world. Although unmentioned in historical record and tardily promulgated by the Holy See, this dogma makes it possible for Jesus to have been sired by the Holy Spirit, even though neither party had sexual desire.

This "infallible" dogma shows that it is possible for moderns to go even beyond Aquinas in abnegating sex. Although he followed Augustine closely on doctrines of sex and marriage, he rejected what has come to be called the Immaculate Conception: "If the soul of the blessed Virgin had never contracted the stain of original sin it would have diminished the dignity of Christ. . . . The blessed Virgin did indeed contract original sin."[123] Although Pope Leo XIII has declared that Aquinas' theology is unsurpassed in giving knowledge of the truth his Marian doctrine is held to be in error.[124]

On the surface the Immaculate Conception may appear to exalt womankind, but by removing Mary's feet of clay it accentuates the innate sinfulness of the rest of Eve's children. Not only does it deprecate those women who participate in normal marital sexuality, but it also slurs the purity of virgins. While the Church continually praises to high heaven virgins who are "unblemished" in mind and body, it nevertheless assumes that they are, in comparison to Mary, defiled. The standard work on Mariology states that had not the "Lily among thorns" been immaculately conceived, then "the devil would have been in her and she would have been offensive to her spouse, the Holy Spirit."[125]

The dogma of the Immaculate Conception also erects one more obstacle to a rational understanding of the earliest and most reliable historical records pertaining to Jesus. Nonconjugal marriage was a contradiction in terms in the Hebrew culture. Regarding Jewish marriage, Marcus Cohn states: "The most important common obligation of the married couple is the performance of the marital act."[126] Thus it would have made no sense for the Gospels to claim that Mary was Joseph's wife if she was immune from sexual desire and did not enter into marital relations with her husband. Actually, it would be more in accord with the biblical ethic for the church to declare that the libido is without "stain" when serving the companionship, recreative, and procreative purposes of marriage, and that all infants born from such a union are "immaculate" conceptions.

In the twentieth century coitus has been debased for both the laity and the clergy by papal encyclicals. During the Depression Pope Pius XI asserted that poverty-stricken couples should "preserve in wedlock their chastity unspotted." They were warned to "take care lest the calamitous state of their material affairs should be an occasion for a much more calamitous error."[127] Since scientific birth control was banned (and is still), the cruel implication was that only those who could support children should indulge in sexual intercourse. Moreover, in a quite un-Pauline manner, the encyclical assured the poor that God would give continence to all who asked for it.

In 1935 Pope Pius XI informed his priests that they were nobly following non-Christian standards of celibacy. Although Jesus had rejected Levitical notions of ceremonial purification, Pius appealed to Leviticus 8:33–35 to prove that the Hebrew priests were sexually abstinent before performing sacred functions. Actually, there is no explicit reference to sexual abstinence in those verses. Moreover, since all of those priests were required to marry,[128] it is absurd to appeal to them in buttressing a doctrine of priestly celibacy. However, Pius argued that since priests of the Old Testament dispensation were required to abstain from coitus when engaged in temple ritual, it was even more incumbent upon priests of the superior Christian dispensation who were consecrated continually to abstain permanently.[129] In the same passage Pius also cited Cicero's reference[130] to sexual abstinence among pagan Roman priests. As has been shown earlier, the appeal to pagan practices in justifying ecclesiastical celibacy is the only honest historical ground on which to establish a sacerdotal system of celibacy.

In the present generation, the document of Vatican II on sex and marriage shows implicitly a bent toward exorcising the tradition of sexual asceticism embedded in the Latin church. In a subtle manner less emphasis is placed upon procreation as the principal end of marital relations.[131] As liberal Catholics remove some of their church's medieval strait-jacket, they are beginning to reach out to the authentic humanizing role of sexuality. Yet the Augustinian tone is by no means dissipated. For example, Genesis 2:18: "It is not good for man to be alone," is interpreted in a manner that the celibate fathers would have found commendable. Ambrose and Augustine were puzzled by that verse and its context because nonascetics had interpreted it to mean that it is good for a man to have a wife for purposes other than procreation. They asked: "If woman is the source of guilt for man, how can we think she was given for a good?" Ambrose answered and Augustine quoted with approval the following: "Since the propagation of the human race could not be from man alone, God said it is not good for man to be alone. . . . Therefore, woman was given to man for the sake of the generation of human posterity."[132] Vatican II likewise interprets Genesis 2:18 to mean that marriage is good because of the children produced.[133]

Pope Paul VI has been ambiguous in his encyclicals on marriage and the priesthood. In 1967 he stated: "When the inalienable right of marriage and of procreation is taken away, so is human dignity."[134] Commenting on the implications of that general pronouncement, Father Peter J. Riga writes: "If there is but one exception—albeit in the service of the apostolate—that right cannot be 'inalienable.'"[135] Pope Paul's position reinforces an encyclical of Pope Leo XIII in 1890 that declared: "No human law can deprive man of the natural and original right to marry."[136] It would seem to follow that the human law that infringes on the privilege of priests to marry is thereby annulled. Yet the church still enforces canon law 1072, which trenchantly rules: "A marriage is invalid when attempted by clerics in sacred orders." But Paul VI drew no such implication, and later in 1967 he issued another encyclical that dredged up most of the old arguments for proving the dignity of required celibacy. His defense was studded with over one hundred citations wrested from Scripture. The prime motivation given for celibacy is that through it the priest can imitate Jesus' rejection of sexual activity. Matrimony, Paul asserted, "continues the work of the first creation." But Jesus instituted celibacy, which has "opened a new way, in which the human creature adheres wholly and directly to the Lord and is concerned only with him."[137]

What, in fact, have been the practical consequences of the church law that expels from the ministry and excommunicates from the church the priest who becomes married?[138] Does it tend to increase, as Pope Paul and his predecessors claim, the moral purity of the clergy? Enforced bachelorhood does not cure the lack of sexual discipline any more than abstention from the use of the right eye suppresses the lustful glances of a man with a good left eye. As one who has worked with fellow priests on several continents, Leo H. Lehmann has written of the unhealthy psychological effects of mandatory clerical celibacy:

Its victims have to confess that, far from freeing them from the sexual urge, it actually breeds a very ferment of impurity in the mind. It is the boast of the Roman Catholic Church that priestly celibacy makes its clergy something more than men—that it makes them supernatural, almost angelic. The simple people readily believe this. In truth it makes them something less than men.[139]

Prurience, the reverse side of the prudery coin, is evidenced in writings of celibate ethicists. A text by Father Heribert Jone entitled *Moral Theology* exemplifies this preoccupation. This contemporary book, which has been translated into seven languages, contains a summary of Roman Catholic moral standards. An analysis discloses that several times as much discussion is given to sexual offenses as to war, suicide, capital punishment, and murder combined. Different types of kisses are meticulously described, with the severity of the sin indicated for each.[140]

Celibacy has produced not only an erogenous mentality but has also caused some gross sexual practices. Strange as it may seem, a priest cannot marry according to canon law, but his vow of celibacy is not broken by liaisons that are customarily deemed immoral. A priest who prefers not to conceal sexual irregularities can obtain absolution from an ordinary confessor, but pardon for marriage can be obtained only from the Supreme Pontiff and on the condition that he abandon his wife. Taylor describes the medieval outlook: "In the eyes of the church, for a priest to marry was a worse crime than to keep a mistress, and to keep a mistress was worse than to engage in random fornication—a judgment which completely reverses secular conceptions of morality, which attach importance to the quality and durability of personal relationships."[141] This value scale is also the reversal of mores in the biblical era.

That the medieval hierarchy's attitude was not different from the official view in the present age is seen in criticisms by those who have been Roman Catholic clergymen. With understandable sarcasm Edward F. Henriques asks: "Is it not significant that canon law imposes no punishment whatever upon such extra-parochial diversions as clerical fornication, adultery, sodomy, flagrant promiscuity, or any other form of sexual aberration, nor even for continual and prolonged concubinage, but only for 'committing' matrimony?"[142] Judging from the testimony given by another contemporary who has served as a priest, such illicit indulgences are not at all rare. Emmett McLoughlin writes: "No priest who has heard priests' confession and has any respect for the truth will deny that sexual affairs are extremely common among the clergy. The principal concern of the hierarchy seems to be that priests should keep such cases quiet and refrain from marriage."[143]

Evidently marriage by priests is considered more of a crime by canon law than promiscuity because marriage is by its very nature an open expression of cohabitation intention. Thus the church officially tends to wink at clandestine affairs. Condoning them is possible because they are usually kept discreetly silent and are thereby not damaging to the church's virginal public image. The harm done to the personalities of the individual men and women involved in this exploitative and surreptitious behavior seems to be secondary to keeping the establishment's sepulcher whitewashed. All of this is done in the name of the one who warned against ravenous wolves who wear lambskins.[144] Hypocrisy, which was for Jesus the most deadly of vices, has become commonplace in the celibate system that tends to esteem outward respectability more than inward character.

Chapter IX

THE SIGNIFICANCE OF
THE QUESTION

The hypothesis being defended in this study is three-pronged. Accordingly, one conclusion is that lifelong celibacy was completely foreign to the biblical outlook, both in theory and in practice. Another is that the traditions about Jesus' life recorded in the authoritative New Testament sources point toward a married Jesus. The third is that the Hellenistic sexual asceticism that infiltrated Gentile Christianity in the postapostolic era has been responsible for the dogma that Jesus was perpetually virginal.

RESIDUAL ASCETICISM AND DOCETISM

It is difficult for Christians even today to weigh judiciously the telling shreds of evidence about Jesus' marital status. The virus of pagan sexual asceticism has eaten like a cancer into the body of Christ, causing sick attitudes and practices. Although sporadic attempts have been made to cure the church of this foreign growth, the malignancy has never been fully arrested. Beginning with Gentile Christianity in the second century and continuing to the present day, a perverse moral dualism has penetrated into the church. After reviewing the history of sex in Christianity, William G. Cole draws this severe but sound conclusion: "The church has been guilty of preserving and preaching a point of view not generic to Christian faith, an attitude which originated in Hellenistic dualism and which is not only un-biblical but also anti-biblical."[1]

Earthly passion and divine love have consequently been treated by orthodox theologians as polar concepts. Reinhold Niebuhr writes:

It is something of a mystery that the Christian faith is consistently embarrassed by all efforts to relate love to eros. Those of us who cherish the Hebraic concept of the unity of human personality in body and soul may be inclined to ascribe this embarrassment to Greek, particularly to Platonic dualism. . . . Augustine, who combined biblical with Neoplatonic thought, defines "love of God" as the object of the heavenly eros. This love, rather than love of neighbor, becomes the chief object of religion. Thus Jesus' double-love commandment is defied and heresy has found a nest in Christian orthodoxy.[2]

That Niebuhr's judgment is accurate can be detected in the perspective of some modern writers from a variety of backgrounds. Søren Kierkegaard, believing that divine and human loves are exclusive, entered in his *Journal:* "God wishes to be loved, and therefore he wishes man to abandon the egoism of giving life. . . . Every time we see celibacy from love of God we see an effort to comply with God's intention."[3] Leo Tolstoy expressed a similar viewpoint: "Sexual love, marriage, is a service of self, and consequently in any case an obstacle to the service of God and man, and therefore from a Christian point of view a fall, a sin."[4] In a major theological book of this century entitled *Agape and Eros*, Bishop Anders Nygren postulated, without biblical warrant, a fundamental opposition between human passion and divine love.[5] The Jesuit Wilhelm Bertrams defends celibacy in our day by affirming that "it is more precious to give all one's love to God than to share it with a human being."[6] As long as this Augustinian ethic persists Christians cannot rediscover the full-orbed meaning of love as an ancient Jew viewed it or view realistically the life of Jesus.

The damage that the fissure between the spiritual and the physical has caused is reflected in contemporary docetism. Although this heresy was repeatedly condemned in early church history, few even now actually think that Jesus had full human nature. There are unlovely ascetic skeletons hidden in the inner sanctum of most Christians, ancient and modern. The Jesus buried there is more of a stained-glass window figure surrounded by an unearthly halo than a Jewish male who was totally involved in Palestinian society.

A theologian who believes that Jesus' full humanity includes sexuality is hard to find. Donald M. Baillie, in his famous essay on the Incarnation, naïvely assumed that docetism was dead in the twentieth century. He asserted that there was no more "explaining away of the human character of the life that Jesus lived, but a full and unreserved recognition of his human nature as *homoousios* with our own, which means 'essentially the same as ours': that lesson of the historical movement has been well learnt on all hands, and it is common ground today."[7] However, he did not discuss sexuality vis-à-vis Jesus either in his writings or orally. Although well read in modern theories of personality, Baillie made no suggestion in his seminars (which I attended for two years) that sexuality was in any way associated with Jesus.

Tom F. Driver's judgment is penetrating:

Docetism was early condemned as a heresy, but it has never disappeared. In our day it may be suggested that a docetism lingers with regard to Jesus' sexuality. This means, if it is true, that Christians are not sure about the humanity of him whom they call True Man. And this uncertainty results in a confusion about what it means for us to be human. One of the signs of this confusion is the chaos in sexual mores at the present time, which the church has not been able to overcome and which it has actually helped to bring about because it had no adequate teaching with regard to the relation between sex and humanity.[8]

Indeed, Christians have failed to relate adequately a basic aspect of Jesus' human nature to a fundamental aspect of their own human nature.

The dogma that Jesus is the Incarnate One is faithfully proclaimed in the church, but talk about what constitutes his carnality is generally a taboo topic. In Christological discussions much attention is devoted to treating Jesus as the embodiment of ideal humanity, but the figure that emerges is more an epiphany of a nebulous Platonic form of man than a psychophysical entity. Although Jesus is recognized as the archetypal generic man, he is only incidentally thought of as a particular man with all the distinctive qualities of his sex. It seems that the "stumbling-block" (skandalon) of Christianity is not only that it centers in a bloody Jewish Messiah,[9] but also that the light of God is focused in a red-blooded male with sensuous and sexual potentialities.

The doctrine of the Incarnation, which points toward the immanence of the divine in human life, makes little sense if the process of human generation is not sanctified and if purity is associated with abstinence from fleshly passion. Far from being intrinsically connected with the doctrine of the Virgin Birth, the doctrine of the Logos made flesh is at loggerheads with it. Throughout the patristic era the divine enfleshment theory was clouded by the pagan view that a perfect hero could be born only by a miraculous avoidance of the natural processes of creation. If Jesus' conception came about by an asexual Spirit fertilizing an ovum, then he would have been freakish from the outset and would have had only a quasi-human nature.

Much of Christian thought today is incongruous with the biblical doctrine of the goodness of creation set forth in Genesis and endorsed by Jesus. Those who champion priestly celibacy and/ or believe sexual desire to be essentially shameful drive a wedge between the God who created all things good and the God who saves evil men. If marriage seems second best to the single life and sex appears defiled, it is more likely that the source of this attitude is in one's individual nurture and not in universal human nature. Too long have personal phobias about sex been blamed on alleged religious history—to the curse effected by Adam and Eve, or even to the Creator who ordained sexual life. The truth may be that the shame associated with organs that have both a sexual and an eliminative function is derived more from unwise toilet training than by the "fall of our first parents." Apropos is a biblical proverb: "To the pure all things are pure."[10]

Sex and religion are two areas of human life that are very disturbing emotionally. Overlaid with taboos, it is difficult to make rational judgments about either one separately, not to mention both together. Even so it is imperative to try to remove the neurotic stance that most Christians have had toward sex. Clarity of thought is acutely needed since both sex and religion are as destructive as dynamite when used foolishly.

THE OFFENSIVENESS OF CELIBACY

Celibacy is a major block to fraternal relations among the major religions that share the Hebrew Scripture. "There are few aspects of Christianity more difficult for Jews to understand than the principle of celibacy," Rabbi Herbert Weiner confesses. He goes on to affirm that for Jews "spiritual and physical love not only do not conflict with each other, but to diminish one is to diminish the other."[11] Leo Jung also expresses the characteristic Jewish repulsion toward the sexual attitudes of ascetic Christians:

The ancient Hebrews and the later Jewish scholars have not been troubled by the fantastic imbalance of attitudes that, springing in part from the vicious and repugnant idea of original sin, has so harassed Christian marriage in the past, and works havoc still. False modesty in the realm of sex seems to be a comparatively modern development, and is confined largely to Western civilization. Also, the theory that enthrones celibacy has always been to Judaism alien and abhorrent.[12]

Some Christians have also found sexual asceticism offensive. J. Middleton Murry writes:

Celibate son and virgin mother, conceiving not by human intercourse, but by the Holy Ghost: they are not the true objects of a modern reverence. . . . They leave in a weird limbo of silence and obscurity the crucial process of earthly generation. Is the limbo obscene—a terrible and loathsome wilderness whose passage had to be endured by a reluctantly incarnate God? . . . The impulse of an asceticism which was no essential part of the Christian Gospel has been incessantly at work to diminish the virtue of the Incarnation. The process began early with the doctrine of the Virgin Birth, which was intended to exalt the deity of Jesus by enshrouding him in miracle—as though the fact of his mortal birth were not miracle enough!—till we have reached at last the complicated refinements of the Immaculate Conception.[13]

It is trite but true to say that religions with Semitic roots will come closer in understanding when there is a mutual appreciation of those elements that belong to their common history. An important element in the source of Western religions as well as the Moslem religion is the Torah's glad acceptance of marital sexuality as an untainted gift of God. The splits between the Eastern and Western church in the eleventh century and between Protestantism and Roman Catholicism in the sixteenth century were historically occasioned in part by conflict over involuntary priestly celibacy and the moral principles on which it was based and enforced. Consequently, a prerequisite for major ecumenical advance is papal willingness to rescind the eight-hundred-year-old ban on clerical marriage and a jettisoning by all Christians of views on sex that are contrary to the wholesome Hebraic viewpoint.

It is encouraging to realize that in the present century the drive toward recovering a long lost outlook on sexuality has come in large part from many within the Catholic priesthood. In 1920 a group of Czechoslovakian priests audaciously attacked the Vatican in an effort to reclaim the right to marry. They were turned back by this countercharge of Pope Benedict XV:

The Latin church owes its flourishing vitality . . . to the celibacy of the clergy. . . . Never will the Holy See in any way even lighten or mitigate the obligation of this holy and salutary law of clerical celibacy, not to speak of abolishing it. We also deny . . . that the innovations of a "democratic" character for whose introduction into ecclesiastical discipline some are agitating, can ever be approved by the Holy See.[14]

During the half-century since that confrontation, opposition to mandatory celibacy has smoldered in the growing liberal sector of the Catholic clergy. Due principally to the relative openness of Pope John XXIII this grave internal conflict is now widely discussed. Etienne Gilson has reported that Pope John said to him: "Would you like to know what distresses me most, not as a man, but as Pope? The thought of those young priests who bear so bravely the burden of celibacy causes me continual suffering." At that audience the Pope went on to confess that it often seemed as though he was hearing "voices demanding that the church relieve them of this burden." He admitted that it would be easy for him to sign a decree permitting priests to marry but then the church would, in his opinion, no longer be worthy to be called "holy and chaste."[15] Yet officially Pope John spoke of celibacy in the church as "one of the purest and noblest glories of her priesthood"[16] and did not advocate reevaluating the law of priestly celibacy at Vatican II.

Indirectly however, Vatican II has stimulated much debate on celibacy by moving in the direction of decreasing papal author-itarianism. Latent antagonisms have been much aired, and polls have indicated that the majority of priests favor having the free-dom to marry.[17] Were the issue to be decided by secret ballot it is probable that priests would vote to reject the medieval celibacy requirement. James Kavanaugh speaks for many fellow priests when he calls it "a senseless law" and claims that it "hides the very Christian love it once was meant to serve."[18]

An exodus of thousands of priests to marry and the correspond-ing critical worldwide shortage of candidates for the priesthood has made the prelates increasingly uneasy. Some of the vital leader-ship has defected in order to wed, including a chaplain to Pope Paul VI. The papacy has anxiously reacted to the crisis by issuing statements filled with exaggerated rhetoric and by making the vow of celibacy more humiliating. Although the celibacy law has been a thorn in the flesh of modern Catholicism Pope Paul has unrealis-tically called it "a brilliant jewel" of the church that is as precious as ever.[19]

The Dutch Jesuit Jan V. Kilsdonk expresses the bitter estrange-ment that has resulted from the intransigence of the present pon-tiff:

When the questions of birth control and celibacy offered the Pope a priceless opportunity for true leadership in proclaiming the human nature of human sexuality in the face of erotic disorientation and com-mercialism, he only had the stones of Humanae Vitae and Sacerdotalis Caelibatus to offer. His every utterance is negative: he forbids, warns, refuses, rejects, condemns.[20]

In 1970 Pope Paul expressed repeatedly his irritation over opposi-tion spearheaded by the Dutch clergy. When they made an over-ture to make celibacy optional he unequivocally asserted: "It is a capital law in our Latin church. It cannot be abandoned or subjected to argument."[21] The Holy See has also recommended for all priests an annual public reaffirmation of their celibacy vows.

If the bishops of Roman Catholicism were to reevaluate the dogma regarding Jesus' marital status, they might well find a way to escape the impasse that has developed over their law of celibacy. The appeal to Jesus' alleged celibacy is now, as always, the main

crutch that keeps the law from collapsing. Deprived of that justi-
fication for priestly celibacy, the ban on clerical marriage in the
largest branch of the Christian church could, in good conscience,
go the way of all flesh. The religious basis for voluntary as well
as involuntary celibacy would also be removed for Christians. Pope
Paul's values regarding the splendor of celibacy should more appropriately be applied to the state of holy wedlock. He has called
celibacy a "sign of the values of faith, of hope, of love, an incom-
parable condition for full pastoral service."[22] If prelates recognized
that Jesus was virile and probably married, then they could more
clearly perceive, as he did, that the Yahwist's theology of marriage
is abidingly true. "It is not good for man to be alone" is not just
a rationale for marriage in the Jewish society. Anthropological
investigations disclose that marriage is universally valued as a
means for obtaining self-fulfillment.[23]

Within the next few decades the law of priestly celibacy will
probably be eliminated, and Christians will look back on the papal
denial of marriage in the same way as we now look on the denial
of freedom to minorities in bondage by ancient Pharaohs or by
modern racists. In spite of Pope Paul's attempt to set back the
clock, one of the successors to his throne, allegedly first occupied
by a married man, will probably someday be married. This will
come about when a future pope resolves the dilemma of Pope
John and others by recognizing that the purity of the church is
not subverted by married priests. A French priest, Jean P. Audet,
writes:

There are many of us, both clergy and laity, whose outlook on life is
no longer such that we perceive any inherent "impurity" in the expression of sexuality. And for the future, one needs no especial prophetic insight to foresee that mankind as a whole is gradually moving,
slowly but inevitably, towards a complete elimination of this spiritual
archaism.[24]

THE RELEVANCE OF JESUS' MARITAL ETHIC

Vance Packard and other sociologists have documented that in
Europe and in the United States there is now a chaotic upheaval
in male-female relationships.[25] Contemporary practices are often at
fisticuffs with old principles. The church tradition has been so

heavily tinged with asceticism that Christians are often unable to respond in a relevant way to the new sexual freedom that has been made possible by birth control technology and by the wider acceptance of sexual equality. Opinion polls show that religion is rapidly losing its influence in Western civilization.[26] The view that sex is a deplorable necessity for human survival—inaccurately named the "Puritan" outlook[27]—is indubitably one cause of the moribund impact of the church on society.

Western man is now in the predicament of having rejected the old pattern before formulating new norms for guiding him out of the "sexual wilderness." While groping for orientation, society has allowed the pendulum to swing from one extreme to another. The historical tendency to mishandle sex is seen in movements of self-indulgent hedonism or self-mortifying asceticism, neither of which fulfills the human need for love. Today a predominantly sensual aim is being substituted for a predominantly spiritual aim. The spirit-body dichotomy of the old moral dualism is retained but the imperative is reversed. An inverted asceticism is displayed by those who equate the good with the earthy and treat transcendent qualities with contempt. A pathetic expression of this in our culture is the frenzied effort to make the pleasurable orgasm the goal of marital and extramarital relations.

To get out of the permissive wilderness we must replace both expressions of moral dualism with the integrated outlook on the self characteristic of biblical culture. One of the least appreciated but most abiding features of that culture was the sane way in which the spiritual, mental, emotional, and biological aspects of sexuality were treated. The full flowering of the Hebraic outlook is articulated by Jesus, who witnessed in word and deed that the one-flesh fellowship of male and female was inseparable from permanent marital fidelity. Within the context of that bond the values of joy and companionship reach their finest human expression.

If my position as defended here is true, it should have practical consequences extending far beyond the correction of a detail in the record of the life of a prominent historical figure.[28] Christianity is the most widespread of world religions and its life style is more closely associated with the historical life style of its founder than in any other world religion. If Jesus blessed marriage by personal practice as well as by lofty tribute, then more should result from this discovery than the removal of the celibacy excrescence that has disfigured the body of Christ since the patristic era. Recognition of Jesus' libido and its expression in a heterosexual bond should encourage a more healthy climate of opinion toward our own sexuality and toward sex education for others. Such a revitalized environment would benefit both the clerical and the lay members of society regardless of whether they marry or remain single.

There is a parallel between the hedonism-asceticism extremes in sexuality and the radical-reactionary extremes in government. Irrational exploitation of the physical body or of the body politic often results from those who hold those polar positions, even though their actions are usually defended as a noble pursuit of freedom. But at neither extreme is the delicate balance between privilege and responsibility maintained. Love that is truly free should indeed be the aim of all who follow the biblical tradition. Jesus affirmed that he, like the Hebrew prophetic religion, had liberty as his theme.[29] "Where the Spirit of the Lord is," Paul wrote to the Corinthians, "there is freedom."[30] But truly free love is neither sexual anarchy nor sexual abnegation. Such polarization, Paul maintained, is the negation of authentic love. Free love is the full expression of spirit through flesh which gives partners long-range obligations as well as delightful liberties.

Niebuhr, perhaps the wisest prophet of our century, has pointed out that an urgent task facing all branches of the Christian church in the 1970s is the long overdue reconciliation of the erotic with Christian love.[31] We need to come to terms with these two dynamic forces both in abstract theological theory and in concrete social practice. Now is the opportune time to yoke together what has long been disjoined: the love of God and the love of spouse-offspring. Transcendent-immanent love is the heart of both true religion and true sexual partnership. Moreover, the awe-ful agony and ecstasy of marital companionship is, as Paul claimed, a marvelous symbol of the love of Jesus. By imitating his example we may at last attain "to mature manhood, measured by nothing less than the full stature of Christ."[32]

NOTES

CHAPTER I TACKLING A TABOO QUESTION

1. Philip Schaff, *History of the Christian Church* (New York, 1914), 2, 397.
2. D. Sherwin Bailey, *Sexual Relation in Christian Thought* (New York, 1959), 10.
3. Helmut Thielicke, *The Ethics of Sex* (New York, 1964), 120.
4. *Sacerdotalis Caelibatus* 21.
5. William E. Phipps, "Did Jesus or Paul Marry?" *Journal of Ecumenical Studies* 5 (1968): 741–44.
6. Cf., e.g., G. Bornkamm, *Jesus of Nazareth* (New York, 1960); E. Fuchs, *Studies of the Historical Jesus* (London, 1964); J. Peter, *Finding the Historical Jesus* (New York, 1965); J. M. Robinson, *A New Quest of the Historical Jesus* (London, 1959).
7. Albert Schweitzer, *The Quest of the Historical Jesus* (1906).
8. Thomas Aquinas, *Summa Theologica* 1–2, q. 94, 2.
9. Aquinas, *Commentary on the Nicomachean Ethics* 8, 12.
10. Emil Brunner, *Man in Revolt* (Philadelphia, 1947), 345, 347.
11. Brunner, *The Divine Imperative* (Philadelphia, 1947), 365.
12. Cf. Brunner, *The Mediator* (London, 1934), 216–76.
13. Brunner, *Man in Revolt*, 348.
14. Hugh Montefiore, in *Newsweek*, Aug. 7, 1967, 83; *Times* (London), Aug. 7, 1967, 2.
15. Montefiore, *For God's Sake* (Philadelphia, 1969), 182.
16. Donald J. West, *Homosexuality* (Chicago, 1967), 264.

198   WAS JESUS MARRIED?

17. Marc Oraison, The Celibate Condition and Sex (New York, 1967), 148.
18. Lev. 20:13.
19. Rom. 1:26–27; 1 Cor. 6:9–10.
20. John Erskine, The Human Life of Jesus (New York, 1945), 27–28.
21. Tom F. Driver, "Sexuality and Jesus," Union Seminary Quarterly Review 20 (1965): 243, 240.
22. Orson Hyde, Journal of Discourses of Brigham Young 2 (1854): 79–83.
23. Ibid., 4 (1857): 259.
24. A. E. Young, Wife No. 19 (Hartford, 1876), 307.
25. Louis M. Epstein, Marriage Laws in the Bible and the Talmud (Cambridge, 1942), 3–33.
26. Nikos Kazantzakis, The Last Temptation of Christ (New York, 1960), 257.
27. Michael Novak, in Commonweal 72 (1960): 502.
28. Kyle Haselden, in The Christian Century 77 (1960): 1149.
29. Cf. Mark 14:36.
30. John Schlaginhaufen, in Luther's Works, ed. H. T. Lehman (Philadelphia, 1957), 54, 154, Table Talk no. 1472.
31. Arnold Lunn, The Revolt Against Reason (London, 1950), 234.
32. Martin Luther, in Letters of Spiritual Counsel, ed. T. G. Tappert (Philadelphia, 1955), 273.
33. Luther, in O. Lähteenmäki, Sexus und Ehe bei Luther (Turku, 1955), 28–33.
34. Luther, in Luther's Works, ed. J. Atkinson (Philadelphia, 1966), 44, 178.
35. Luther D. Martin Luthers Werke (Weimar, 1891), 12, 94, 14.
36. George F. Moore, Judaism in the First Centuries of the Christian Era (Cambridge, 1927), 1, 183; 2, 85, 90, 118, 151–53, 168, 267, 392.
37. Samuel Sandmel, The First Christian Century in Judaism and Christianity (New York, 1969), 63–66, 82–86.
38. Ibid., 85, 88, 94.
39. Joseph Klausner, Jesus of Nazareth (New York, 1925), 368.
40. Frederick C. Grant, Ancient Judaism and the New Testament (New York, 1959), 109.

CHAPTER II   SEXUAL ATTITUDES
IN ANCIENT JUDAISM

1. 1 Cor. 15:45–47.
2. David Mace, *Hebrew Marriage: A Sociological Study* (London, 1953), 144.
3. *Kiddushin* 66d.
4. Johannes Pedersen, *Israel* (Copenhagen, 1926), 1–2, 61.
5. Israel Abrahams, *Studies in Pharisaism and the Gospels* (Cambridge, 1917), 78.
6. *Yebamoth* 6, 6.
7. Edward Schillebeeckx, *Marriage* (New York, 1965), 19.
8. E.g., Ezek. 44:9, Lev. 25:49, Gen. 6:3; cf. E. D. Burton, *Spirit, Soul, and Flesh* (Chicago, 1918), 68–70.
9. Ruud J. Bunnik, "The Question of Married Priests," *Cross Currents* 16 (1966): 91.
10. Sigmund Freud, *Collected Papers* (New York, 1959), 4, 206.
11. David Bakan, *Sigmund Freud and the Jewish Mystical Tradition* (Princeton, 1958), 272.
12. E.g., Ambrose, *Letters* 45, 10.
13. Gerhard von Rad, *Genesis* (Philadelphia, 1961), 85; cf. Gen. 3:1.
14. Cf. Matt. 10:16; regarding serpent symbolism, see Erwin R. Goodenough, *Jewish Symbols in the Greco-Roman Period* (New York, 1952), 13, 181.
15. *Genesis Rabbah* 15, 7; 18, 6; *Sanhedrin* 38b; Rashi, *On Genesis* 4, 1; cf. L. Ginzberg, *The Legends of the Jews* (Philadelphia, 1925), 5, 134.
16. Theodor H. Gaster, *Myth, Legend, and Creation in the Old Testament* (New York, 1969), 34.
17. *Zohar* 1, 55b; cf. *Yebamoth* 62b.
18. *Zohar Hadash* 4, 50b.
19. *Yebamoth* 64a.
20. Rom. 3:1–2.
21. Martin Buber, *Israel and the World* (New York, 1948), 181.
22. Gen. 24:53, 34:12.
23. Roland de Vaux, *Ancient Israel: Its Life and Institutions* (New York, 1961), 29.
24. Alfred Bertholet, *History of Hebrew Civilization* (New York, n.d.), 151.
25. Exod. 21:7; Neh. 5:5; Deut. 21:18–21.
26. Exod. 21:15, 17.

27. Code of Hammurabi 166; G. R. Driver, The Middle Assyrian Laws (Oxford, 1935), 182.
28. A. C. Johnson, et al., Ancient Roman Statutes (Austin, Tex., 1959), 3, 4, 10.
29. Raphael Patai, Sex and the Family in the Bible and the Middle East (New York, 1959), 49, 51.
30. E. Neufeld, Ancient Hebrew Marriage Laws (London, 1944), 139.
31. Approximate ages of some kings at the birth of their successors are: Jehoshaphat, 23; Jehoram, 23; Ahaziah, 22; Amaziah, 15; Jotham, 21; Ahaz, 16; Amon, 16; Josiah, 16; Jehoiakim, 19.
32. Neufeld, op. cit., 141.
33. Vendidad 14, 15.
34. W. K. Lacey, The Family in Classical Greece (Ithaca, 1968), 162.
35. L. Friedländer, Roman Life and Manners Under the Early Empire (London, n.d.), 1, 229.
36. V. R. Jones, Woman in Islam (Lucknow, 1941), 93.
37. Hilma Granqvist, Marriage Conditions in a Palestinian Village (Helsingfors, 1931), 1, 33.
38. Gen. 26:8.
39. Prov. 5:18–19 (Anchor Bible).
40. Deut. 24:5.
41. Robert H. Pfeiffer, Introduction to the Old Testament (New York, 1941), 713.
42. Song of Songs 8:6–7.
43. O. Eissfeldt, The Old Testament: An Introduction (New York, 1965), 89.
44. "The Song of Solomon," Peake's Commentary on the Bible (London, 1962), 469.
45. Cf. N. K. Gottwald, "Song of Songs," Interpreter's Dictionary of the Bible (New York, 1962).
46. Prov. 12:4.
47. Judg. 11:37.
48. Lev. 21:13–15.
49. Num. 6.
50. Gen. 30: 1; cp. 19:30–38; Isa. 4:1.
51. W. G. Lambert, "Celibacy in the World's Oldest Proverbs," Bulletin of the American School of Oriental Research 169 (1963): 63.
52. Ludwig Köhler, Hebrew Man (London, 1956), 89.

53. *Mishkatu* 13, 1.
54. Alfred Guillaume, "The Influence of Judaism on Islam," in *The Legacy of Israel*, ed. E. Bevan (Oxford, 1927), 165.
55. *Vendidad* 4, 47.
56. N. H. Snaith, "Leviticus," *Peake's Commentary, op. cit.*, 246.
57. Norman P. Williams, *The Ideas of the Fall and of Original Sin* (London, 1927), 19, 224, 304, 378.
58. David M. Feldman, *Birth Control in Jewish Law* (New York, 1968), 86–87.
59. Jerome, *Letters* 22, 21.
60. Cassian, *Conferences* 21, 4.
61. Lucien Legrand, *The Biblical Doctrine of Virginity* (New York, 1963), 23–26.
62. Jer. 28.
63. Jer. 16:9; M. D. Goldman, professor of Semitic studies at the University of Melbourne, plausibly interprets several passages in the prophecy as alluding to Jeremiah's wife ("Was Jeremiah Married?" *Australian Biblical Review* 2 (1952): 43–47).
64. Cf. Josephine M. Ford, *A Trilogy on Wisdom and Celibacy* (London, 1967), 24.
65. Jer. 32:6–15.
66. Jer. 29:5–6.
67. *Hypothetica* 11, 14.
68. Philo, *Apology for the Jews*, excerpted in Eusebius, *Praeparatio Evangelica* 8, 11.
69. Pliny, *Natural History* 5, 15.
70. Josephus, *Wars* 2, 8.
71. *Damascus Document* 7, 6–9.
72. *Ibid.*, 4, 21.
73. *Rule of the Congregation* 1, 6–11.
74. Cf. Num. 1.
75. Y. Yadin, *The Scroll of the War of the Sons of Light Against the Sons of Darkness* (London, 1962), 290.
76. *War of the Sons of Light* 7, 4–6.
77. Josh. 5:2–12.
78. 1 Sam 21:5; cf. 2 Sam. 11:11.
79. Abel Isaksson, *Marriage and Ministry in the New Temple* (Lund, 1965), 55–56.
80. Ford, *op. cit.*, 30–31, 34.
81. B. Walter, *The Hindu World* (New York, 1968), 1, 84–85.

82. E.g., George F. Moore, *Judaism in the First Centuries of the Christian Era* (Cambridge, 1927), 2, 120.
83. *Yebamoth* 63b.
84. *Kethuboth* 63a; *Sotah* 4b.
85. Moore, *op. cit.*, 2, 119.
86. Louis M. Epstein, *Sex Laws and Customs in Judaism* (New York, 1948), 14–15.
87. *Mishnah Torah*, Deut. 3, 1.
88. *Sirach* 7:25; 26:1–4; 36:18–26.
89. *Tobit* 8:4–9.
90. *Sibylline Books* 3, 595.
91. Cf. Goodenough, *Introduction to Philo Judaeus* (New Haven, 1940), 9.
92. Hirschel Revel, "Celibacy," *Universal Jewish Encyclopedia* (New York, 1948); cf. Ford, *op. cit.*, 59.
93. *Yebamoth* 62b.

CHAPTER III   THE SEXUALITY OF JESUS

1. "He has never been seen to laugh" is included in a clumsy forgery ascribed to a Publius Lentulus, the governor of Jerusalem in Jesus' day. Cf. Charles Guignebert, *Jesus* (New York, 1935), 166–68.
2. E.g., Matt. 7:3–5; 23:24; John 16:33; cf. J. Jonsson, *Humor and Irony in the New Testament* (Reykjavik, 1965), 95–207.
3. Quoted in Clement, *Miscellanies* 3, 7, 59.
4. Kaufmann Kohler, "Essenes," *The Jewish Encyclopedia* (New York, 1903).
5. Upton C. Ewing, *The Essene Christ* (New York, 1961), 194.
6. Theodor H. Gaster, *The Dead Sea Scriptures* (New York, 1956), 12.
7. Jean Carmignac, *Christ and the Teacher of Righteousness* (Baltimore, 1962), 128; cf. Adolf Harnack, *What Is Christianity?* (New York, 1901), 35.
8. Luke 2:46–47; 4:16.
9. (Jerusalem) *Kethuboth* 32c; *Aboth* 5, 21; *Shabbath* 1, 3; Josephus, *Against Apion* 2, 171–78; George F. Moore, *Judaism in the First Centuries of the Christian Era* (Cambridge, 1927), 3, 104.
10. E. Schürer, *A History of the Jewish People in the Time of Jesus Christ* (New York, 1891), 2, 2, 46–52.

11. W. Schneemelcher, ed., *New Testament Apocrypha* (Philadelphia, 1963), 1, 391–2.

12. *Gospel of Thomas* 6 and 14.

13. Jean P. Audet, *Structures of Christian Priesthood* (New York, 1967), 41.

14. Tertullian, *On Monogamy* 8; Jerome (*Letters* 22, 21), Cassian (*Conferences* 21, 4), and John of Damascus (*Exposition of the Orthodox Faith* 4, 24) assert that Elijah lived a virginal life. John of Damascus believed that Elisha also was a celibate because he received from Elijah a double share of his spirit (cf. 2 Kings 2:9).

15. Lucien Legrand, *The Biblical Doctrine of Virginity* (New York, 1963), 25.

16. Cf. C. Y. Glock, *Religion and Society in Tension* (Chicago, 1964), 94.

17. Matt. 1:18; Luke 1:27.

18. Matt. 1:8–9; *Kiddushin* 3, 8.

19. Cf. E. P. Blair, "Joseph, husband of Mary," *Interpreter's Dictionary of the Bible* (New York, 1962).

20. Deut. 22:23–24; 2 Samuel 3:14; E. Neufeld, *Ancient Hebrew Marriage Laws* (London, 1944), 144.

21. Gen. 24:52–67.

22. John 2:1–11; Matt. 25:1–13; L. Finkelstein, *The Pharisees: The Sociological Background of their Faith* (Philadelphia, 1938), 47.

23. Louis M. Epstein, *Sex Laws and Customs in Judaism* (New York, 1948), 126.

24. Luke 1:35.

25. Diogenes Laertius, *Lives of the Philosophers* 3, 2; Plutarch, *Life of Alexander* 2; Suetonius, *The Lives of the Caesars* 2, 94.

26. Justin Martyr, *Apology* 1, 21. Justin probably did not get his ideas on virginal conception from the New Testament. See Thomas Boslooper, *The Virgin Birth* (Philadelphia, 1962), 31–32.

27. Ps. 139:14.

28. E.g., Deut. 14:1; 2 Sam. 7:14; Isa. 43:6; Hos. 1:10.

29. *Genesis Rabbah* 8, 9.

30. *Kiddushin* 30b.

31. "Marriage (Jewish)," *Encyclopedia of Religion and Ethics* (Edinburgh, 1905).

32. M. M. Dawson, ed., *The Basic Teachings of Confucius* (New York, 1942), 145.

33. Matt. 13:55; Luke 2:33; 4:22.

34. For unhistorical and ascetic reasons Origen ingeniously suggested this solution (*Romans Homilies* 1, 3).
35. E.g., Mark 8:11–13; Luke 16:31.
36. Cf. G. B. Caird, *The Gospel of Luke* (New York, 1963), 31; T. Walker, *Is Not This the Son of Joseph?* (London, 1937), 24–5.
37. Cf. "Mary," *Encyclopaedia Biblica* (New York, 1902); Frederick C. Grant, *An Introduction to New Testament Thought* (New York, 1950), 230.
38. B. H. Streeter, *The Four Gospels* (London, 1936), 268; R. Bultmann, *The History of the Synoptic Tradition* (Oxford, 1963), 296. In Latin MS "b" Luke 1:38 follows immediately after 1:33.
39. Judg. 13:2–24; Luke 1:8–24.
40. E.g., Acts 13:2; 15:28.
41. *Dialogue with Trypho* 49 and 68; cf. Isa. 11:1; Jer. 23:5; John 7:42.
42. Guignebert, *op. cit.*, 116.
43. Athanasius, *The Incarnation of the Word of God* 8, 5.
44. Grant, "Jesus Christ," *Interpreter's Dictionary*.
45. Emil Brunner, *The Christian Doctrine of Creation and Redemption* (Philadelphia, 1952), 354; cf. H. von Campenhausen, *The Virgin Birth*, 13–18.
46. Especially John 1:1–18; Phil. 2:5–11.
47. Brunner, *op. cit.* 354.
48. Brunner, *The Mediator* (London, 1934), 325.
49. Paul Tillich, *Theology of Culture* (New York, 1959), 66.
50. Cf. J. G. Machen, *The Virgin Birth of Christ* (New York, 1930).
51. Brunner, *The Christian Doctrine of Creation and Redemption*, 233.
52. Tertullian, *Against Marcion* 4, 10.
53. Clement, *Miscellanies* 3, 10, 68.
54. Cf. W. Eichrodt, *Theology of the Old Testament* (Philadelphia, 1961), 1, 152.
55. Neufeld, *op. cit.*, 143.
56. *Kiddushin* 29b–30a.
57. *Aboth* 5:21; *Sanhedrin* 76b; *Kiddushin* 76b.
58. *Kiddushin* 29a; Moore (*op. cit.*, 2, 127) believes that this law was in effect in the era in which Jesus lived.
59. Luke 2:21–25.
60. Matt. 13:55; Mark 6:3.
61. Joseph Klausner indicates that the custom in Jesus' day was that the son learned the father's trade (*Jesus of Nazareth*, New York, 1925, 233).

62. Yebamoth 62b, quoted in Israel Abrahams, "Family (Jewish)," Encyclopedia of Religion and Ethics.
63. Louis Cassels, The Real Jesus (New York, 1968), 77.
64. Joseph Blenkinsopp, Celibacy, Ministry, Church (New York, 1968), 34–37.
65. E.g., N. Schmidt, The Prophet of Nazareth (New York, 1905), 255–56; G. Vermes, The Dead Sea Scrolls in English (Baltimore, 1962), 30.
66. Otto Betz, "Dead Sea Scrolls," Interpreter's Dictionary.
67. Rule of the Congregation 1, 6–8; Josephus, Wars 2, 8, 2.
68. Mark 1:6; Damascus Document 12, 14.
69. Manual of Discipline 8, 14; 9, 19.
70. Luke 3:3–16; Manual of Discipline 3, 8.
71. Luke 3:9, 17; Manual of Discipline 4, 9–26.
72. Josephus, Antiquities 18, 5, 2.
73. Matt. 11:18–19; Luke 5:33.
74. Luke 7:33–34; Matt. 6:16–18.
75. Thomas Aquinas, Summa Theologica 3a, q. 40, 2.
76. Manual of Discipline, 9, 19.
77. Cf. Luke 7:24.
78. E.g., Mark 2:15; Luke 14:1, 19:5.
79. Josephus, Wars 2, 8, 3.
80. Erwin R. Goodenough, Jewish Symbols in the Greco-Roman Period (New York, 1952), 6, 158.
81. J. B. Lightfoot, Saint Paul's Epistles to the Colossians and to Philemon (London, 1879), 412.
82. Cyprian, On the Dress of Virgins 18 and 23.
83. Algernon C. Swinburne, "Hymn to Proserpine."
84. Luke 3:17.
85. Luke 4:16–21.
86. Luke 7:18–22; Isa. 29:18–19, 35:3–5.
87. Cf., e.g., Luke 17:21; Mark 4:26–32.
88. Luke 7:28.
89. Luke 7:23–35.
90. Guignebert, op. cit., 140.
91. H. H. Rowley, The Dead Sea Scrolls and the New Testament (London, 1957), 28–32.
92. Xenophon, Memorabilia 2, 1, 6.
93. Epictetus, Discourses 3, 12.
94. Matt. 7:14.
95. Cf. Matt. 5:3–12, 16:24–26.

96. Harnack, op. cit., 94, 90.
97. Rudolf Bultmann, Jesus and the Word (New York, 1934), 99.
98. Hans von Campenhausen, Tradition and Life in the Church (Philadelphia, 1968), 102–6.
99. F. Homes Dudden, "Asceticism," A Dictionary of Christ and the Gospels (New York, 1908).
100. Moore, op. cit., 2, 264–65.
101. Leo the Great, Sermons on the Nativity 7.
102. Matt. 4:2; John 19:28, 4:6.
103. Luke 7:9, 22:42–44; John 12:27.
104. Mark 15:34; Ps. 22:1.
105. Mark 10:21; John 15:15.
106. John 19:26; Luke 19:42.
107. Luke 10:21; John 15:11, 11:35; Matt. 9:36; Mark 3:5.
108. Heb. 2:10, 5:7–9.
109. Heb. 5:8.
110. Luke 2:52; cp. 1 Sam. 2:26.
111. Theodore H. Robinson, The Epistle to the Hebrews (New York, 1933), 51.
112. Oscar Cullmann, The Christology of the New Testament (Philadelphia, 1959), 95.
113. Irenaeus, Against Heresies 3, 19, 3; 5, 21, 1.
114. Ibid., 2, 22, 4.
115. Plato, Laws 835c.
116. Athanasius, Life of Anthony 5.
117. Jerome, Letters 22, 7.
118. Gregory the Great, Dialogue 2, 2.
119. Thomas of Celano, Lives of St. Francis of Assisi 2, 116, 7.
120. D. H. Lawrence, A Propos of Lady Chatterley's Lover (London, 1931), 14.
121. Alexander B. Bruce, The Humiliation of Christ (New York, 1887), 267.
122. Paul Tillich, Systematic Theology (New York, 1967), 2, 127.
123. Tom F. Driver, "Sexuality and Jesus," Union Seminary Quarterly Review 20 (1965): 239.
124. In a cartoon on the cover of The Christian Century (April 8, 1970), a celibate priest remarks, "I look at every old biddy and say to myself, 'There, but for the grace of God, goes my mother-in-law!'"
125. Diogenes Laertius, Lives 2, 36–37.
126. Cassius Dio, Roman History 56.

127. Clement, *Miscellanies* 7, 12, 70.
128. Cyprian, *On the Discipline and Advantage of Chastity* 7.
129. Chrysostom, *Letters to Theodore* 2, 5.
130. Jeremy Taylor, *Works* (London, 1828), 5, 254.
131. Martin Buber, *Between Man and Man* (London, 1947), 60–62.
132. Matt. 14:21; Mark 6:25–34, 7:25–30, 14:3–9; Luke 13:11–13, 18:1–5, 23:27–29; John 4:7–26.
133. Luke 7:11–17, 7:36–50, 8:1–3, 10:38–64, 13:10–17, 23:27–28.
134. Gal. 3:28.
135. Mary Daly, *The Church and the Second Sex* (New York, 1968), 37.
136. *Gospel of Thomas*, Saying 114.
137. *Maha-Parinibbana-Sutta* 5, 23.
138. Charles S. Braden, *Jesus Compared* (Englewood Cliffs, N.J., 1957), 39.
139. *The Analects* 17, 25.
140. John 8:3–11.
141. Isa. 42:3.
142. John 4:7–30.
143. For evidence that Jesus was more considerate of women than was customary among Jewish rabbis of his day, see *Aboth* 1, 5; cf. Claude G. Montefiore, *Rabbinic Literature and Gospel Teaching* (London, 1930), 47, 217.
144. R. C. Leslie, *Jesus and Logotherapy* (New York, 1965), 47–54.
145. Cf. A. Plummer, "The Woman that was a Sinner," *The Expository Times* 27 (1915–16): 42–43.
146. Matt. 21:31–32.
147. Cf. Montefiore, *op. cit.*, 222.
148. Mark 2:17.
149. *Midrash Rabbah on Lamentations* 2, 2.
150. Mark 15:40.
151. John 20:11–18.
152. Mark 15:40–41; Matt. 27:56; Luke 8:2, 24:10.
153. Joseph N. Sanders, "Those Whom Jesus Loved," *New Testament Studies* 1 (1955): 38–41.
154. John 11:5. Liddell and Scott indicate that *agapaō*, the verb employed in reference to this relationship, could refer to erotic passion; cf. Eph. 5:25.
155. The Synoptics do not inform us where they lived, but Luke 17:11 suggests that the section beginning with 9:51 and including the first meeting (10:38–42) occurred in the northern

part of Palestine. The traditional association of the sisters with Bethany, a suburb of Jerusalem, is due to John 11:1. However, the Greek prepositions there may be read: "Lazarus of (apo) Bethany, from (ek) the village of Mary and her sister Martha." According to Tertullian these women were "constantly attending him"; indeed, their relationship with Jesus was closer than that of his mother, whom Tertullian described as being like the unbelieving synagogue and deserving the indignation of her son (*On the Flesh of Christ* 7).

156. Luke 10:38–42.

157. John 12:3–8.

158. Richard F. Hettlinger, *Living with Sex* (New York, 1966), 63.

159. Robert M. Grant, *After the New Testament* (Philadelphia, 1967), 193; cf. Tertullian, *On Purity* 11.

160. Cf. "Mary Magdalen," *The Catholic Encyclopedia* (New York, 1910).

161. V. Hawtrey, trans., *The Life of Saint Mary Magdalen* (New York, 1904).

162. J. H. Bernard, *Gospel According to St. John* (New York, 1929), 412; J. Middleton Murry, *Jesus, Man of Genius* (New York, 1926), 328.

163. Dorothy Sayers, *The Man Born to Be King* (London, 1943), 183.

164. Francis C. Burkitt, "Mary Magdalene and Mary, Sister of Martha," *The Expository Times* 42 (1931): 158–59; cf. B. H. Branscomb, *The Gospel of Mark* (London, 1937), 301.

165. Mark 3:31–35.

166. Luke 4:29.

167. *Yebamoth* 6, 6.

168. Cf. 2 Kings 4:1.

169. Isa. 7:3, 8:3, 8:18.

170. Mark 7:14–23.

171. Driver, *op. cit.*, p. 245.

CHAPTER IV   TRADITIONAL ARGUMENTS FOR JESUS' CELIBACY

1. *Miscellanies* 3, 6, 49.

2. J.-J. von Allmen, *A Companion to the Bible* (New York, 1958), 256.

3. Joachim Jeremias, "*Numphē*," in *Theologisches Wörterbuch zum*

Neuen Testament, ed. G. Kittel (Stuttgart, 1933–) (hereafter cited as *TWNT*).
4. Cf. Mark 2:19; Matt. 22:1–12.
5. Jer. 2:2; Isa. 62:5.
6. 2 Cor. 11:2; Mark 2:19b.
7. Max Thurian, *Marriage and Celibacy* (London, 1959), 50.
8. Tertullian, *An Exhortation to Chastity* 9.
9. Jerome, *Letters* 22, 5; *Against Jovinian* 1, 49.
10. Gregory of Nyssa, *On Virginity* 21.
11. Augustine, *Against Julian* 4, 14.
12. George F. Moore, *Judaism in the First Centuries of the Christian Era* (Cambridge, 1927), 2, 267.
13. *Pesikta Rabbati* 24, 2; Job 24:15.
14. "Gunē," *TWNT, op. cit.*; J. H. Moulton and G. Millikan, *Vocabulary of the Greek Testament* (London, 1949).
15. Frederick C. Grant, *An Introduction to New Testament Thought* (New York, 1950), 321.
16. William G. Cole, *Sex in Christianity and Psychoanalysis* (New York, 1955), 17.
17. Lactantius, *Divine Institutes* 6, 23.
18. Martin Luther, *Commentary on the Sermon on the Mount* (Philadelphia, 1892), 158–60.
19. David Mace, *Whom God Hath Joined* (Philadelphia, 1953), 30–31.
20. Edward Schillebeeckx, *Celibacy* (New York, 1968), 24; cf. Lucien Legrand, *The Biblical Doctrine of Virginity* (New York, 1963), 53–60.
21. Karl Barth, *Church Dogmatics* (Edinburgh, 1961), 3, 4, 144.
22. E.g., Matt. 5:29–30, 7:5–6; 19:24, 23:24.
23. *Leviticus Rabbah* 19, 1.
24. Matt. 8:22.
25. Matt. 10:37.
26. Cf. Gen. 29:30–31.
27. Matt. 15:4–6.
28. Luke 2:7; Rom. 8:29.
29. Luke 3:23; Mark 6:3.
30. Cf. Mark 9:43–48.
31. Moore, *op. cit.*, 2, 131.
32. Exod. 20:3; Mark 12:29.
33. Luke 2:43–50.

34. Mark 3:21, N.E.B.
35. John 2:4.
36. John 7:5.
37. Matt. 10:36; Micah 7:6.
38. Mark 6:4.
39. Jer. 11:21, 12:6.
40. Mark 3:33, 35; a recently discovered apocryphal source stresses Jesus' alienation from his mother and his brothers. See S. Pines, "The Jewish Christians of the Early Centuries of Christianity According to a New Source," *The Israel Academy of Sciences and Humanities Proceedings* 2 (1966): 61.
41. Clement, *Who Is the Rich Man That Shall Be Saved?* 14, 22, 27.
42. Athanasius, *Life of Anthony* 2.
43. Matt. 19:21.
44. Luke 16:13, 12:15–21.
45. 1 Timothy 6:10.
46. Athanasius, op. cit., 45.
47. Irenaeus, *Against Heresies* 1, 24; 2, 35; Clement, *Miscellanies* 7, 17, 106.
48. Clement, op. cit., 3, 1, 1.
49. Eusebius, *Ecclesiastical History* 4, 7.
50. Irenaeus, op. cit., 1, 24, 4.
51. Clement, op. cit., 3, 1, 1.
52. Tertullian, *On Monogamy* 3.
53. Cyprian, *On the Dress of Virgins* 4 and 23.
54. Methodius, *Symposium* 2, 7.
55. Jerome, *Commentary on Matthew* 19:12.
56. Augustine, *On Holy Virginity* 37.
57. Jerome, *Sacra Virginitas* 3.
58. Vatican II, *Presbyterorum Ordinis* 3, 2, 16.
59. Paul VI, *Sacerdotalis Caelibatus*, sect. 5, 12, 22.
60. Karl Rahner, *Servants of the Lord* (New York, 1968), 155.
61. Floyd V. Filson, *A Commentary on the Gospel According to St. Matthew* (New York, 1960), 207.
62. T. H. Robinson, *The Gospel of Matthew* (London, 1928), 158.
63. Josephus, *Antiquities* 4, 8, 40; *Against Apion* 2, 38.
64. Deut. 23:1.
65. Deut. 24:1.
66. *Gettin* 9, 10.

67. A. E. Cowley, ed., *Aramaic Papyri of the Fifth Century B.C.* (Oxford, 1923), 46.
68. *Sirach* 25:26.
69. Philo, *On the Special Laws* 3, 30, 35.
70. Josephus, *Life* 414–15, 426–27; cf. *Antiquities* 4, 253.
71. Rabbi Akiba, *Gettin* 9, 10.
72. L. Friedländer, *Roman Life and Manners under the Early Empire* (London, 1928), 1, 241.
73. Seneca, *On Benefits* 3, 16, 2.
74. Josephus, *Antiquities* 18, 5, 1.
75. *Mark* 6:17–29.
76. Thurian, *op. cit.*, 49; cf. Barth, *op. cit.*, 3, 4, 141–44.
77. Cf. *Mal.* 2:14.
78. Moore, *op. cit.*, 2, 125, 152.
79. *Genesis Rabbah* 68, 4.
80. Israel Abrahams, "Marriages Are Made in Heaven," *Jewish Quarterly Review* 2 (1890): 173.
81. *Sota* 2a.
82. Alan H. McNeile, *The Gospel According to St. Matthew* (London, 1957), 274.
83. Cf. B. W. Anderson, *Understanding the Old Testament* (Englewood Cliffs, N.J., 1966), 246.
84. *Ezek.* 16; a similar motif is in *Isa.* 54:5–6, 62:4–5.
85. Reinhold Niebuhr, *An Interpretation of Christian Ethics* (New York, 1956), 2.
86. *2 Chron.* 33:13.
87. Shakespeare, Sonnet 116.
88. Hermas, *Mandatum* 4, 1.
89. Tertullian, *Against Marcion* 5, 7.
90. Tertullian, *On Modesty* 7–10.
91. McNeile, *op. cit.*, 275.
92. Cf. W. Lillie, *Studies in New Testament Ethics* (Edinburgh, 1961), 127.
93. Cf. S. E. Johnson, "The Gospel According to St. Matthew," *The Interpreter's Bible* (Nashville, 1951), 481.
94. *Yebamoth* 8, 2–4.
95. "Eunouchos," *TWNT*, *op. cit.*
96. Chrysostom, *Homilies on Matthew* 62.
97. *1 Cor.* 7:10–11, 39.
98. *1 Cor.* 7:25, N.E.B.
99. *Apology* 1, 15.

100. *Miscellanies* 3, 6, 50.
101. Jacques Dupont, *Mariage et Divorce dans l'Evangile* (Bruges, 1959), 161–222.
102. Quentin Quesnell, "Made Themselves Eunuchs for the Kingdom of Heaven," *The Catholic Biblical Quarterly* 30 (1968): 357–58.
103. Otto Borchert, *The Original Jesus* (New York, 1933), 318–19.
104. Tertullian, *Against Marcion* 4, 38.
105. *On the Dress of Virgins* 22; *Sacra Virginitas* 2, 1954 encyclical.
106. Jerome, *Against Jovinian* 1, 36.
107. Augustine, *On the Good of Marriage* 8; *On Holy Virginity* 12.
108. Ambrose, *Concerning Virgins* 1, 9, 52.
109. *Presbyterorum Ordinis* 3, 2, 16.
110. Paul VI, *Sacerdotalis Caelibatus* 34, 1967 encyclical.
111. Marc Oraison, *The Celibate Condition and Sex* (New York, 1967), 158.
112. John of Damascus, *Exposition of the Orthodox Faith* 4, 24.
113. Thurian, *op. cit.*, 115.
114. Tertullian, *Against Marcion* 4, 38.
115. Clement, *Miscellanies* 3, 12, 87.
116. *Ibid.*, 3, 6, 48.
117. Moore, *op. cit.*, 2, 384, 394–95.
118. *Sanhedrin* 92b; *Shabbath* 30b; "egeirō," *TWNT*, *op. cit.*, but cp. *Berakoth* 17a.
119. Emanuel Swedenborg, *Marriage and the Sexes in Both Worlds* (Philadelphia, 1881), 14, 23, 28, 31, 38.
120. *Tobit* 12:19; *1 Enoch* 15:4–7.
121. *1 Enoch* 104, 6; *2 Baruch* 51:10.
122. D. H. Lawrence, *A Propos of Lady Chatterley's Lover* (London, 1931), 65.
123. *Acts* 23:6–7.
124. *1 Cor.* 6:13, 15:50; *Rom.* 14:17.
125. *1 Cor.* 15:42–53; *2 Cor.* 5:1.
126. *1 Cor.* 2:9.
127. *1 Cor.* 13:13.
128. Maurice Wiles, "Studies in Texts: Luke 20:34–36," *Theology* 60 (1957); 501–2.
129. Jeremy Taylor, *Works* (London, 1828), 5, 253.
130. Sidney C. Callahan, *Beyond Birth Control: The Christian Experience of Sex* (New York, 1968), 52–54.
131. Ruud J. Bunnik, "The Question of Married Priests," *Cross Currents* 15 (1965): 426–27.

CHAPTER V PAUL AND SEXUAL RELATIONS

1. 1 Cor. 9:5.
2. Cp. Rom. 16:1; 1 Cor. 7:15, etc.
3. E.g., in the King James version *gunē* is translated 121 times as "woman" and 89 times as "wife."
4. J. B. Bauer, "Uxores Circumducere," *Biblische Zeitschrift* 3 (1959): 94–102.
5. Mark 1:30; 1 Pet. 5:13 may allude to Peter's wife; Clement wrote: "We are told that the blessed Peter when he beheld his wife on her way to execution, rejoiced on account of her call and her homeward journey" (*Miscellanies* 7, 11, 63; repeated by Eusebius, *Ecclesiastical* History 3, 30).
6. Clement, *op, cit.*, 3, 6, 53.
7. Basil, *On Renunciation of the World* 1.
8. 1 Cor. 9:5, N.E.B.
9. Tertullian, *On Monogamy* 8.
10. E.g., *The Jerome Biblical Commentary* (Englewood Cliffs, N.J., 1968), 2, 267.
11. "Gunē," in *Theologisches Wörterbuch zum Neuen Testament*, ed. G. Kittel (Stuttgart, 1933–) (hereafter cited as *TWNT*).
12. Acts 1:12–14.
13. K. Lake and H. J. Cadbury in *The Beginnings of Christianity*, ed. F. J. Foakes-Jackson (London, 1933), 4, 1, 11; G. W. H. Lampe, "Acts," in *Peake's Commentary on the Bible* (London, 1962), 887.
14. John 1:45–2:11, 21:2.
15. Luke 9:51–58.
16. Cf. Luke 6:13, 10:1, 24:13.
17. Mark 15:40–41.
18. *Sirach* 36:24–26.
19. Clement, *op. cit.*, 3, 6, 53.
20. Rom. 16:3; Acts 18:2, 26; 1 Cor. 16:19.
21. *Ioulia*, according to p46; or *Iounia*, another feminine name, in other manuscripts.
22. Cf. J. A. Fitzmyer, S.J., "The Letter to the Romans," *Jerome Biblical Commentary*, op. cit., 2, 330.
23. Chrysostom, *Homilies on Romans* 31.
24. John A. O'Brien, "Why Priests Marry," *The Christian Century* 87 (1970): 417.
25. Along with Johannes Jeremias (*Die Briefe an Timotheus und Titus*, Göttingen, 1953, 7) and C. F. D. Moule ("The Problem

of the Pastoral Epistles: A Reappraisal," *John Rylands Library Bulletin* 47 (1965): 430–52), I reject the judgment that these letters were written in the second century. Before Paul's death one of his amanuenses, such as Tychicus or Luke, possibly wrote the letters. However, they may have been composed after Paul's death by a disciple of Paul who utilized fragments of his letters. Since the contents of the Pastorals are essentially Pauline, they will be referred to, for convenience, as having been written by Paul.

26. 1 Tim. 3:2, 12; Titus 1:6.
27. E.g., P. T. Camelot, "Virginity," *New Catholic Encyclopedia* (New York, 1966).
28. 1 Cor. 7:8–9, 39; Rom. 7:2–3.
29. 1 Tim. 5:14.
30. Jean P. Audet, *Structures of Christian Priesthood* (New York, 1967), 60.
31. Arthur C. McGiffert, *A History of Christian Thought* (New York, 1932), 1, 291; cf. F. W. Farrar, *History of Interpretation* (New York, 1886), 210–18.
32. H. B. Swete, ed., *Theodori Episcopi Mopsuesteni Commentarii* (Cambridge, 1882), 2, 99–108; cf. M. Dibelius, *Die Pastoralbriefe* (Tübingen, 1931), 33.
33. Walter Lock, *The Pastoral Epistles* (Edinburgh, 1924), 36–37; cf. "gunē," *TWNT*, op. cit.
34. 1 Tim. 3:5.
35. 1 Cor. 4:15; Gal. 4:19; 1 Thess. 2:11.
36. Rom. 16; Gal. 6:10.
37. Clement, op. cit., 3, 12, 79.
38. *Codex Justinian* 1, 1, Title 3, law 41.
39. Phil. 3:5; Gal. 1:14.
40. E.g., T. R. Glover, *Paul of Tarsus* (London, 1925), 1–23.
41. W. C. van Unnik, *Tarsus or Jerusalem: The City of Paul's Youth* (London, 1962).
42. Rom. 7:12.
43. Phil. 3:3–11.
44. Rom. 3:31.
45. Rom. 4.
46. Rom. 14:14, N.E.B.
47. 1 Cor. 10:25–31.
48. Clement, op. cit., 3, 6, 53. A witty editor comments: "No doubt she would not have fitted comfortably into the basket when her

husband escaped from Damascus over the city wall." (J. E. L. Oulton and H. Chadwick, eds., *Alexandrian Christianity*, Philadelphia, 1954, 34n).

49. Origen, *Romans Homilies* 1, 1.
50. Acts 16:14–15.
51. Ernest Renan, *Saint Paul* (New York, 1875), 115.
52. Edward Schillebeeckx, *Marriage* (New York, 1965), 128.
53. Cf. Acts 23:6.
54. Rom. 9:2–3.
55. Kenneth J. Foreman, *The First Letter of Paul to the Corinthians* (Richmond, 1961), 85.
56. Methodius, *Symposium* 3, 12.
57. Martin Luther, in *Luther's Works*, ed. H. T. Lehman (Philadelphia, 1957), 54, Table Talk no. 3777; cp. T. G. Tappert, ed., *Select Writings of Martin Luther* (Philadelphia, 1967), 353–54.
58. E.g., Farrar, *The Life and Work of St. Paul* (New York, 1880), 44–46.
59. *Yebamoth* 6, 6.
60. *Kiddushin* 4, 13.
61. *Kiddushin* 29b.
62. Acts 9:1–2, 22:3, 26:10; Gal. 1:14.
63. Jeremias, "War Paulus Witwer?" *Zeitschrift für die Neutestamentliche Wissenschaft* 25 (1926): 310–12 and 28 (1929): 321.
64. 1 Thess. 4:17; 1 Cor. 15:51.
65. C. T. Craig, "First Epistle to the Corinthians," *The Interpreter's Bible* (New York, 1953), 10, 76.
66. 1 Cor. 7:26–31.
67. 1 Cor. 7:20–23.
68. 1 Cor. 7:9, 38.
69. 1 Cor. 7:36.
70. J. A. T. Robinson, *Jesus and His Coming* (London, 1957), 160–85; C. H. Dodd, New Testament Studies (Manchester, 1953), 113–17.
71. 1 Cor. 7:32–35.
72. Francis Bacon, "Of Marriage and Single Life," *Essays* (1597).
73. Thomas Aquinas, *Summa Theologica* 2-2, q. 186, 4.
74. Pius XII, *Sacra Virginitas* 1, 1954.
75. Cf. Clement, *op. cit.*, 3, 12, 88.
76. John Calvin, *Opera* (Brunswick, 1871), 10a, 228.
77. Jeremy Taylor, *Works* (London, 1828), 5, 253.
78. 1 Cor. 7:25.

79. E. D. Burton, *The Epistle to the Galatians* (Edinburgh, 1921), 302–310.
80. Burton, *Spirit, Soul, and the Flesh* (Chicago, 1918), 186.
81. Gal. 5:22.
82. Robinson, *The Body* (London, 1952), 20–26.
83. Raymond T. Stamm, "The Epistle to the Galatians," *The Interpreter's Bible* (New York, 1951), 10, 561.
84. K. G. Kuhn, "New Light on Temptation, Sin, and Flesh in the New Testament," in *The Scrolls and the New Testament,* ed. K. Stendahl (New York, 1957), 101–4.
85. W. D. Davies, "Paul and the Dead Sea Scrolls: Flesh and Spirit, in *ibid.,* 162.
86. Rom. 16:16; 1 Cor. 16:20; 2 Cor. 13:12; 1 Thess. 5:26.
87. E. Venables, "Kiss," *A Dictionary of Christian Antiquities* (London, 1880).
88. Tertullian, *To His Wife* 2, 4.
89. "The kiss of love," 1 Pet. 5:14.
90. K. M. Hofmann, *Philema Hagion* (Gütersloh, 1938), 94–147.
91. *Gospel of Philip* 55; *Pistis Sophia* 138.
92. E.g., Justin, *Apology* 1, 65.
93. Athenagoras, *A Plea Regarding Christians* 32.
94. Clement, *The Instructor* 3, 12.
95. *Apostolic Constitution* 2, 57.
96. Cf. Harvey Cox, *The Secular City* (New York, 1965), 184.
97. 1 Cor. 6:12–20.
98. D. Sherwin Bailey, *Sexual Relation in Christian Thought* (New York, 1959), 10.
99. Arguments against authenticity are overly subjective and are not so weighty as to counterbalance the unanimous judgment of antiquity that the letter is by Paul. Style differences can be explained by the use of amanuenses. Cf. L. Cerfaux, "En faveur de l'authenticite des epitres de la captivite," *Litterature et Theologie Pauliniennes* (Burges, 1950), 60–71; G. H. P. Thompson, *The Letters of Paul to the Ephesians, to the Colossians, and to Philemon* (Cambridge, 1967), 4–16.
100. Eph. 5:32.
101. Paul VI, *Sacerdotalis Caelibatus* 26.
102. Ruud J. Bunnik, "The Question of Married Priests," *Cross Currents* 15 (1965): 427.
103. Dorothea Krook, *Three Traditions of Moral Thought* (Cambridge, 1959), 346.

104. 1 Cor. 11:2–12, 14:34.
105. The verb *sunoikeō*, "dwells," and the verbal form of *gnōsis*, "knowledge," are used for marital intercourse in the Septuagint.
106. Westermarck, *Christianity and Morals* (London, 1939), 127.
107. J. Moffatt, *The First Epistle of Paul to the Corinthians* (London, 1938), 74.
108. E.g., 1 Cor. 1:19, 8:1, 13:2; cf. Rudolf Bultmann, "*ginōskō*," *TWNT*, op. cit.
109. Irenaeus, *Against Heresies* 1, 24, 5; 1, 18, 2.
110. Clement, *Miscellanies* 3, 1, 1–3; 3, 5, 40.
111. J. Weiss, *Der Erste Korintherbrief* (Göttingen, 1910), 169; A. Robertson and A. Plummer, *First Epistle of St. Paul to the Corinthians* (Edinburgh, 1914), 132.
112. Henry Chadwick, "All Things to All Men," *New Testament Studies* 1 (1955): 261–75.
113. Tertullian, *On Monogamy* 3; Jerome, *Letters* 48, 14; *Against Jovinian* 1, 7. Also, E. V. Arnold speaks of "the unconquerable repugnance of St. Paul to the sexual relation under any condition whatever," and cites the opening of 1 Cor. 7 as proof (*Roman Stoicism*, Cambridge, 1911, 426).
114. J. C. Hurd cites many scholars who think 1 Cor. 7:1b to be Paul's quotation of his adversaries' position (*The Origin of 1 Corinthians*, London, 1965, 68); C. K. Barrett, *A Commentary on the First Epistle to the Corinthians* (London, 1968), 154.
115. Col. 2:21–22.
116. Emil Brunner, *The Divine Imperative* (Philadelphia, 1947), 367.
117. *Ketuboth* 5, 6.
118. Augustine, *On Marriage and Concupiscence* 1, 16; cf. Origen, *On Prayer* 31, 4; Methodius, *Symposium* 3, 12.
119. Cf. Acts 26:5.
120. J.–J. von Allmen, *Pauline Teaching on Marriage* (London, 1963), 15.
121. E.g., H. Achelis, *Virgines Subintroductae* (Leibniz, 1902), 21–28; Weiss, op. cit., 206–9.
122. Cf. H. Weinel, *St. Paul* (New York, 1906), 267.
123. Werner G. Kümmel, *Neutestamentliche Studien für Rudolf Bultmann* (Berlin, 1954), 275–95.
124. Chadwick, op. cit., 265–67.
125. Cf. P. H. Menoud, "Mariage et celibat selon Saint Paul," *Revue de Theologie et de Philosophie* 39 (1951): 21–34.

126. Eph. 5:28–30.
127. 1 Tim. 6:20.
128. Col. 2:8, 21.
129. Irenaeus, *Against Heresies* 1, 24.
130. Calvin, *Institutes* 4, 12, 23.
131. Von Allmen, *A Companion to the Bible* (New York, 1958), 256.

CHAPTER VI   SEXUAL ATTITUDES IN SECOND-CENTURY CHRISTIANITY

1. Michael Novak, "Closing the Gap Between Theology and Marital Reality," *Commonweal* 80 (1964): 343.
2. Paul Ricoeur, "Wonder, Eroticism, and Enigma," *Cross Currents* 14 (1964): 135.
3. Plato, *Cratylus* 400c.
4. Aristotle, *Metaphysics* 986a.
5. Diogenes Laertius, *Lives of Eminent Philosophers* 8, 9.
6. *Lives* 8, 54.
7. Eric R. Dodds, *The Greeks and the Irrational* (Berkeley, 1951), 155.
8. J. M. Robinson, *An Introduction to Early Greek Philosophy* (Boston, 1968), 227–30.
9. *Lives*, 10, 118 and 132.
10. Lucretius, *The Nature of the Universe* 4:1052–1120.
11. Plato, *Phaedrus* 233.
12. G. M. A. Grube, *Plato's Thought* (Boston, 1958), 114.
13. Plato, *Phaedrus* 250, 253.
14. *Lives* 6, 29.
15. M. I. Finley, *Aspects of Antiquity* (New York, 1968), 94.
16. *Lives* 6, 104.
17. Epictetus, *Discourses* 3, 4, 51.
18. Cf. Samuel Sandmel, *Philo's Place in Judaism* (Cincinnati, 1956), 211; F. W. Farrar, *History of Interpretation* (New York, 1886), 137–38, 142; Erwin R. Goodenough, *An Introduction to Philo Judaeus* (New Haven, 1940), 160.
19. *Ecclesiastical History* 2, 4.
20. Philo, *On the Migration of Abraham* 9.
21. Cf. *Allegorical Interpretation* 3, 45 and 129; Harry A. Wolfson, *Philo* (Cambridge, 1962), 2, 251.
22. Philo, *On the Creation* 56, 165; *Questions and Answers on Genesis* 1, 31.

23. Philo, *On the Creation* 151.
24. F. C. Conybeare, *Philo about the Contemplative Life* (Oxford, 1895), 317, 302.
25. K. S. Guthrie, *Numenius of Apamea* (London, 1917), 145–48.
26. *Ibid.*, 2, Fragment 13.
27. *Ibid.*, 97, Fragment 16.
28. *Ibid.*, 133.
29. Plutarch, *On the Control of Anger* 464b.
30. Strabo, *Geography* 7, 3, 3.
31. J. Müller, *Das Sexuelle Leben der Völker* (Paderborn, 1935), 139, 156.
32. Friedrich Nietzsche, *Genealogy of Morals* 3, 7.
33. R. J. Devine, *Holy Virginity* (Rome, 1964), 82.
34. Max Thurian, *Marriage and Celibacy* (London, 1959), 46, 59.
35. Johannes Leipoldt, *Griechische Philosophie und Früchristliche Askese* (Berlin, 1961), 31, 60.
36. Emil Brunner, *The Divine Imperative* (Philadelphia, 1947), 364.
37. Morton S. Enslin, *The Ethics of Paul* (New York, 1930), 180; Havelock Ellis had earlier said essentially the same thing (*The Dance of Life*, New York, 1923, 249).
38. Joseph W. Swain, *The Hellenic Origins of Christian Asceticism* (New York, 1916), 143.
39. 1 Cor. 16:22.
40. Roland H. Bainton, *What Christianity Says About Sex, Love, and Marriage* (New York, 1957), 25.
41. R. Walzer, *Galen on Jews and Christians* (Oxford, 1949), 65.
42. George F. Moore, *Judaism in the First Centuries of the Christian Era* (Cambridge, 1927), 1, 187–89.
43. Clement, *To the Corinthians* 1, 38.
44. Clement, *Letter to Polycarp* 5 (shorter recension).
45. Cf. Josephine M. Ford, *A Trilogy of Wisdom and Celibacy* (London 1967), 139.
46. Hermas, *Vision*, 1, 1.
47. *Ibid.*, 2, 2.
48. Hermas, *Similitude* 9, 11.
49. Irenaeus, *Against Heresies* 4, 20, 2; Origen, *First Principles* 4, 2, 4.
50. *Acts of Paul* 5–6.
51. Tertullian, *An Exhortation to Chastity* 12; *On Monogamy* 16.
52. Irenaeus, *op. cit.*, 1, 6, 3.
53. Cyprian, *Letters* 61.

54. Prov. 6:27; *Letters* 22, 14.
55. "Gunē," in *Theologisches Wörterbuch zum Neuen Testament,* ed. G. Kittel (Stuttgart, 1933–) (hereafter cited as TWNT).
56. Sextus, *Sentence* 230.
57. E. Wynne-Tyson, *Porphyry* (London, 1965), 7.
58. Justin, *Apology* 1, 26; Tertullian, *Against Marcion* 5, 19.
59. Clement, *Miscellanies* 3, 3, 12.
60. Tertullian, *Against Marcion* 4, 6.
61. Irenaeus, *op. cit.*, 27, 2.
62. Tertullian, *On the Flesh of Christ* 1.
63. Tertullian, *Against Marcion* 4, 7.
64. Tertullian, *On Prescription Against Heretics* 30; *Against Marcion* 5, 7.
65. Tertullian, *Against Marcion* 4, 29 and 34.
66. *Ibid.*, 5, 15.
67. Clement, *Miscellanies* 3, 6, 46.
68. Irenaeus, *op. cit.*, 1, 27, 1.
69. Tertullian, *Against Marcion* 4, 6; *On Prescription Against Heretics* 30.
70. Tertullian, *The Refutation of All Heresies* 7, 17.
71. Clement, *Miscellanies* 3, 3, 18; Plato, *Republic* 329c.
72. Guthrie, *op. cit.*, 151.
73. Clement, *Miscellanies* 3, 17, 102.
74. *Ibid.*, 3, 13, 91.
75. *Ibid.*, 3, 9, 63.
76. Justin, *Dialogue with Trypho* 2.
77. Justin, *Apology* 2, 13, 1.
78. Arthur C. McGiffert, *A History of Christian Thought* (New York, 1932), 1, 100.
79. Justin, *Apology* 1, 29.
80. Minucius Felix, *Octavius* 31.
81. Justin, *Dialogue with Trypho* 100; cf. Erwin R. Goodenough, *The Theology of Justin Martyr* (Jena, 1923), 181, 238.
82. Justin, *Dialogue with Trypho* 66–84.
83. *Ibid.*, 54.
84. Origen, *On Prayer* 24, 5; Eusebius, *Ecclesiastical History* 4, 29.
85. Irenaeus, *op. cit.*, 1, 28, 1.
86. Martin Elze, *Tatian und Seine Theologie* (Göttingen, 1960), 61–68.
87. Tatian, *Address to the Greeks* 21.
88. Philostratus, *Life of Apollonius of Tyana* 1, 8 and 13.

89. Hippolytus, The Refutation of all Heresies 8, 13.
90. 1 Tim. 3:22.
91. Epiphanius, Against Heresies 45, 2.
92. Clement, Miscellanies 3, 12, 80–81.
93. A. Vööbus, Celibacy, a Requirement for Admission to Baptism in the Early Syrian Church (Stockholm, 1951), 17–19.
94. Quoted in Jerome, Commentary on Galatians.
95. Clement, Miscellanies 3, 12, 81.
96. Ibid., 3, 6, 49.
97. Theodoret, Treatise on Heresies 1, 20.
98. Clement, Miscellanies 3, 12, 81.
99. Vööbus, History of Asceticism in the Syrian Orient (Louvain, 1958), 1, 37.
100. E. Peterson, Frühkirche, Judentum und Gnosis (Freiburg, 1959), 211.
101. Acts of Andrew (Codex Vaticanus) 5.
102. Acts of Thomas 12.
103. Acts of John 113, 93.
104. Vööbus, History of Asceticism, op. cit., 1, 69.
105. "Manichaeism," in Sacramentum Mundi, ed. Karl Rahner (New York, 1969).
106. A. V. W. Jackson, Researches in Manichaeism (New York, 1932), 19.
107. H. J. Warner, The Albigensian Heresy (London, 1922), 1, 32.
108. Denis de Rougemont, Passion and Society (London, 1956), 80–85.
109. Tertullian, Against the Valentinians 4.
110. Clement, Miscellanies 3, 1, 3.
111. Tertullian, Against the Valentinians 30.
112. Cf. Irenaeus, op. cit., 1, 1.
113. J. E. L. Oulton and H. Chadwick, Eds., Alexandrian Christianity (Philadelphia, 1954), 30.
114. J. Leipoldt and H. M. Schenke, Koptisch-Gnostische Schriften aus den Papyrus-Codices von Nag-Hamadi (Hamburg, 1960), 34–38.
115. Robert M. Wilson, The Gospel of Philip (New York, 1962), 4–11.
116. Wilson, "The Gospel of Philip," in Studies in Church History, eds. C. W. Dugmore and C. Duggan (London, 1964), 1, 99, 103.
117. Gospel of Philip, Sayings 72 and 108.

222 WAS JESUS MARRIED?

118. Jack Finegan, *Hidden Records of the Life of Jesus* (Philadelphia, 1969), 277.
119. *Gospel of Philip*, Saying 17.
120. *Ibid.*, Sayings 91, 82; cf. G. L. Borchert, *An Analysis of the Literary Arrangement and Theological Views in the Coptic Gnostic Gospel of Philip* (Unpublished dissertation, Princeton University, Speer Library, 1967), 102, 481.
121. Hans von Campenhausen, *The Virgin Birth in the Theology of the Ancient Church* (Naperville, Ill., 1964), 19.
122. Justin, *Dialogue with Trypho* 48.
123. Eusebius, *Ecclesiastical History* 3, 27.
124. C. J. DeCatanzaro, "The Gospel According to Philip," *Journal of Theological Studies* 13 (1962): 42–43.
125. Liddell and Scott show that *koinōnos* refers to one with whom a man has sexual intercourse.
126. *Hōtre* literally means "yoke-partner" and is derived from *hōt(e)r*, meaning "be joined" (in marriage); cf. W. E. Crum, *A Coptic Dictionary* (Oxford, 1939), 726.
127. Robert M. Grant, *Gnosticism: A Source Book* (New York, 1961), 67.
128. *Pistis Sophia* 36.
129. *Ibid.*, 17, 19.
130. Cf. Irenaeus, *Against Heresies* 3, 11, 7; C. H. Dodd, *The Interpretation of the Fourth Gospel* (Cambridge, 1965), 105–8.
131. John 1:45.
132. John 2:1, 12, 19:25.
133. John 11:5, 32, 12:3, 20:1–18.
134. C. C. Richardson, *Early Christian Fathers* (Philadelphia, 1953), 291, 295.
135. Athenagoras, *A Plea Regarding Christians* 33.
136. Plato, *Laws* 840d; Clement, *Miscellanies* 3, 3, 24.
137. Philo, *The Special Laws* 3, 112.
138. Athenagoras, *op. cit.*, 33.
139. Gen. 25:1; Rom. 7:2; 1 Cor. 7:39.
140. Henry C. Lea, *History of Sacerdotal Celibacy in the Christian Church* (New York, 1907), 1, 25.
141. Tertullian, *An Exhortation to Chastity* 13.
142. Jerome, *Against Jovinian* 1, 49.
143. Canon 38.
144. Rom. 5:14; 1 Cor. 15:45.
145. Eph. 1; Irenaeus, *Proof of the Apostolic Preaching* 32.

146. Irenaeus, *Against Heresies* 3, 19, 3.
147. *Ibid.*, 3, 21, 10.
148. *Ibid.*, 3, 22, 4.
149. Irenaeus, *Proof of the Apostolic Preaching* 14.
150. *Ibid.*, 32.
151. Ireneaus, *Against Heresies* 5, 19, 1.
152. *Ibid.*, 3, 22, 4.

CHAPTER VII SEXUAL ATTITUDES IN EARLY ORTHODOXY

1. Tertullian, *Against Marcion* 1, 29.
2. Tertullian, *To His Wife* 1, 1; *On the Resurrection of the Flesh* 63.
3. Tertullian, *An Exhortation to Chastity* 13.
4. Tertullian, *To His Wife* 1, 5.
5. Tertullian, *An Exhortation to Chastity* 13.
6. Tertullian, *On Monogamy* 17.
7. Tertullian, *On Prescription Against Heresies* 7.
8. Tertullian, *An Exhortation to Chastity* 1; *Against Marcion* 5, 15.
9. E.g., Jerome, *Letters* 22, 15; *Against Jovinian* 1, 3, 4, 20, 40.
10. Tertullian, *On the Flesh of Christ* 20.
11. Tertullian, *On Monogamy* 3, 8.
12. Pseudo-Clement, *Letters on Virginity* 1, 6.
13. Tertullian, *On the Resurrection of the Flesh* 27.
14. Cyprian, *On the Dress of Virgins* 4; Jerome, *Letters* 48, 10; 77, 12; 84, 2; *Against Jovinian* 1, 40; *Letter to Pammachius* 34.
15. Augustine, *Holy Virginity* 27.
16. Thomas Aquinas, *Summa Theologica* 2–2, q. 152, 5.
17. Pius XII, *Sacra Virginitas* 2, 1954 encyclical.
18. G. B. Caird, *A Commentary on the Revelation of St. John the Divine* (London, 1966), 179.
19. Jean L. D'Aragon, "The Apocalypse," *The Jerome Biblical Commentary* (Englewood Cliffs, N.J., 1958), 2, 484; for a similar Catholic interpretation, see W. J. Harrington, *The Apocalypse of St. John* (London, 1969), 184.
20. Hans von Campenhausen, *Tradition and Life in the Church* (Philadelphia, 1968), 119.
21. Tertullian, *On the Apparel of Women* 1, 1.
22. *Ibid.*, 2, 2.
23. Tertullian, *On the Veiling of Virgins* 12.
24. Clement, *Miscellanies* 1, 28, and 29.

25. Tertullian, An Exhortation to Chastity 6.
26. Clement, op. cit., 3, 6, 46.
27. Clement, The Instructor 1, 4.
28. Clement, Miscellanies 4, 8, and 19.
29. Ibid., 1, 1, 11.
30. Ibid., 3, 12, 84; 3, 9, 66; The Instructor 2, 10, 83.
31. Clement, Miscellanies 2, 23.
32. Ibid., 7, 12, 70.
33. Ibid., 3, 17, 103.
34. Clement, The Instructor 2, 6.
35. Arnobius, The Case Against the Pagans 3, 9; 2, 37.
36. A. Roberts and J. Donaldson, eds., The Ante-Nicene Fathers (Edinburgh, 1885), 2, 381.
37. Clement, Miscellanies 3, 5, 40.
38. Ibid., 3, 4, 25; 3, 2, 10.
39. Ibid., 3, 7, 60.
40. Ibid., 3, 12, 83.
41. Ibid., 3, 12, 84.
42. Morton S. Enslin, "A Gentleman Among the Fathers," Harvard Thelological Review 47 (1954): 240.
43. Quoted in Eusebius, Ecclesiastical History 6, 19.
44. Ibid., 6, 9.
45. Henry Chadwick, Early Christian Thought and the Classical Tradition (New York, 1966), 90–91.
46. Eric R. Dodds, Pagan and Christian in an Age of Anxiety (Cambridge, 1965), 119–20.
47. Origen, Against Celsus 1, 4.
48. Origen, Commentary on Rom. 5:9 and on 1 Cor. 6:12.
49. Clement, Miscellanies 3, 17, 102.
50. Eusebius, op. cit., 6, 8.
51. Luther added: "For my part I'd rather have two pair added than one pair cut off" (H. T. Lehmann, ed., Luther's Works, Philadelphia, 1957, 54, 177, Table Talk no. 2865b.)
52. Origen, Matthew Homilies, 15, 1–3.
53. Chadwick, The Sentences of Sextus (Cambridge, 1959), 138.
54. Sextus, Sentence 13.
55. Philo, The Worse Attacks the Better 176.
56. Arnobius, op. cit., 5, 17; J. Frazer, Adonis, Attis, Osiris (New York, 1961), 263.
57. Strabo, Geography 14, 1, 23; Lucian, The Goddess of Syria 15, 27, 51.

58. Origen, *First Principles* 1, 8, 1.
59. Origen, *Leviticus Homilies* 8, 3.
60. Porphyry, *Life of Plotinus* 1; 2, 37.
61. Origen, *Leviticus Homilies* 12, 4; cf. H. Crouzel, *Virginite et Mariage Selon Origene* (Paris, 1963), 49–53.
62. Origen, *On Prayer* 17, 2.
63. Heb. 5:7; cf. J. Danielou, *Origen* (New York, 1955), 263–68.
64. Origen, *Genesis Homilies* 3, 6.
65. *Ibid.*, 5, 4.
66. Origen, *Numbers Homilies* 6, 3; *Orations* 31, 4.
67. Origen, *Ezekiel Selections* 7.
68. Origen, *Commentary on 1 Cor.* 7:5.
69. Origen, *Matthew Homilies* 14, 25.
70. Origen, *Romans Homilies* 9.
71. Origen, *Genesis Homilies* 17.
72. Origen, *Matthew Homilies* 10, 17.
73. "Priest," *Encyclopedia of Religion and Ethics* (Edinburgh, 1905).
74. M. Pfliegler, "Celibacy," in *Life in the Spirit*, ed H. Küng (New York, 1968), 109–15.
75. Joseph W. Swain, *The Hellenic Origens of Christian Asceticism* (New York, 1916), 9.
76. Albrecht Oepke, "gunē," in *Theologisches Wörterbuch zum Neuen Testament*, ed. G. Kittel (Stuttgart, 1933–) (hereafter cited as *TWNT*).
77. 1 Pet. 2:9.
78. L. E. Elliott-Binns, *The Beginnings of Western Christendom* (London, 1948), 329.
79. Origen, *Leviticus Homilies* 1, 6.
80. Origen, *Against Celsus* 7, 48.
81. Cf. E. Molland, *The Gospel in Alexandrian Theology* (Oslo, 1938), 134.
82. Cf. *Symposium* 180–5.
83. Origen, *Romans Homilies* 7, 8.
84. Origen, *Song of Songs Homilies* 1, 2.
85. *Ibid.*, 1, 4.
86. Origen, *Commentary on Song of Songs* 1, 1.
87. Cf. Tertullian, *On the Veiling of Virgins* 16.
88. Cf. Hippolytus, *Commentary on Song of Songs*.
89. Cyprian, *Letters* 61, 3.
90. Jerome, *Letters* 53, 7–8.

91. Jerome explains that "hand" refers to coitus (*ibid.*, 22, 19).
92. *Ibid.*, 22, 25.
93. *Ibid.*, 22, 20.
94. Ambrose, *On Virginity* 1, 2, 9; 1, 7, 52.
95. Pius XII, *Sacra Virginitas* 1, 1954 encyclical.
96. Chrysostom, *Letters to Theodore* 2, 3; 1, 14; The Roman Catholic F. Getlein, in his chapter on "The Anti-sex League of the Catholic Church," parodies a folk song in reference to priestly celibacy: "You can't get to heaven in the married life/ 'Cause the Lord don't like your earthly wife" (*The trouble with Catholicism*, Baltimore, 1964, 146).
97. Jan van Ruysbroek, in *The Spiritual Espousals* (London, 1952), 2, 21; 3, 9.
98. Teresa, *Conceptions of the Love of God* 4.
99. Teresa, *Life* 29, 17.
100. Mary Alacoque, quoted from her autobiography in J. H. Leuba, *The Psychology of Religious Mysticism* (London, 1925), 113–14.
101. William James, *The Varieties of Religious Experience* (New York, 1902), 12.
102. Bernhard Häring, S.J., *A Sacramental Spirituality* (New York, 1962), 167–70.
103. Lucien Legrand, *The Biblical Doctrine of Virginity* (New York, 1963), 108–11.
104. A. Bea, *Canticum Canticorum Salomonis* (Rome, 1953), 4–5.
105. E.g., R. E. Murphy, "Canticle and Canticles," *Jerome Biblical Commentary*, 1, 507; A. M. Dubarle, "L'amour humain dans le Cantique des cantiques," *Revue Biblique* 61 (1954): 67–86.
106. Methodius, *Symposium* 3, 8.
107. *Ibid.*, 1, 4.
108. James Mackinnon, *From Christ to Constantine* (London, 1936), 418.
109. Methodius, op. cit., 4, 2; 5, 3.
110. 1 Cor. 13:3.
111. Mark 4:20.
112. Cyprian, *On the Dress of Virgins* 21.
113. Methodius, op. cit., 7, 3.
114. Athanasius, *Letters* 48.
115. Jerome, *Letters* 48, 2.
116. Chrysostom, *On Virginity* 80.
117. Robert Briffault, *The Mothers* (New York, 1927), 3, 372.

118. Gregory the Great, *Homilies on the Gospels* 1, 3, 4.
119. Pius XII, *Sacra Virginitas* 3, 1954 encyclical.
120. Legrand, *op. cit.*, 80.
121. G. J. Laing, *Survivals of Roman Religion* (New York, 1931), 92–93.
122. Cicero, *De Domo Sua* 53, 136.
123. Tertullian, *On Prescription Against Heretics* 40.
124. Gerhard Delling, "Parthenos," *TWNT*, op. cit.
125. H. Cherniss, *The Platonism of Gregory of Nyssa* (Berkeley, 1930), 62.
126. Gregory of Nyssa, *On Virginity* 3.
127. *Ibid.*, 4 and 14.
128. *Ibid.*, 21.
129. Gregory of Nyssa, *The Great Catechism* 16.
130. Cf. E. V. McClear, "The Fall of Man and Original Sin in the Theology of Gregory of Nyssa," *Theological Studies* 9 (1948): 184.
131. Gregory of Nyssa, *On Creation of Man* 16.
132. Gregory of Nyssa, *On Virginity* 19.
133. *Ibid.*, 6.
134. *Exposition of the Orthodox Faith* 4, 24; cf. Dan. 3:50, 6:22.
135. H. Lietzmann, *A History of the Early Church* (New York, 1961), 4, 148.
136. Socrates, *History of the Church* 4, 23.
137. John T. Noonan, *Contraception* (Cambridge, 1965), 81.
138. Richard Lewinsohn, *A History of Sexual Customs* (New York, 1958), 101.
139. Porphyry, *On Abstinence* 4, 6–9; cf. H. I. Bell, *Cults and Creeds in Graeco-Roman Egypt* (Liverpool, 1953), 21.
140. E. Zeller, *Outlines of the History of Greek Philosophy* (London, 1931), 258.
141. Hippolytus, *The Refutation of All Heresies* 1, 2.
142. Porphyry, *On Abstinence* 1, 36.
143. Jerome, *Against Jovinian* 2, 9.
144. William Lecky, *History of European Morals* (New York, 1872), 1, 109.
145. Dodds, *op. cit.*, 31.
146. Johannes Leipoldt, *Griechische Philosophie und Früchristliche Askese* (Berlin, 1961), 26.
147. Philo, *On the Contemplative Life* 8, 65–68.
148. *Ibid.*, 3, 18, 32–33.

149. Herbert Workman, *The Evolution of the Monastic Ideal* (London, 1913), 37.
150. E.g., Palladius, *Lausaic History* 8, 4; 48, 3.
151. E. Preuschen, *Analecta* (Tübingen, 1909), 1, 16.
152. Eusebius, *op. cit.*, 2, 17.
153. "Maximus, the Cynic," *Dictionary of Christian Biography*.
154. Gregory of Nazianzus, *Oration* 23.
155. Basil, *Letters* 4 and 9.
156. D. R. Dudley, *A History of Cynicism* (London, 1937), 211.
157. Nemesius, *On the Nature of Man* 18, 37.
158. Plato, *Republic* 559.
159. Pseudo-Justin, *On the Resurrection* 3.

CHAPTER VIII   SEXUAL ATTITUDES IN
ROMAN CATHOLICISM

1. Jerome, *Letters* 84, 6; 22, 30.
2. Jerome, *Against Jovinian* 1, 41.
3. *Ibid.*, 1, 47.
4. Jerome, *Letters* 48, 20.
5. *Ibid.*, 22, 30.
6. *Ibid.*, 123, 13.
7. Jerome, *Against Jovinian* 1, 3.
8. Jerome, *Letters* 22, 20.
9. Jerome, *Against Jovinian* 1, 12.
10. *Ibid.*, 1, 3.
11. *Ibid.*, 1, 26.
12. Jerome, *Letters* 118, 4.
13. Jerome, *Against Jovinian* 1, 26.
14. *Ibid.*, 1, 36.
15. *Ibid.*, 1, 16.
16. *Ibid.*, 1, 22.
17. Siricius, *Letters* 2; Ambrose, *Letters* 42.
18. P. Delhaye, "Le Dossier Anti-matrimoniale de l'Adv. Jov. et son Influence sur Quelques Ecrits Latins du XIIieme Siecle," *Medieval Studies* 13 (1951): 65–86.
19. Gerald J. Campbell, "St. Jerome's Attitude Toward Marriage and Women," *The American Ecclesiastical Review* 143 (1960): 384, 386.
20. Tertullian, *On the Flesh of Christ* 23; *On Monogamy* 8.
21. Jerome, *Against Helvidian* 11.
22. *Ibid.*, 18.

23. *Ibid.*, 21.
24. *Protevangelium of James* 9, 2.
25. Tertullian, *Against Marcion* 4, 19; *On the Flesh of Christ* 7.
26. Jerome, *Letters* 49, 21.
27. E.g., Leo XIII, *Quamquam Pluries*, 1889 encyclical; Pius XI, *Ad Catholici Sacerdotii* 2, 2, 1935 encyclical.
28. E.g., J. B. Mayor, *The Epistle of St. James* (London, 1897), vi-xlv; V. Taylor, *The Gospel According to St. Mark* (New York, 1966), 248–49.
29. Jerome, *Against Jovinian* 1, 36.
30. Augustine, *The Good of Marriage* 10.
31. Augustine, *On Marriage and Concupiscence* 1, 14.
32. Augustine, *Confessions* 6, 12, 22.
33. *Ibid.*, 6, 15, 25.
34. *Ibid.*, 8, 7, 17.
35. *Ibid.*, 8, 12, 30.
36. Augustine, *On Marriage and Concupiscence* 2, 7 and 15.
37. E.g., T. J. Bigham and A. T. Mollegen, "The Christian Ethic," in *A Companion to the Study of St. Augustine*, ed. R. W. Battenhouse (Oxford, 1955), 384; Adolf Harnack, *History of Dogma* (London, 1898), 5, 219.
38. Peter Brown, *Augustine of Hippo* (Berkeley, 1967), 394.
39. Augustine, *Against Julian* 4, 14, 72; cf. Cicero, *On Offices* 1, 30.
40. T. Taylor, *Porphyry* (London, 1965), 7.
41. Plotinus, *Ennead* 3, 5, 1.
42. John P. Kenny, "Concupiscence," *New Catholic Encyclopedia* (New York, 1966).
43. Augustine, *On Marriage and Concupiscence* 1, 7.
44. *Ibid.*, 1, 6.
45. Augustine, *Against Julian* 4, 16.
46. *Ibid.*, 5, 8.
47. Augustine, *City of God* 14, 18–19.
48. Augustine, *On Marriage and Concupiscence* 2, 5.
49. Augustine, *City of God* 14, 24.
50. *Ibid.*, 14, 26.
51. Norman P. Williams, *The Ideas of the Fall and of Original Sin* (London, 1927), 366.
52. Augustine, *On Marriage and Concupiscence* 1, 13.
53. Augustine, *Against Julian* 5, 14.
54. *Ibid.*, 5, 15.
55. *Ibid.*, 5, 11.

230   WAS JESUS MARRIED?

56. Augustine, *On Marriage and Concupiscence* 1, 12.
57. Augustine, *Against Julian* 5, 16.
58. Augustine, *Soliloquies* 1, 10; quoted with approval in Thomas Aquinas, *Summa Theologica* 2–2, q. 151, 3.
59. Augustine, *Sermons* 354, 9, 9.
60. Augustine, *On Genesis* 8, 5.
61. Cf. M. H. Pope, *Job* (New York, 1965), 22.
62. Mary Daly, *The Church and the Second Sex* (New York, 1968), 46.
63. Augustine, *City of God* 15, 22.
64. Brown, *op. cit.*, 389.
65. Augustine, *The Lord's Sermon on the Mount* 1, 15, 41.
66. Augustine, *Incomplete Work Against Julian* 4, 39–41.
67. *Ibid.*, 1, 48.
68. Augustine, *Against Julian* 5, 9 and 15.
69. *Ibid.*, 4, 14.
70. Augustine, *Incomplete Work Against Julian* 4, 45–64.
71. Williams, *op. cit.*, 343.
72. George F. Moore, *Judaism in the First Centuries of the Christain Era* (Cambridge, 1927), 1, 479.
73. Augustine, *Against Julian* 5, 15.
74. J. S. MacArthur, *Chalcedon* (London, 1931), 18.
75. Paul Lehmann, "The Anti-Pelagian Writings," in *A Companion to the Study of St. Augustine*, 221.
76. John A. O'Brien, "Why Priests Marry," *The Christian Century* 87 (1970): 417.
77. D. Sherwin Bailey, *Sexual Relation in Christian Thought* (New York, 1959), 59.
78. Friedrich Nietzsche, *Beyond Good and Evil*, preface.
79. Paul Tillich, *Systematic Theology* (Chicago, 1957), 2, 52.
80. Nicholas Berdyaev, *The Destiny of Man* (London, 1937), 233.
81. Waldemar Molinski, "Marriage," in *Sacramentum Mundi*, ed. Karl Rahner (New York, 1969).
82. Aquinas, *Summa Theologica* 1, q. 98, 2.
83. *Ibid.*, 3, supp. 81, 3.
84. *Ibid.*, 1, q. 92, 1.
85. *Ibid.*, 1, q. 93, 4.
86. *Ibid.*, 3, supp. 39, 3.
87. Aristotle, *On Generation of Animals* 2, 3; Aquinas, *op. cit.*, 1, q. 92, 1.
88. *Ibid.*, 3, q. 28, 1.

89. *Ibid.*, 2–2, q. 154, 4.
90. *Ibid.*, 2–2, q. 152, 1.
91. *Ibid.*, 3, supp. q. 44, 2.
92. *Ibid.*, 3, supp. 49, 6.
93. C. S. Lewis, *The Allegory of Love* (Oxford, 1936), 14; cf. Peter Lombard, *Sentences* 4, 31, 6; Albert, *On Sentences* 4, 26, 8.
94. Aquinas, *op. cit.*, 3, supp., q. 42, 4.
95. *Ibid.*, 3, q. 29, 2.
96. Eusebius, *The Proof of the Gospel*, 1, 8 and 9.
97. *Ibid.*, 1, 8; 4, 10.
98. Henry C. Lea, *History of Sacerdotal Celibacy in the Christian Church* (New York, 1907), 1, 43.
99. Socrates, *History of the Church* 1, 11.
100. Cf. *ibid.*, 5, 22.
101. *Council of Rome* 386, canon 9.
102. Ambrose, *Duties of the Clergy* 1, 258.
103. "Adrian II," *New Catholic Encyclopedia*.
104. "Celibacy, History of," *ibid.*
105. Lea, *op. cit.*, 1, 289.
106. *Ibid.*, 1, 235.
107. *Ibid.*, 1, 385, 388.
108. Joseph Blenkinsopp, *Celibacy, Ministry, Church* (New York, 1968), 61–62.
109. Joseph H. Fichter, *America's Forgotten Priests* (New York, 1968), 210.
110. Theodosius, *The Theodosian Code* 16, 2, 44.
111. Jerome, *Letters* 117, 7.
112. Gregory the Great, *Dialogues* 4, 11.
113. Lea, *op. cit.*, 1, 86 and 164.
114. "John XII," *The Catholic Encyclopedia* (New York, 1907).
115. U. Richental, "Chronicle," in *The Council of Constance*, eds. J. H. Mundy and K. M. Woody (New York, 1961), 190.
116. Lea, *op. cit.*, 2, 251–58.
117. Horace, *Letters* 10, 24.
118. James Cleugh, *Love Locked Out: An Examination of the Irrepressible Sexuality of the Middle Ages* (New York, 1964), 298.
119. W. Nigg, *The Heretics* (New York, 1962), 286.
120. Gordon R. Taylor, *Sex in History* (London, 1953), 49–50.
121. Cf. J. B. Carol, ed., *Mariology* (Milwaukee, 1955), 1, 389.
122. Augustine, *On Nature and Grace* 42.

123. Aquinas, op. cit., 3, q. 27, 2, 2.
124. Leo XIII, Aeterni Patrias, 1879 encyclical.
125. Carol, ed., op. cit., 1, 338, 353, 375.
126. Marcus Cohn, "Marriage," The Universal Jewish Encyclopedia (New York, 1948).
127. Pius XI, Casti Connubii 2, 1930 encyclical.
128. Lev. 21:13–15.
129. Pius XI, Ad Catholici Sacerdotii 2.
130. Cicero, The Laws 2, 8.
131. Cf. Peter J. Riga, Sexuality and Marriage in Recent Catholic Thought (Washington, 1969), 8–15.
132. Ambrose, On Paradise 10, 47; Augustine, Against Julian 2, 7, 20.
133. Vatican II, Pastoral Constitution on the Church in the Modern World 51.
134. Paul VI, Populorum Progressio 37.
135. Riga, "Pope Paul VI and Celibacy," in Married Priests and Married Nuns, ed. J. F. Colaianni (New York, 1968), 86.
136. Leo XIII, Rerum Novarum 9.
137. Paul VI, Sacerdotalis Caelibatus 20.
138. Canon Law 985, 3; 2388, 1.
139. Leo H. Lehmann, The Soul of a Priest (New York, 1933), 122.
140. Heribert Jone, Moral Theology (Westminster, Md., 1956), 155.
141. Taylor, op. cit., 69.
142. Edward Henriques, "Committing Matrimony," in Married Priests, 147.
143. Emmett McLoughlin, People's Padre (Boston, 1954), 93–94.
144. Matt. 7:15.

CHAPTER IX   THE SIGNIFICANCE OF THE QUESTION

1. William G. Cole, Sex in Christianity and Psychoanalysis (New York, 1955), 285.
2. Reinhold Niebuhr, "Toward Intra-Christian Endeavors," The Christian Century 86 (1969): 1666.
3. R. G. Smith, ed., Søren Kierkegaard (New York, 1965), 93.
4. Leo Tolstoy, "Afterward," in A. Maude, The Life of Tolstoy (London, 1965), 2, 271.
5. Anders Nygren, Agape and Eros (London, 1953), 200–19.
6. Wilhelm Bertrams, The Celibacy of the Priest (Westminster, Md., 1963), 21.

7. Donald M. Baillie, *God Was in Christ* (New York, 1948), 10.
8. Tom F. Driver, "Sexuality and Jesus," *Union Seminary Quarterly Review* 20 (1965): 236.
9. 1 Cor. 1:23.
10. Titus 1:15.
11. Herbert Weiner, *The Wild Goats of Ein Gedi* (New York, 1961), 89–90.
12. Leo Jung, *The Jewish Library* (New York, 1934), 362.
13. J. Middleton Murry, *Adam and Eve* (London, 1944), 95–96, 108.
14. Benedict XV, *Address*, Dec. 16, 1920.
15. Etienne Gilson, "Souvenir du Pere," *La France Catholique*, 862, July 7, 1963.
16. John XXIII, *Address*, Jan. 26, 1960.
17. Cf., e.g., Joseph H. Fichter, *America's Forgotten Priests* (New York, 1968), 164.
18. James Kavanaugh, *A Modern Priest Looks at his Outdated Church* (New York, 1967), 10–11.
19. Paul VI, *Sacerdotalis Caelibatus* 1.
20. Jan V. Kilsdonk, in F. Franck, "Pontificate of Lost Opportunities," *Commonweal* 92 (Mar. 20, 1970): 31.
21. Paul VI, *Address*, Feb. 1, 1970.
22 *Ibid.*
23. Cf. R. Linton, "Universal Ethical Principles: An Anthropological View," in *Moral Principles of Action*, ed. R. Anshen (New York, 1952), 652.
24. Jean P. Audet, *Structures of Christian Priesthood* (New York, 1967), 106.
25. Vance Packard, *The Sexual Wilderness* (New York, 1968).
26. *Ibid.*, 17.
27. Cf. "The Teachings of Classical Puritanism on Conjugal Love," *Studies in the Renaissance* 2 (1955): 155.
28. In order that a verified hypothesis regarding Jesus' marital status may emerge, a mutual exchange of insights is needed. I share Charles Peirce's position that scientific truth on any issue is that eventual position that emerges as unchallenged after competent investigators have reviewed the evidence, contributed their individual half-truths, and have corrected one another. For this reason the candid criticism of readers from various religious traditions is solicited. All responses will be cordially received and carefully

considered. I would be especially interested to learn of errors of fact or of judgment contained in this volume and suggestions of other ramifications and new sources of information.

29. Luke 4:18; John 8:32.
30. 2 Cor. 3:17.
31. Niebuhr, in *The Christian Century* 86 (1969): 1666.
32. Eph. 4:13.

Indexes

BIBLICAL TEXTS

Genesis 1–5   15–20, 68, 83, 113, 184
24   21, 84, 113
Leviticus 8:33–35   183
15:18   26–27
Deuteronomy 24:5   23, 30
Psalms 51:5   27
Song of Songs 23–24, 151–154
Jeremiah 16:1–4   27–29
Hosea 2   85, 91
Matthew 1:16–25   43
5:27–28   72–74
19:3–12   79–91, 130, 133, 149, 165
Mark 2:19   71–72
3:21–31   41, 77
Luke 1:34   40–42
2:42–52   36, 47–48, 56

7:36–50   63–66
8:2–3   101
14:26   75–77
18:29   78
20:34–36   92–98
Acts 1:14   100
Romans 16   102, 114
I Corinthians 7   89, 106–117
9:5   48, 99–100, 165
Galatians 5:16–24   111
Ephesians 5:21–33 86, 113–114
Philemon 4:3   107
I Timothy 4:1–5   118–119, 132
Hebrews 4:15   11, 56
13:14   178
I Peter 3:7   114
Revelation 14:4   144–145

Index

GENERAL

Adam, Jesus the last, 15, 139–140

Allmen, J. von, 71, 117, 119

Ambrose, 93, 153, 166, 178, 184

Anthony, 57, 78–79, 160, 162

Aquinas, 5, 50, 110, 144, 175–177, 182

Athanasius, 43, 156–157, 162

Augustine, 72, 80, 93, 116, 144, 167–177, 182, 184, 188

Audet, J. P., 38, 103, 194

Bailey, D. S., 1, 113, 175

Barth, K., 75, 83

Basilides, 79, 134

Betrothal, 21–23, 39–40, 46–48

Blenkinsopp, J., 48–49, 179

Brunner, E., 5–6, 44–45, 116, 124–125

Buber, M., 21, 61

Bultmann, R., 42, 54

Bunnik, R. J., 18, 97, 113

Calvin, J., 100, 110, 119

Campenhausen, H. von, 54, 145

Chadwick, H., 117, 135, 148

Chalcedon creed, 6, 45, 55

Chrysostom, 60–61, 89, 153, 157

Cicero, 164, 169, 183

Clement of Alexandria, 46, 59–61, 78, 90, 94, 100, 102, 104, 107, 128–130, 133, 145–147, 148–149

Cole, W. G., 74, 187

Cynics, 53, 122, 132, 162

Cyprian, 60, 80, 92, 128, 152, 156

Daly, M., 62, 172

Digamy, 103, 139

Docetism, 11, 37, 45, 79, 188–189

Dodds, E. R., 121, 148, 162

Driver, T. F., 9, 58–59, 69, 189

Dual paternity, 40–42, 45–46, 136

Elijah, 38, 144, 159–160

Empedocles, 121, 130, 164

Encratites, 132–134, 147

Enslin, M. S., 125, 147

Epictetus, 53, 122, 130

Erskine, J., 8–9, 91

Essenes, 29–32, 35, 49–53, 111

Flesh, 17–18, 111
Freud, S., 5, 18

Gnostics, 79, 115, 118–119, 126,
    129–130, 135
Gospel of Philip, 64–65, 135–
    138
Grant, F. C., 14, 44, 74
Gregory of Nyssa, 72, 158–160
Guignebert, C., 43, 52–53

Hermas, 86, 126–128

Ignatius, 126
Incarnation, 44–45, 189–190
Irenaeus, 57, 128, 129–130,
    132, 139–141

Jeremias, J., 71, 108
Jerome, 28, 57, 80, 92–93, 100,
    115, 128, 152–153, 157, 162,
    164–167, 178
John of Damascus, 93, 160
John the Baptist, 49–52, 82,
    144, 166
Joseph, 46–49, 70, 76, 167,
    182–183
Josephus, 29, 31, 82
Julian, 173–174
Justin Martyr, 40, 89–90, 131–
    134

Kazantzakis, N., 10–11
Kierkegaard, S., 124, 188

Lawrence, D. H., 58, 95
Legrand, L., 28, 38, 154, 157
Leipoldt, J., 124, 135
Luther, M., 12–13, 74, 108, 149

Mace, D., 15–16, 74–75
Manicheism, 134, 168–169
Marcion, 92–93, 128–130, 142–
    143, 147

Marriage, Jesus' view of, 76–78,
    82–85, 94–98
Mary Magdalene, 64–67, 101,
    136–138
Mary, mother of Jesus, 39–46,
    70, 77, 136, 150–151, 158,
    159, 166–167, 172, 181–183
Methodius, 80, 108, 155–158
Montefiore, H., 6–7, 12
Moore, G. F., 13, 32, 55, 73,
    84, 173–174
Moral dualism, 3, 121–123,
    151–152, 187, 195

Neoplatonism, 122, 128, 131–
    133, 148, 151, 155, 169, 188
Niebuhr, Reinhold, 85, 188,
    196
Nietzsche, F., 124, 175
Novak, M., 11, 120–121

Oraison, M., 7, 93
Origen, 107, 147–151
Original sin, 171, 176, 181, 191

Paul VI, 1, 80, 93, 113, 184–
    185, 193–194
Paul, the apostle, 89, 95–96,
    99–119, 125, 156, 196
Philo, 29, 33, 82, 123, 138–139,
    149
Pius XII, 80, 92, 109–110, 144,
    153, 157
Plato, 40, 124, 130, 163
Polygamy, 9–10, 19–20
Priestly celibacy, 150–151, 177–
    181, 183–186, 191–194
Pythagoreanism, 121–123, 131,
    138, 161–162

Quesnell, Q., 90–91

Ricoeur, P., 121

Saturninus, 118–119, 132
Schillebeeckx, E., 75, 107
Socrates, 53–54, 59, 91

"Spiritual" marriage, 117, 127, 172
Stoicism, 106, 122, 162, 171

Tatian, 131–134, 147
Taylor, J., 61, 96, 110
Tertullian, 46, 72, 86–87, 93–94, 100, 112, 115, 127–129, 142–145, 167
Therapeutae, 33, 162
Theodore of Mopsuestia, 103–104, 153, 154, 174

Thurian, M., 83, 93, 124
Tillich, P., 45, 58, 175

Vatican II, 80, 93, 183–184, 192
Virginity, 39–46, 143–145, 155–160, 165–167

Woman's status, 17, 20, 61–63, 114, 145, 164–165, 172–173, 176, 182